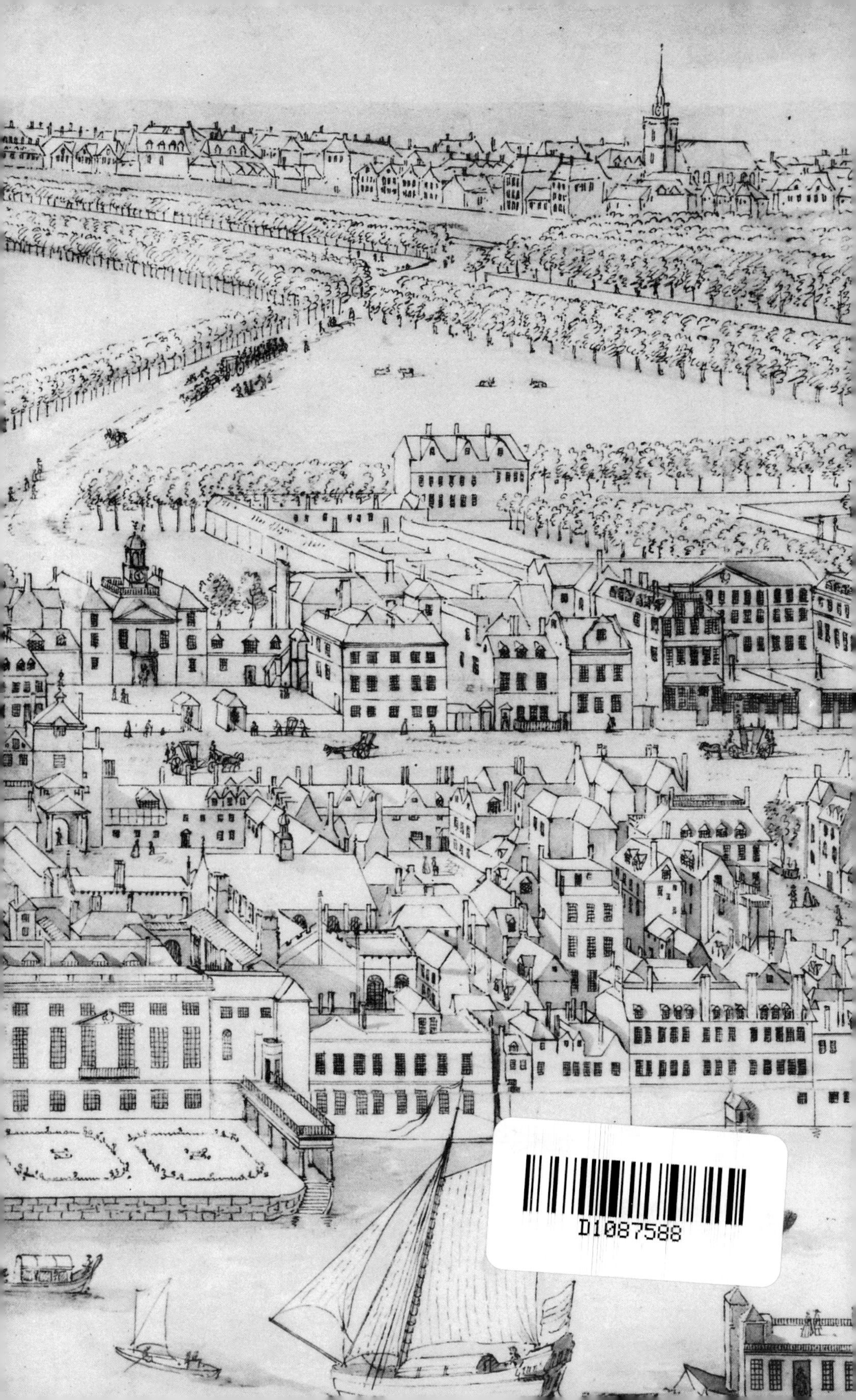

Henry
Purcell

Henry
Purcell

Maureen Duffy

FOURTH ESTATE · *London*

First published in Great Britain in 1994 by
Fourth Estate Limited
289 Westbourne Grove
London W11 2QA

A catalogue record for this book is available from the British Library.

ISBN 1–85702–098–7

Typeset by York House Typographic Ltd
Printed in Great Britain by the Bath Press Ltd, Avon

A Rebus on Mr Henry Purcell's Name

The mate to a cock, and corn tall as wheat
Is his Christian name who in music's compleat;
His surname begins with the grace of a cat,
And concludes with the house of a hermit, note that;
His skill and performance each auditor wins,
But the poet deserves a good kick on the shins.

Richard Tomlinson (set to music by John Lenton)

Contents

Acknowledgements

THERE ARE SO many people who have helped me, many of whom I don't know by name, that I must first ask them to forgive me for the starkness of these acknowledgements.

I should like to acknowledge throughout the invaluable assistance of Dr Andrew Ashbee's *Records of English Court Music* vols i–ii and v. I have also drawn heavily on the kindness and patience of the staff of the British Library, particularly Dr Parker and those in the music department, and of the Public Record Office, both in Chancery Lane and Kew. I am equally indebted to the staff of the Westminster Library Archives and Local Studies department, Westminster Abbey Muniments, the Chapter Office, Windsor Castle, the Society of Genealogists and Chelsea Library Local Studies department. I must also express my thanks to the county record offices of Berkshire, Buckinghamshire, Northamptonshire, Surrey and Wiltshire for their help, also to Guildhall Library, Corporation of London and Greater London Record Offices and the London Library.

I was assisted by several individual researchers: Maurits Verhoeff of Amsterdam for Belgian archive researches, Hilary Marshall for probate translations, Mrs Christine Hawker for researches in Hereford and Worcester and Duncan W. Harrington for Kent ecclesiastical material. I am also grateful to Mrs Jean Tsushima of the Honourable Artillery Company and her assistant Mrs Sally Hofmann, to Dr Robin Myers of the Stationers' Company, and the archivist of the Drapers' Company, and particularly to Dr Brian Boydell of the University of Dublin for answering my questions relating to the Trinity centenary ode.

I gratefully acknowledge the financial assistance of the Society of Authors bursary scheme towards the writing of this book.

I should also like to thank Richard Huijing who typed a difficult manuscript with great expertise and Helen Jeffrey who spotted my mistakes and inconsistencies. Finally I would like to express my gratitude to the musicians and scholars whose skill and devotion make it possible through modern technology to hear more of Purcell's music than at any time since his death, in particular Robert King's invaluable fine series of recordings of the odes and anthems, and Christopher Hogwood's delightful compilation of the occasional theatre music.

List of Illustrations

With thanks also to the British Library, the Holburne Museum University of Bath, the Public Records Office and the Westminster Public Libraries

Prologue

IT'S THE BITTER winter of 1946, so cold that we're allowed to stay in the school hall at break and dinner-time, huddled over the iron radiators, drinking our warm, near-curdled milk. Outside, as well as the ice and snow, is immediately post-war Britain: rationed, exhausted and grey. The new look, with its long anti-utility skirts, hasn't reached us yet, but ill-cut demob suits have. My best friend and I, however, have another world beyond this that occupies half our waking thoughts and conversations: of gallantry, poetry, music. We are ardent royalists, though our royals have been dead for over two hundred years. Sometimes we pay the one shilling and ninepence to see them reincarnate on the screen. When in music lessons we sing 'Fairest isle' with knowing enthusiasm, we're transported to the 'seat of pleasure and of love', the mythologised England of Charles II, where men pursue and women are 'grateful'. We know perfectly well that this means sex, and that the last thing we can do if we're to have a career and a better life than our parents, by which we mean richer in every sense, more daring, is to be 'grateful' to any of the boys in grey flannels and tweed sports jackets who might pursue us in those pre-pill, virtually pre-condom days.

My best friend has a good soprano and plays the piano. I can oompah in the bass, always useful in a girls' school, and I play, alone and self-taught on a recorder handed down to me by a cousin, the top line of *Henry Purcell: Short Duets*, with varying accuracy.

A little later, taken by a perceptive French mistress, I hear a 'restored' *Messiah* in Bath Abbey. When it comes to 'He was despised', a well-built man in his thirties stands up, opens his mouth and out comes the most ravishing human sound I have ever heard. It's Alfred Deller and I've succumbed to my first countertenor. Two years later still I'm back in London after the long exile of evacuation, I've changed schools and am in the grip of the English folk dance and song revival, dancing Playford, and I'm taken, this time by the Latin mistress, to hear Flagstad sing Dido in the Mermaid Theatre production, which in memory is all purple, and black, and gold. My subjugation to Purcell's music is complete.

When, a further thirty years on, I came to research and write a biography of Aphra Behn, I found myself stumbling over Henry Purcell at every turn, not simply as the composer of his music, but as an actor in that extraordinary theatrical composition that's the world of the post-Restoration seventeenth century, at times a painted baroque stage set, at others a well of creativity in every sphere of the arts, science, philosophy and commerce.

The period itself wasn't one for biography. A few 'brief lives' had begun to appear, but biographical facts mostly have to be dug for and then speculated on, rather in the manner of a Holmesian sleuthing. Valuable material has been lost even in modern times. Only the codicil to Edward Purcell's will survived a wartime evacuation. Pictures of the young Henry, supposedly, in the uniform of a Chapel boy, extant in 1928 are now untraceable. Archives have to be forced to give up dusty secrets; references like that to Purcell's naval surgeon brother Joseph, previously known only as the administrator of their brother Daniel's meagre estate, have to be followed like Ariadne's thread through labyrinthine search procedures before they yield any new information. In the attempt to flesh out the picture of my Purcell, I have preferred to speculate and then opt for an interpretation rather than leave all the questions open. Others can and will open them up again for their Purcells. Reluctantly, for example, I have come to the conclusion that the fine music to *The Tempest* wasn't composed by him for that play, or at least not for any performance in his lifetime, although whoever did write it may have reused existing Purcell material (as Tom D'Urfey often did), which would make sense if the composer is indeed his pupil John Weldon.

For me, perhaps because that was how I first began my love affair with his music, an affair in which the age itself was both backdrop and go-between, Purcell remains supremely the musical exponent of desire, of yearning in all its manifestations, whether it's the longing for peace of 'O solitude' or for sexual fulfilment of 'Still I'm wishing', and even when longing breaks down into the madness of 'Bess of Bedlam'. As his fellow student Henry Hall put it:

> *Who e'er like Purcell could our passions move,*
> *Whoever sang so feelingly of love?*

· 1 ·

Curtain Tune

ON 21 FEBRUARY 1660 Samuel Pepys set out after dinner, together with John Crew (father-in-law of his patron, the Earl of Sandwich), in Crew's coach for Westminster Hall. They had been there in the morning when General Monck had used his troops to have the MPs, who had been excluded by the Council of State in Pride's Purge of 1648 (when it was feared they might come to an agreement with Charles 1), readmitted to the House. Demands for a free parliament were growing daily, although Monck was still recommending a commonwealth to the House and had spoken against the restoration of Charles Stuart. That afternoon there was no more information to be got at Westminster Hall, but Pepys met two others who had also come in search of it: 'Mr Lock and Pursell, Maisters of Musique; and went with them to the Coffee-House into a room next the Water by ourselfs. Here we had variety of brave Italian and Spanish songs and a Canon for 8 *Voc:*, which Mr Lock had newly made on these words: *Domine salvum fac Regem*, an admirable thing.'

They were joined after a couple of hours by Captain Silas Taylor, an old acquaintance of Pepys who was sequestrator for the parliament in Herefordshire, where his brother Sylvanus had estates. He brought them news of the latest developments: Monck had persuaded the House to restore the gates of the city that had been torn down by his soldiers eleven days before and to release the members of Common Council who had been arrested at that time. Silas Taylor was an amateur musician, composer and performer, of some pretension. He probably knew Matthew Locke through his wife, Mary Garnons, also from Herefordshire, and he had been at Shrewsbury School with members of the Shropshire–Welsh branch of the Purcell clan. The four of them must have divided up the eight parts of Locke's new canon, 'God save the King', between them. As they sang they could see, out of the coffee-house window, the light of the bonfires like 'a glory' about the city and hear the ringing of the bells that marked Londoners' rejoicing because their gates and liberties were to be restored.

Locke's canon was a little premature: the ground swell for restoration had hardly begun. Across the water, Charles and his supporters watched events unfolding from exile in Brussels. Parliament was dissolved on 16 March and fresh elections were called. Monck had gradually moved towards acceptance that the monarchy should be restored, and late in March he sent word to Charles that he should move to Breda, over the border in the Dutch Republic, a city which supported Charles's nephew, William of Orange. Charles reached Breda on 4 April. The negotiations to restore him were to drag on until May, but by then it had become clear that his return was inevitable, and Pepys noted as early as 21 April that 'formerly great cavaliers' were crossing the Channel to sue for posts and favours. Their petitions began to appear in state papers from the end of April, which, because of the ten-day discrepancy between English and Continental dating, appears as May in the Breda records.

On 13 May (Breda style), five days before his proclamation in Westminster Hall and three weeks before he landed in England, King Charles wrote to the Lord Chamberlain: 'Our will is that you cause Thomas Purcell to be admitted Groom of Our Robes in Ordinary.'[1] There's no record of a petition which might have contained useful details of Thomas Purcell's claim to this post, the kind of job that Secretary Nicholas described as one 'of great trust'. Thomas Purcell, the composer's uncle, must have been in Breda to advance his cause. His fellow appointees, Lancelot Thornton as clerk of the robes and

John Duncombe, Tobias Rustat and Paul Ferine as grooms, all had family connections with the royal household or government. Thornton's family held the strangely named post of 'Chafe-wax to the Great Seal' in the Chancery, Duncombe's father had been sewer to Charles I, Rustat had been yeoman of the robes to Charles in exile and Ferine's father had been the late King's perfumer.

It's possible, but unlikely, that Thomas Purcell and his family had no previous court service and that he was appointed simply because of his personal qualities and his support for the King's cause. A Purcell appears in the state papers for 1649 among a group of high-ranking royalist officers going from the court, then in exile at St Germain, to Ireland, where the royalist cause was in disarray under the much criticised command of the Duke of Ormonde, but this may be one of the Duke's own Purcell relatives. What's clear is that Thomas Purcell's first appointment was not as a musician, but to the intimate post of royal servant.

The Purcell whom Pepys met and sang with was almost certainly Henry senior, who at that time was appearing with Matthew Locke in the proto-opera *The Siege of Rhodes* at the Cockpit theatre in Drury Lane. It had first been performed in the autumn of 1656 at Sir William Davenant's residence, Rutland House, in Charterhouse Yard, as part of his attempts to circumvent the laws against public theatres by staging entertainments 'by Declamations and Music'. The authorities were, quite rightly, suspicious that this might be theatre by the back door. Earlier that year a government spy in the audience of *The First Day's Entertainment* on 23 May reported back on the 'opera'[2] and, rather surprisingly, it was allowed to continue, perhaps because of Oliver Cromwell's own delight in music.

This work had more of declamation than opera about it, and the music, composed by Henry Lawes, Charles Coleman, Captain Henry Cooke and George Hudson, was mainly instrumental. Cooke had earned his title fighting for Charles I, while Henry Lawes's brother William had been killed on the royalist side at the siege of Chester.

Charles Coleman on the other hand had been given a doctorate by the Commonwealth reformed University of Cambridge, although he had originally been a member of Charles I's Chapel Royal. Music could cross the political divide. Davenant himself was a known royalist and had even been converted to Roman Catholicism by the Queen Mother, Henrietta Maria. The spy reported that those involved were 'Henry Lawes, Dr Coleman, Capt Cook, Ned Cole[man] and wife and others'. It's probable that these 'others' already included Locke and Purcell.

The Siege of Rhodes was a much more elaborate affair, with solos, recitatives and sets designed by John Webb, an assistant of Inigo Jones, showing 'the art of prospectives in scenes'; the dances were the work of Luke Channel, Davenant's regular choreographer. It is a direct descendant of the court and Commonwealth masques.[3]

The published version gives a date of 17 August 1656 and, conveniently, has a list of the composers and performers at the back. As well as those known to be involved in the first entertainment, the vocal music, from the list of composers for that in the 1657 edition, now included Matthew Locke, who also sang the part of the Admiral. Captain Cooke sang the role of Solyman, Mrs Catherine Coleman, the wife of Edward Coleman (Charles's son), played Ianthe to his Alphonso; John Harding sang Pyrrhus, Gregory Thorndall Villerius, and the part of Mustapha was sung by 'Mr Henry Persill'.

In his preface to the printed edition Davenant wrote: 'The Music was composed, and both the Vocal and Instrumental is exercis'd, by the most transcendant of England in that Art, and perhaps not unequal to the best Masters abroad, but being *Recitative*, and therefore unpractis'd here; though of great reputation among other Nations, the very attempt of it is an obligation to our own.'

The work proved so successful that Davenant was able to transfer it to the Cockpit, where it played daily at the usual time of three in the afternoon. It was followed there in 1658 by *The Cruelty of the Spaniards in Peru* and the next year by *The History of Sir Francis Drake*, which was advertised in the printed version as having many places for a shilling.

There's little scope in *The Cruelty of the Spaniards in Peru* for soloists, but *The History of Sir Francis Drake* is more elaborate, although the company had to reuse the scenery from the previous production. Perhaps this meant there was more money for the performers. Unfortunately, there's no cast list, but there are certainly roles which 'Henry Persill' could have played. His appearing together with Locke at the encounter with Pepys suggests that they were both involved in this production too, as well as in the expanded second part of *The Siege of Rhodes*, which was registered in May 1659 and is almost certainly the 'new opera' that Evelyn saw in the same month. He compares it unfavourably with what he had seen in Italy, but mentions the use of recitative and the 'prospective' scenery exactly as it appears in the Stationers' Register. There was, however, no part for Catherine Coleman. In 1658, and after some protests, Richard Cromwell had announced a commission of enquiry into these operatic goings-on. No doubt the appearance of a woman on stage had added to the complaints, and the only female appearance in *Sir Francis Drake* is a painted scene of a captive bride tied to a tree. That this device was designed to counter some outcry against women acting in public is made clear when the news is brought that she has been set free and her father and bridegroom come on to dance together to 'castanetts'. The timely restoration of Charles II at least saved the theatre from further such absurdity.

On 17 March 1660 Sir William Davenant was given a pass to go to France. He was almost certainly hurrying to reassure the court in exile that, even if the content of some of the 'operas' might be interpreted as supporting the present government, he remained a royalist. The day before Pepys had noted the great bonfire at the Exchange and people crying out 'God Bless King Charles the Second'. Davenant seems to have been living partly in the parish of St Andrew's, Holborn, at this period, for his second wife, Anne, was buried there in March 1655 'out of Eagle Court'. He must have remarried almost at once, as Charles, the first child of his new wife, was born in 1656. By his third marriage Davenant had what Pepys described at his funeral as 'many children, by five or six in the first mourning coach, all boys', yet their baptisms don't appear in the appropriate registers. The government had issued an ordinance in 1653 that all births, marriages and deaths were to be recorded by a secular registrar. Davenant's children were certainly baptised, but probably not registered, in defiance of this order. John Evelyn's children, for example, were baptised in the drawing-room of his home, Sayes Court. Whether to register or not must have been a difficult decision for many people, especially those who had been in the royal service or that of the church before the Civil War. Burial, however, couldn't be other than a public act.

A number of musicians lived in the part of London close to the Inns of Court, in the parishes of St Andrew's, Holborn, and St Clement Danes. The Yockney family lived in Robin Hood Court in St Andrew's parish, where Simon Burr and John Cuddenham, both described as 'musiconer', and at least three trumpeters also lived. There was a John Pursell in Shoe Lane. The attraction of this area for musicians lay in the opportunities for private and public music, with subsequent payment, provided by the Inns of Court and their members. Given their close association with Sir William Davenant and the need to be in easy reach of the Cockpit, Locke and Henry Purcell senior are most likely to have been living in this part too, but there is no record of either of their marriages or the births of their children.

Their friendship could be explained by their working together for Davenant, but it seems to me to be of longer date. Neither of them appears in John Playford's list of recommended teachers of music in London included in his *Musicall Banquet* of 1651, unless they are part of the 'Cum multis aliis' at the end of the two lists, divided into 'For the Voyce or Viole' and 'For the Organ or Virginall'. Several of those who were to take part in the operas at the Cockpit are there: the Colemans, Henry Lawes, Captain Cooke, John Harding and George Hudson.

Matthew Locke's life demonstrates the vicissitudes of the professional musician at this period. Trained at Exeter, in the cathedral school, he spent some time abroad 'in the Low Countries' in the late 1640s, presumably at the exiled court. He returned to England and contributed most of the music to the masque *Cupid and Death* by James Shirley, acted before the Portuguese ambassador in 1653. The rest of the music was by Christopher Gibbons, son of Orlando, the Elizabethan composer. Gibbons lived in the parish of St Clement Danes, where he had moved from St Giles, Cripplegate (another favourite parish with musicians), after his marriage to Elizabeth Filbridge and where their children were registered: Orlando in 1656, Christopher and Elizabeth, twins, in the following year and Mary the next; Ann is listed in June 1660, just when the restored King was appointing Gibbons organist and musician in ordinary for the virginals over supper in Baynard's Castle.

Locke was still at Exeter when Charles I was forced to execute Strafford in 1641, setting in motion the forces that led to the Civil War and the republicanism of the next twenty years. He could have expected a cathedral or court appointment to follow his training. Instead, with the rest of the church and court musicians, he was thrown on the world to make a living as best he could. Some of them went over to the parliament, and trumpeters found it easy to get places in the army. Some, like Matthew Locke's 'dear friend' Christopher Simpson, were taken into private homes as tutors and providers of domestic music. Simpson never forgot his patron, Sir Robert Bolles of Leicestershire, and his 'affording me a cheerful maintenance when the iniquity of the times had reduced me, with many others in that common calamity, to a condition of needing it'.[4]

Music, of course, didn't die. In fact, the closure of the avenues of court and church can be interpreted as having spread it wider and deeper, as Thomas Fuller understood, writing of the musicians in 1661 in his *Worthies*: 'Right glad I am when music was lately shut out of our churches . . . it hath since been harboured and welcomed in the halls, parlours and chambers of the primest persons of this nation.' The rapidly expanding middle class, whose new money came from trade, were anxious for all the bourgeois refinements. Their sons and daughters were taught, both at home and at school, to dance and sing and play a variety of instruments, all of which required the employment of professional teachers. Girls' schools in particular had a high standard of musical training. Robert Perwich's school at Hackney, which educated eight hundred girls during the Commonwealth years, included among its music masters Edward Coleman for the voice, John Rogers for the lute, William Gregory for the lyra viol, Albertus Brian for the organ and harpsichord and also Simon Ives, who with William Lawes had composed the great masque *The Triumph of Peace*, acted before Charles I and Henrietta Maria in 1634. Locke certainly seems to have done some teaching, and it seems safe to assume, from his being appointed master of choristers at Westminster Abbey on the Restoration, that Henry Purcell senior had a reputation as a teacher as well as a singer. It's also a fair assumption that he was Chapel or cathedral trained to be given such an appointment.

John Harding, who had taken part in *The Siege of Rhodes* in 1656, had been in the Abbey choir before its closure and was among those petitioning the Council of State that they should be paid their arrears as they had wives and children in want. The petition was signed by all those of 'the late Chore' resident in town. Harding was among the first musicians to be appointed to the Chapel Royal on 16 June 1660.

Another member of the opera's original cast to be given a royal post was Gregory Thorndall. He was born in New Windsor in 1618, the son of a tailor, Walter; by 1648 Walter had moved to Wapping, where he apprenticed another of his sons to a member of the Drapers' Company. Gregory Thorndall most likely received his training either in or through St George's Chapel in Windsor.

On 5 August 1624, also in New Windsor, a Henry Purcell, son of Francis, was baptised, to be followed on 25 February 1627 by his brother Thomas. Five more children are recorded in the registers: Francis in 1630, Hester and Anne in 1633, and, after a long gap, John in 1639 and Sara in 1642. In 1655 Francis, probably the father, died. There are no other Purcell entries except an isolated one in 1730.[5] The family seems to have moved to Windsor in the early 1620s and to have left before the Restoration. If these are the forebears of the composer, then it's most likely that his father at least received his musical education in or through St George's Chapel. The records of choristers are unfortunately both sparse and patchy, but the organist and master of the choristers who would have been responsible for Henry Purcell senior's training was either Nathaniel Giles or his successor in 1632, William Child. Having been reappointed to Windsor as organist in 1660 and joined the Chapel Royal as both composer for the wind instruments and organist, Child was well placed to put in a good word for his boys. He might have continued to teach them in the Commonwealth, when he's said to have retired to a farmhouse near Windsor.[6]

Giles, as master of the choristers in both the Chapel Royal and St George's, had powers to seek out boys for the King's service and for Windsor, where he was to be 'Governer of the same tenne children or choristers to be instructed taught and brought up in the knowledge of Musicke that is to say in singing pricksongs descant and such as be apt to the instruments.' He was to supply them with 'good and sufficient meate drinke apparrel bedding and lodging'. It would have been easy for him too to transfer particularly promising boys to the Chapel Royal.[7]

Thomas Purcell must have received the same early education as his brother. If he joined the King in exile for at least part of the time, this could account for the emphasis on the violin in his appointment as composer, since it was the King's favourite instrument – a taste that had been encouraged, if not picked up, while in France.

I have been unable to find any records which give a clue to Francis Purcell's means of livelihood. Windsor was an obvious place to be for anyone who had court connections or aspirations. The lack of any other Purcell entries in registers or documents reinforces the impression that he had come to the town to take advantage of the opportunities it offered, and had not been born there. The Thorndall family's limited appearance in the records of a place where a tailor could prosper may be interpreted in the same way.

St George's Chapel wasn't the only source of music in the town. According to the Chamberlain's Accounts, there seem to have been town waits and trumpeters who provided music on civic occasions, such as the Mayor's Feast, and organs were 'set up' at the town hall. But it was a deeply divided town – divided politically from the royal castle and chapel which suffered much damage during the Commonwealth. It was certainly no place for royalists to linger after the outbreak of the rebellion, when Henry Purcell senior would have been sixteen and his brother Thomas thirteen.

When he published his *Sonatas of Three Parts* in 1683, Henry Purcell junior, then aged twenty-four, had as frontispiece a portrait of himself looking like a grim forty-year-old (more indeed like his father or uncle), with a coat of arms underneath. It must be assumed that he had a right to these arms. Few musicians had such a right: Byrd, Gibbons and the Mundys are the best known among the previous generation. It's worth examining, then, whom and what he was laying claim to.

The arms are those of the Purcells of Shropshire, granted to Thomas Purcell, father of a member of parliament for Shrewsbury, in 1597. The three boars' heads derive from the French *pourceau* (a boar). The family's fortunes in the time of Elizabeth I were founded in the wool trade and they were closely connected with the Drapers' Company. During the sixteenth and early seventeenth centuries the Purcells spread into Wales, Staffordshire, Berkshire and London. Mostly they remained Roman Catholic, although the Welsh branch seems to have gradually conformed to the state religion.

In 1571 Richard Purcell had acquired the manor of Overgarther, straddling the border between Shropshire and Montgomery, from the impoverished Edward, Lord Stafford. The manor and its lands included several hamlets in both counties. By 1660, when the last parliament of the Commonwealth was elected, this part of the family was Protestant, for John Purcell Esquire stood for Montgomery County with, as his stable-mate for Montgomery Borough, Sir Thomas Middleton, who had led a recent but failed royalist rebellion in the region.[8] John Purcell was elected again to Charles II's first parliament after the Restoration. He may be the John Purcell who turns up in Westminster parochial records about this time. He was also entitled to the Purcell arms. He sat on several committees and was related to Sir Henry Herbert, master of the revels. The state papers record his death in 1665.

By the beginning of the seventeenth century the main English branch consisted of Edward of Onslow, Shropshire, who died in 1607, Humphrey, his brother, who held lands in Staffordshire and Berkshire and died in 1608, and Thomas, an unmarried attorney of the King's Bench who lived in London and Berkshire, all recorded in the *Heralds' Visitations* of Shropshire and Staffordshire. Edward was succeeded by his eldest son, another Edward, while two of the younger sons, Thomas and Richard, were apprenticed to London drapers. Humphrey's only surviving son, Francis, who inherited the Berkshire property, married and lived in Burghfield near Reading. His wife was Mary Gifford, daughter of Richard Gifford of Chillingham and therefore closely related to the Charles Gifford who was instrumental in rescuing Charles II after the battle of Worcester and helping to conceal him in one of the family's properties, White Ladies in Shropshire. Afterwards he joined the King in exile.

There has often been speculation about Henry Purcell senior's religion. Charles II accepted the offer of refuge from Catholics because, it was said, he knew that they were used to concealing people, principally priests. Humphrey Purcell had been part of a Catholic enclave in Berkshire, which included lands held by the Earl of Shrewsbury (whose son Francis, Lord Talbot, was part of the King's escape party too) and the Plowden family. By the beginning of the war this enclave had largely dissolved and Francis Purcell had moved to Staffordshire, where his children were brought up by their Gifford grandparents. Two of his sons, Francis and Walter, fled abroad in the early 1640s and spent some time at the English College in Rome, where Francis died. At least one of their sisters was a nun.

Both Edward and the elder Francis were heavily fined as papists and recusants, and some of their property was sequestrated during the Commonwealth period. The family continued to practise their faith. At least two Shropshire Purcells were educated at Lisbon College in the 1690s, and several were buried in the Catholic cemetery at White Ladies. Yieldfields Hall, where the Staffordshire Purcells lived, was said to have a chapel and a resident priest.

It's unlikely that a young man of twenty-four, in the royal service, would have invented such a dangerous pedigree for himself merely out of snobbery, and such behaviour is entirely at odds with all the testimony of friends, which emphasised Purcell's unassuming 'humble' demeanour and his hatred of pride.[9] At the same time it is hard to believe that Henry senior would have been appointed master of the choristers at Westminster Abbey if he had been a known Roman Catholic. Thomas's position is more equivocal since he was groom to first the Queen Mother and then the Queen, both Catholics, at Somerset House (also known as the Savoy Palace). He appears on a list of Henrietta Maria's retainers paid off at her death. Matthew Locke too, who became organist in her chapel, was either already or became a Catholic; at least, in his *Observations* of 1672 he made no effort to deny the charge levied against him by Thomas Salmon: 'Thou smellst of popish superstition . . . O Brat of Rome.'

Thomas Purcell and his wife, Katherine, must have been living in Somerset House from 1663 to at least 1668, when four of their children, Charles, Matthew, William and Katherine, were baptised in St Mary Le Strand. The building had needed restoring completely under the supervision of Henrietta Maria herself, so that by 1665

Each part with just proportion graced,
And all to such advantage placed,
That the fair view her window yields,

The town, the river and the fields,
Entering, beneath us we descry,
And wonder how we came so high.[10]

Thomas already had a son Francis, and his eldest son was named Edward, like his brother Henry's eldest son, which makes another connection with the Shropshire Purcells. Had Thomas been a Roman Catholic, his children would presumably have been baptised in the Savoy Chapel at Somerset House. It looks as though he was trying to keep his religious sheet clean by these baptisms in the parish church.

As a resident in a royal palace Thomas paid no hearth tax or poor rates. Henry and his wife, Elizabeth, did, although they rented their house in the Little Almonry, otherwise known as Great Almonry South, 'by virtue of his place' as a singing man of the Abbey. The new prebendaries had been installed in July 1660, but the choir had to wait until the following February. Henry Purcell senior was among the first to be made a singing man, or lay clerk, and master of the choristers. Instead of his installation fee of five shillings he donated the still extant Treasurer's book in which the accounts were kept. As yet there were no boys for him to be master of and one of his jobs must have been to find some. Perhaps his eldest son, Edward, was among them. Reckoning back from the information on his tombstone, he must have been born in 1655 and just about old enough for the choir; the usual age of admission was nine, but these were desperate times. At least four more children had been born after Edward: Joseph, Charles, Henry and Daniel, but no records of their baptisms have come to light. Joseph and Charles probably came next after Edward and before Henry (who must have been born in 1659 to be twenty-four in 1683). Daniel probably followed in 1660 or 1661. Katherine was baptised in the Abbey in March 1662, the first child to be christened there since 1645. The rubric at the head of the baptismal register, whose earlier entries seem to have been made up by Philip Tynchare, the chaunter, from a few remaining fragments of a previous book, says that he had also included private baptisms 'of the children of parents as were members of the church or dwelt within the verge thereof'. Daniel's birth must have occurred before the family were installed in the Little Almonry, or surely his baptism would have been recorded in the registers of either the Abbey or St Margaret's, Westminster. The exact date of the family's move into the Little Almonry is hard to pin down. The entry for the year 1661–2 in the poor rates has Henry as simply 'Percell', as if he were so newly arrived his first name and indeed his status were still unknown. Unless the family were in lodgings and not paying rates, they weren't living in St Margaret's parish before this date. Henry Cooke and John Harding, however, were there from no later than the mid-1650s.

Another fact that makes it almost certain that Henry Purcell senior was a Protestant is that his son Henry has a Protestant godfather: John Hingestone, organist to Oliver Cromwell and music teacher of Cromwell's daughters. When he died in 1684, Hingestone left an elaborate will in which, among many bequests, including several to other godsons, he left five pounds 'also to my godson Henry Pursell (son of Elizabeth Pursell)'.[11] His need to make precise which Henry Purcell he meant implies that there was at least one other with whom there might be confusion. It's possible that Thomas had a son called Henry. He and his brother, after all, had an Edward, a Charles and a Katherine apiece, so why not a Henry? The St Mary Le Strand register is missing for the period 1669–80, when such an entry would have been recorded.

The Abbey muniments show the gradual restoration of the services. Christopher Gibbons was paid for tuning the organs and John Playford for a set of Mr Barnard's *Collections of Services and Anthems* and a quire of ruled paper, so that Henry Purcell as copyist could make another set for the boys. Playford also had to supply nine copies of the Book of Common Prayer for the chaunter and the choirmen. Traditionally the master of the choristers had the chamber over the great gate of the Almonry for the boys, and Sarah Spede was employed as 'bedmaker and sweeper of the schollers chamber'. Their master had to supply them with service books and clothes and keep them fed.

By April 1661, in time for the coronation, Henry Purcell must have made up his complement of boys, and he was paid one pound in May for their singing at the burial of the Duke of Cambridge, in addition to his own fee of seven shillings and tenpence. The singing men also had a share of the money from showing visitors the monuments, a practice which had continued even in the Commonwealth period. He was now receiving two annual stipends, and a series of additional fees for copying, for weddings and burials, for the choristers as well as himself, and monument moneys. His signature in the Abbey Treasurer's book shows that he spelt his name 'Purcill'. The collectors of the hearth tax spelt it 'Peirshall'. His income was further augmented, late in 1662, when the ageing court musician Angelo Notari, who had originally come from Italy in the service of Prince Henry as early as 1612, asked to be allowed an assistant for his place of musician in ordinary for the lutes and voices 'because of his unabilities to execute that employment without', presumably splitting his annual salary of forty pounds with the elder Purcell.

It's inconceivable, in view of how influence was exercised in the seventeenth century, that Henry Purcell senior and Angelo Notari were unrelated to each other by close ties of, at the very least, friendship. Notari was a Venetian whose work was first published in England in 1613. He therefore provides a direct link between the younger Purcell and the Italian composers, particularly Monteverdi, whom Purcell so much admired. Notari disappears with the dissolution of the court in 1642, but before that he had been responsible for training 'singing boys' for the royal service, and Henry or Thomas Purcell could have been among them.

The Purcell family were in need of extra money after Katherine's birth in early 1662. Fortunately, the payments for the new post were backdated to summer 1660, though this may have been only for Notari. *The Siege of Rhodes* was revived and revised by Sir William Davenant again in June 1661 and since Henry Purcell still appears in the cast list of the 1663 printed version 'double parted' with Thomas Blagrave in the role of Mustapha, some money must have come his way from this. Blagrave was also a member of the Chapel Royal, as Henry and Thomas Purcell seem to have been, since they appear on a list of Chapel members exempt from paying the tax known as 'lay subsidy', granted in 1661.

In seeking boys to fill the Abbey choir Henry Purcell would have been in competition with Henry Cooke, who was similarly engaged in boosting the complement of both the royal chapel and the King's Private Music. Cooke had a patent which allowed him to take boys from any cathedral or collegiate church 'or any other place within his Majesty's realm of England'. John Hill stood in at first for the missing Abbey choristers on his cornet. Matthew Locke in his *Present Practice of Musick Vindicated* of 1673 alleged that it took a whole year of supplying the upper parts in the Chapel Royal with cornets and 'men's feigned voices there not being one lad for all that time capable of singing the part readily'. This seems a little exaggerated, and surely by the time of the coronation on 23 April the two choirs were in place. Henry Cooke claimed money for the choristers from Michaelmas 1660. Both Pepys and Evelyn describe the ceremony at length and with, in Pepys's case, almost hysterical excitement. It began with a grand entertainment for the city in the form of a procession with pageants. For the concerts with music by Matthew Locke on the day before the actual ceremony in the Abbey all the musicians had special scarlet liveries. Evelyn makes no mention of the twenty-four violin band of the Private Music being part of the music in the Abbey. Perhaps he was affronted by them. Pepys too, who had difficulty hearing the music because of the great noise, only mentions the violins playing at the banquet in Westminster Hall after the ceremonies were over.

The impact of the occasion, both the intense preparations for it and the day itself, on a household of young children whose father was one of the chief protagonists can be imagined. Edward, and perhaps Charles and Joseph too, would have been old enough to be taken to see some of the procession and pageantry, and may, like their mother, have had new clothes for the celebrations. There must have been a conflict of interest for Purcell senior: was he to be part of the Chapel Royal, in all their finery, or of the Abbey? I think the Abbey won. He would have been needed to direct the choristers, and would thus have been among those on the north side of the Abbey, not part of the smaller group on a dais in the south.

The coronation was the most spectacular event for over thirty years. Pepys wrote that after it he could shut his eyes to every thing 'of state or shewe being sure never to see the like again in this world'. It was a brilliant piece of propaganda, emphasising the power and popularity of the restored monarchy, although Charles was already feeling the financial pinch, and doubts about his lifestyle were starting to be expressed. Aside from the brilliance of the spectacle, music was clearly central to the whole extended pageant; beginning at 9.30 in the morning, it was to last well into the night. The music symbolically looked both back to the great days of Elizabeth and James and forward and out towards Italy and France. The anthems, many of whose texts are still used at coronations (*I was glad* and *Zadok the priest*, for example), were set by several composers, including Henry Lawes, who had composed the music for Milton's *Comus* and, now in his sixties, was the most respected of the older generation of musicians. Cooke was responsible for most of the setting of the service: the Epistle, Gospel and Nicene Creed. On at least two occasions the choir and instrumental music were divided after the Italian style, the gentlemen of the Chapel Royal on the south side being answered by the instrumentalists on the north.

The following month Pepys recorded the visit of 'Captain Cooke, Mr Gibbons and others of the King's Musique' to the Earl of Sandwich, when they presented him with 'some songs and Symphonys which were performed very finely' and for which they were no doubt given a substantial present. Perhaps Thomas or Henry Purcell was among the company. In spite of his official position, Cooke was always ready to take part in extra musical events, such as the visit to Sandwich of a semi-official nature or the spontaneous happening Pepys records in July 1661.

Cooke called on Thomas Townshend at the Great Wardrobe after a birthday dinner for Sandwich and went with Pepys and Townshend to a tavern where Cooke sang for them: 'without doubt he hath the best manner of singing in the world'.

If Pepys's experience is anything to go by, the court musicians took as many opportunities as they could for earning money privately, either by teaching or by performing, and though he doesn't mention Henry Purcell senior, it seems unlikely, with such a large family to support and royal wages so often in arrears, that Purcell wouldn't have looked for similar ways of supplementing his income. The King had been voted what seemed a sufficient and even generous sum to run his affairs, but the means to raise it, the hearth tax, was unpopular: the money was slow to come in and never reached the projected total. John Playford in his 1662 edition of his *Introduction to the Skill of Musick* wrote with approval of Charles II's 'bountiful augmentation' of the annual allowance of the gentlemen of the chapel, but by the middle of the 1660s John Hingestone was telling Pepys that the royal musicians were ready to starve. Pepys and his wife had lessons in singing, dancing and playing a whole range of instruments, and Pepys learned composition as well. Many of their teachers were or became royal musicians, for example John Goodgroome, John Birchensha and even Dr William Child.

That Henry Purcell senior engaged in musical activity outside the Abbey and the court can be inferred from a composition of his that survives, collected by John Playford in his 1667 volume of *The Musical Companion*:

Sweet tyranness, I now resign
My heart for ever more tis thine.
Those magic arts force me,
My arts, to slavery.
What need I care? Thy beauty flings
Such flow'ry smiling charms would conquer Kings.

It doesn't seem likely that, although this is the only generally known example of his work, it was the only piece he ever wrote. Playford thought well enough of it to include it in the 1672 edition in a full three-part version.[12]

Henry senior was unequivocally a professional musician. His brother Thomas, however, is a very different matter. Following his initial political appointment as groom of the robes he soon began to amass a whole series of other, apparently musical, positions connected with the court. While I have no evidence to doubt his musical competence, his extraordinary rise seems to me to spring from other causes and talents. From the first he heads the list of musicians to be paid from the Treasury and to be kept in time of retrenchment. Henry Lawes died in October 1662 and Thomas Purcell was appointed to his place of musician in ordinary by royal warrant, yet if the musical achievements of Lawes and his successor are compared in terms of composition and publication, it's hard to see how Thomas could have been thought fit to fill the 'camlet gown guarded with black velvet and furred, the velvet doublet and damask jacket' that went with the job. Lawes's post of composer to the Private Music was given more understandably to Dr Charles Coleman. The only unequivocally acknowledged extant composition by Thomas Purcell is a single burial chant.

Inevitably, the older generation of pre-Commonwealth musicians was coming to an end. On 7 March 1662 Angelo Notari sent a letter to the Clerk of the Great Wardrobe asking for his money to be paid to the bearer, his landlord, because he was 'very ill and weak and not able to come to the wardrobe', but he didn't die until December 1663, when Henry Purcell senior came into full possession of their joint post. Two months later Purcell himself missed a wedding at the Abbey. Perhaps he was already ill. In July 1664 he made the usual cross against his name for his share of the monument moneys. In August someone else made the entry: 'Widow Pursell'. Henry had died on the 11th, just after his fortieth birthday.

He was buried in the east cloister of the Abbey on the 13th as 'Gentleman of His Majesty's Chapel Royal and Master of the Boyes of Westminster . . . near Mr Lawes'; he would have been buried at night as was the custom, with his peers supplying the music and Christopher Gibbons at the organ. His positions were soon filled. Goodgroome, Pepys's tutor and already a member of the Chapel Royal, was given the place Purcell had shared with Notari, although he had to wait until 1669 before his arrears of livery were paid. Thomas Blagrave, Purcell's double part in *The Siege of Rhodes* and one of the royal violins, became a singing man at the Abbey and master of the choristers.

Henry had died intestate, which indicates a failure to recognise the seriousness of an illness, possibly more chronic than acute. Elizabeth Purcell was granted probate on 7 October, but she was required to provide an inventory before 30 November to the Peculiar of St Peter's, Westminster. If she indeed complied with this, it has vanished. The rate books of St Margaret's, Westminster, recorded his death under the entries for the Great Almonry with the sinister term 'ob' (short for *obit*) and the rates were assessed, and paid, at five shillings instead of six.

Elizabeth Purcell had lost not only her husband and the greater part of her income, but her home as well, which went with the job of singing man. She now had six children under the age of ten to support. It would be hard to underestimate the effects of their father's death on them and her, even in an age when death was a constant presence.

· 2 ·

A Child of the Chapel

FROM THE RATE books it looks as if Elizabeth moved just after Christmas. She didn't go far – round the corner, as it were, to Tothill (or Tuttle) Street, where she paid four shillings in rates, which indicates a modest house, neither great nor small.[1] The royal service's only pension was in the form of unpaid arrears and benevolences, for the dependants of deceased musicians, and there are records of payments to her of twenty pounds in 1668 and 1671. The Abbey fees dried up in December.

Elizabeth could, of course, have moved right away. That she didn't indicates that she wanted to stay close to her husband's places of employment in the hope that one day some of her sons might step into his shoes, according to contemporary practice. She was also close to her brother-in-law, Thomas, and his family at Somerset House, and to her friends among the musicians, including Henry junior's godfather John Hingestone, who might be expected to do something for him.

Hingestone – 'my auld acquaintance' as Pepys calls him, meaning from the days of Cromwell, a term he also uses for Captain Silas Taylor – was either a great survivor or indispensable to the reopening and reinstatement of the royal chapels. He was among the first to be appointed, along with Locke, Captain Cooke and Christopher Gibbons. Organist to Cromwell, in 1660 he became tuner and repairer of the organs, virginals and wind instruments to Charles II. Pepys, who calls him 'organist', got him to go to the Dog Tavern and provide a bass part to Pepys's setting of the psalm *It is decreed*. Before the Restoration, when he wasn't at Hampton Court instructing the Protector's daughters, Hingestone seems to have lived in lodgings near or in St James's Park, where Sir Roger L'Estrange joined in a musical evening in the 'little low room'; the company was suddenly discomfited by the silent appearance of Cromwell himself. The location fits well with his being godfather to the infant Henry.

Among his several godsons was the son of his fellow royal musician Humphrey Madge, a wind player, but his favourite was Richard Graham, who was trained in the law and for whom Hingestone obtained the freelance post of solicitor to the newly revived Corporation for Regulating the Art and Science of Music in 1663. Hingestone's will shows how close the family of musicians was, particularly those engaged in the royal service. He leaves gold rings to them all, as other musicians do later, with the rider that they shall attend the funeral so ensuring a good musical send-off. His books and instruments are distributed among his colleagues: Will Gregory, Morgan Harris, Ralph Courtville, 'my beloved friend Mr Thomas Blagrave'. For the music school at Oxford he has a picture of 'my ever honoured master Orlando Gibbons'.

By entering the Chapel Royal musicians became, whatever their position at birth, gentlemen, a status constantly insisted on in class-conscious seventeenth-century society. On Edward Purcell's tombstone over fifty years later and in Daniel's entry in the Magdalen College Registers their father is identified as 'Gentleman of the Chapel Royal'. Although he had died while they were still very young, Henry Purcell senior and his achievements had made a lasting impression on his children.

Henry junior was about five at his father's death. In the late twentieth century a child of that age would probably be judged too young to be deeply and permanently affected, but in earlier centuries children were expected to grow up faster and be aware earlier. Mozart gave his first public performance at six and attempted to write his first opera at four. Even girls, if their parents could afford it, were sent to school to learn to read as soon as 'capable'. The prodigious Susanna Perwich was ready for the serious study of music by the time her parents opened their Hackney School when she was seven.

Unfortunately, no one thought to record even an anecdote about Purcell's childhood. Some things, however, may be inferred and are certainly worth speculating on, since it's these early years which are the most important influence on any artist. In a missing letter from Thomas Tudway to his son which Sir John Hawkins drew on for his *History of Music* Tudway, who was a child of the Chapel from about 1664 to 1668 and claimed to have known the young Purcell, wrote of his 'commendable ambition of exceeding every one of his time'.[2] It's not, I think, too farfetched to see the roots of this ambition in his position as Henry Purcell II, son of a revered and lost father whom he should, and would, try to excel.

His father's death must have had a profound psychological and practical impact. If he was admitted to the Chapel Royal between about 1667 and 1668, his musical education, in a house inevitably devoted to and filled with music, must have begun by late 1664 – not necessarily in any formal sense (though with Mozart and the young J.S. Bach in mind, that may already have been under way), but at least by a kind of osmosis through being in a musical family. The move to Tothill Street out of the immediate neighbourhood of the singing men's houses of the Almonry must have seemed a kind of exile from music itself.

Fortunately, there were plenty at hand to take on his education, and it's entirely possible that Elizabeth Purcell herself might have been able to make a significant contribution. She had grown up during the Commonwealth, when much emphasis had been placed on education, especially that of girls, for whom music was of prime importance. It looks as though, since she outlived him by thirty-five years, Elizabeth was younger than her husband. Certainly she must have had energy, determination and common sense to provide as well for her family as their subsequent positions prove.

In the contemporary accounts of Anthony à Wood, Thomas Ford and others both Christopher Gibbons and John Blow are said to have been

Purcell's masters, yet when he entered the Chapel Royal as a boy, Henry Cooke was master of the choristers and remained so until 1672, when he was succeeded by Pelham Humphreys, who would have overseen Purcell's final year. The references to Gibbons and Blow must therefore be to teaching outside the Chapel Royal either before Purcell was admitted or in parallel with his education there.

Boys were taken into the household of a musician as boarders, for which the term often used, by Anthony à Wood and others, was 'bred under'. Blow, for example, boarded with Captain Cooke when he left the Chapel Royal in 1665. It may be that the young Purcell boarded with Gibbons for his first musical training, which was possibly on the virginals since they were easier for a child to manage. Gibbons was organist at the Abbey (until 1666) and Chapel Royal, and musician in ordinary for the virginals of the Private Music; Blow, who according to his tombstone was also his pupil, became Abbey organist in 1668. It would seem likely that Blow taught Purcell organ from 1668 and that this was in addition to the boy's official training. In their teaching both Gibbons and Blow, and his godfather, Hingestone, concentrated on the organ and the virginals. If his study of these instruments had already begun shortly after his father's death, however, it was to be interrupted in the most dramatic way the following year when the plague began its tidal sweep through London.

Dr Gibbons, as he had become on receiving his degree from Oxford in 1664, was paid for the Abbey choristers in June 1665, but by the following month John Tynchare, the chaunter, was performing services with only five of the singing men, 'the rest of the Quire being absent by reason of plague'. They buried Sir Henry Killigrew with this depleted force, but two of them, Ambler and Corny, later died 'of the sickness'. From July to December no wax lights were used and Tynchare took the services alone by daylight.[3]

The court had already moved: first to Syon House and then on to Oxford via Hampton Court and Salisbury. Matthew Locke was among the musicians who went with them. A new schoolroom had to be prepared at Hampton Court for Captain Cooke's pupils. The town emptied. In Tothill Fields, alarmingly close to the Purcells' new home, the pest-houses were reopened. Music must have been silenced and the family probably left London for a time, although Elizabeth Purcell paid in full the extra rate levied to cover the added expenses incurred by the overseers of the poor for St Margaret's during the plague.

The court didn't return until February the following year and the Abbey choir wasn't back in full strength until April. A Katherine Purcell was buried of the sickness in St Margaret's, but both the Katherines, daughters of Thomas and Henry, seem to have survived, unless Thomas's daughter Katherine who outlived him is a second one born later, in May 1667. The all-enveloping manifestation of death, coming as it did soon after their personal loss, and the passing by their door of the parish sedan carrying those infected to the nearby pest-houses and the dead cart taking others to the pit must have made a strong impression on the whole family, especially on Henry, in whose work death recurs perpetually.

With the court fled and the official business which was its lifeblood at a standstill, Westminster presented a particularly dismal appearance. The grass-grown streets were empty even of cats and dogs, which were killed as part of the parish's attempts to curb the spread of the sickness. The dog killer was paid one pound and eight shillings for six weeks at the height of the summer and a further four shillings for burying 353 dogs. Nearly three thousand poor people were buried in the year at the expense of the parish; it also had to provide, for the humans, care and medicines, shrouds and lime, food, which became very scarce and dear, and warders to patrol the houses which were locked up, either because their occupants were dead or had fled, or because they were sick inside. The system seems to have worked well and the justices of the peace acknowledged that they had had no complaints. Every morning the raker came with his carts and doleful bell to empty the middens and clean the streets, like an image of death himself, and fires were lit in the streets to burn off putrid vapours.[4]

Pepys did complain to his diary that in July they were already burying the dead in the open in Tothill Fields and not in the New Chapel Yard, which was only for those who could 'pay dear'. By October he was recording that he had heard that all the physicians in Westminster were dead and just one apothecary was left. Throughout the summer months the sun burned down mercilessly, day after windless day, so that 'even the birds seemed to pant'.

The total expended by St Margaret's from April to November, which was when the weather changed and the plague abated, was over seventeen hundred pounds, nearly a hundred pounds more than the receipts from all sources, including not only the extra rate, but also large sums in private charity. Not everyone had left Westminster. William Smegergill, alias Caesar, the lutenist and songwriter, told Pepys he had been there 'all this while very well' and how at the height of the plague 'bold people were there to go in sport to one another's burials. And in spite to well people, would breathe in the faces (out of their windows) of well people going by.'

By December the weekly plague bill had fallen from over six thousand dead in a week at the height of the sickness to a mere three hundred. The Purcells would probably have felt able to return home in time for Christmas, as Elizabeth Pepys did; certainly Thomas and Katherine were back in Somerset House by January 1666, when their son William was baptised in St Mary Le Strand. Pepys felt it was music that had seen him through: 'I have never lived so merrily . . . as I have done this plague year . . . by the acquaintance of Mrs Knipp, Coleman and her husband and Mr Laneare; and great store of dancings we have had at my cost (which I was willing to indulge myself and wife) at my lodgings.' The Colemans, of course, were those who had been in *The Siege of Rhodes*. Both Edward and Nicholas Lanier were now royal musicians. It sounds as if the Colemans were staying with Lanier, whose family had been established at Greenwich since the first Nicholas came from Italy to take up service with Queen Elizabeth I.

Perhaps at no other period has music played such an all-pervading role in the national life; it wouldn't do so again until the inventions of modern technology, wireless and gramophone, brought it once more within the orbit of millions. The late seventeenth century saw a great increase in individual wealth and personal freedom, both of which were to be eroded in the following centuries by the revolution first in agriculture and then in the production of what are now called consumer goods, with the consequent descent of thousands into poverty and the regulated life of the factory system. By the 1660s there had been an explosion in trade, consumption and therefore manufacture, which was still home and workshop based. The yeoman freeholder was able to support himself and his family, to exercise his vote and take part in local government, either through the parish church or the council, and to have a say in regulating his profession through his guild or livery company.

The Interregnum had given the population a taste for greater equality and freedom of speech, and the responsibility for running their daily and political life. Along with this went the feeling that everyone who worked for it was entitled to a just reward and a reasonable standard of living, that culture and education weren't simply for the aristocrat. The middle class expanded with the increase in trade and consumption, and the concomitant developments in science and technology. The rise in population, which the improved standards of living were to lead to, contained the seeds for the destruction of this almost idyllic state. But that was in the future.

For people like Pepys and Roger North, a day without music was a day wasted. But even ordinary, less affluent people sang or whistled or played whatever instrument they could lay their hands on. Singing and dancing were part of almost every social occasion, whether in the home, the tavern or the music room, on the water or in the open air. There were private and public music meetings and music was part of all theatrical performances, whether sacred or secular. The general population had the energy, the imagination and the time to practise and take part in a diversity of musical productions to a reasonably high standard.[5]

There were, of course, dud performers and performances, and Pepys is quick to notice them, but he is prepared to record the good even when the music is only from, for example, a solo bagpipe. He makes no distinction between what is now the professional and the amateur, expecting the highest skill whether the occasion is private or public, impromptu or rehearsed.

The Great Fire of the year following the plague can have affected the Purcell family only as a source of excitement, since it was stopped in the Strand, but they might have been diverted by the sight of the Dean of Westminster, John Dolben, who had fought at Marston Moor, marching out at the head of his choristers to stem the advancing flames.[6]

Once the sickness was over, Tothill Street reverted to being a good place for boys to grow up in, as the fields were only the length of Strutton Ground away. Tothill Fields were a combination of pleasure and market garden where the boys from the King's School played games, lovers could pretend to hide and seek in the maze and fruit, including melons, was grown. Its unfortunate aspect was that the ground was marshy and inclined to flood, and there was the added danger of malaria in the summer.

Henry wasn't to be there long, though he must often have visited his mother, for the family house was close to the rooms in the rambling Palace of Whitehall where he took up his lodging with the other Chapel Royal boys. Thomas Tudway, who claimed to be a chorister at the same time as Purcell, left when his voice broke in 1668 so, presuming that they had at least a year as scholars together, Purcell must have joined him in 1666 or 1667 when he was about seven years old. Even after he left the Chapel Tudway would have continued to see Henry Purcell as he went to board at Captain Cooke's and continued to be taught by him, and perhaps this was what he meant.

Edward Purcell, the eldest of Elizabeth's children, aged about twelve, could have found service in somebody's household, possibly even the royal one, while Charles might already have been at sea. Joseph was still at school. In 1668 the house in Tothill Street seems to have been shut up for three quarters of the year. The overseer recorded Elizabeth Purcell as having died because they failed to collect more than a quarter's rate. She must have taken her remaining children and gone away for a time, but by the following year she was in residence again.

That two or three of the family were provided for, at least as far as education and board and lodging went, must have eased the financial difficulties she undoubtedly faced, even if, as has been suggested, her influential brother-in-law Thomas was able to help her out.[7] By this time he had seven children of his own, four of them under five. Payments from the court were badly in arrears, and the King himself was forced to borrow and retrench.

The choristers' education was both musical and general. They were taught to read and write, in English and Latin, as well as to play the organ, lute and violin, to sing, of course, and to copy music. Henry Cooke was paid for fire in the music room, for paper and ink, and for strings for the lutes. Money for nursing sick boys also turns up frequently in the accounts. Three of them had smallpox in 1664. When the court fled the plague, six of the boys and eight of the gentlemen accompanied it on its perambulations.

Twice a year, at Easter and Michaelmas, they were given new clothes – their winter and summer liveries – and ribbons, hats, gloves, shoes and stockings often had to be replaced. On one occasion Cooke refused to let the children appear since, because of the court's slowness in paying, they were in rags. This was due partly to the lack of royal funds and partly to the incompetence of Thomas Townshend, the deputy at the Great Wardrobe, who had to be constantly urged to make up his accounts and pay out on them. In October 1667 things were so bad that Henry Cooke was given permission to arrest and prosecute Townshend, 'who hath often had notice but hath taken up no course to satisfy the petitioner'.

The children's uniforms were in a sumptuous scarlet, their cloaks lined with satin in summer and velvet in winter and their suits trimmed with silver and silk lace. The boys had worsted stockings for ordinary wear and silk for ceremonial, two cuffs laced for best and four plain. They had six new shirts and half-shirts a year, and six handkerchiefs. When his voice broke and he left the Chapel, each boy was given a double set of clothing.

Once a year in April the boys went to Windsor for six days to take part with the other musicians in the garter ceremonies. The full Chapel complement was twelve, but membership changed regularly as boys left for one reason or the other. Writing on music later in the century, Roger North found the system very unsatisfactory, since a boy would be taken up for the quality of his voice alone, regardless of his musical training, and he felt that boys were only just learning to be competent musicians when it was time for them to leave. He floated the revolutionary idea that it would be better to have older girls for the soprano parts, but withdrew it hastily on the grounds that it was against scripture.[8]

The journey from Worcester or Lincoln or Chester in a coach with a new master must have seemed frighteningly long to some of the smaller boys. They probably suffered badly from homesickness until they settled into the companionship of the group and began to find their way about the scatter of buildings and gardens that was more like a little town than a single palace. At least Henry Purcell, who was in a sense returning to his father's second home and had his family close by, was spared that. He belonged to the third generation of children. The first had included John Blow and Pelham Humphreys, who had left in 1665 and were now moving into places of authority. The second was Thomas Tudway's group, which included William Turner and James Hart, both of whom became gentlemen of the Chapel; Tudway moved to Windsor and then to King's College, Cambridge. Of Purcell's own contemporaries the closest to him were Thomas Haywood, also later a gentleman of the Chapel Royal, and Henry Hall, born in Windsor and ultimately organist of Hereford, who wrote of their friendship begun as children:

I loved thee living, and admire thee dead.
Apollo's harp at once our souls did strike,
We learnt together but not learnt alike,
Though equal care our master might bestow
Yet only Purcell e'er shall equal Blow.[9]

Hall's lines mean that although Cooke was responsible for their general musical education, he and Purcell at least were taught organ by Blow. Since Hall left the Chapel only a few months before Purcell, they spent six formative years together – and indeed longer because Hall went to board with Pelham Humphreys when his Chapel service ended.

The master of the children was paid thirty pounds a year for each child to cover food, laundry, board and teaching, though the Latin lessons sometimes seem to have been an extra charge on the Wardrobe. When Hall and Purcell joined, Captain Cooke was master. It's hard to form an estimate of his musical abilities; he clearly had a good voice, although Pepys noted on one occasion that he 'could discern Captain Cooke to overdo his part at singing which I never did before'. Perhaps Cooke felt it was necessary to keep himself in the royal ear.

He was also a prolific composer, but, as Tudway says, in the older, graver style and although he provided much of the music for the coronation, the King was soon looking over his shoulder to France and Italy for the more lively style he was used to in exile. Charles's attention span was short. He became fidgety unless constantly diverted and to him the long sonorities of the English service, with its unaccompanied anthems, must have sounded not much more interesting than Puritan psalm-singing. In 1664 Pelham Humphreys, the most promising of the Chapel graduates of the first post-Restoration wave, was sent to Italy and Paris to study styles there; he returned in 1667 as an 'absolute monsieur'. Pepys records Humphreys's contempt for the old musicians, including Thomas Blagrave and Charles's new find from France, Louis Grabu, the master of the Private Music, who was appointed like Humphreys to one of Nicholas Lanier's places in 1666. 'Little Pelham's' travels had rather gone to his head, but Pepys admitted he was a fine musician and admired his compositions. Pelham had soon introduced instrumental symphonies and ritornellos to break up the vocal line between the verses, though Cooke had begun the process as early as September 1662, when Pepys heard him singing an anthem 'with symphonies' in the Chapel Royal.

According to Tudway, who explained this revolution to his patron Robert Harley, Earl of Oxford, fifty years later, Charles didn't insist on the new style at every service, only when he himself was present on Sunday mornings and 'at great feasts and offerings'. However, 'the old masters of music viz Dr Child, Dr Gibbons, Mr Law, the organists to His Majesty hardly knew how to comport themselves with these new-fangled ways but proceeded in their composition in the old style'. The younger composers, among them Tudway, were deliberately fostered by the King 'so that every month at least and afterwards oftener they produced something new in this kind' and 'followed their youthful fancies . . . for otherwise it was in vain to hope to please His Majesty'.[10]

Cooke certainly encouraged his boys in composition, and several of them were capable of writing anthems good enough to be performed in the Chapel Royal during Blow's and Humphreys's period as choristers. As the lists of anthems and services which were copied at this time show, they were required to master both the old and the new styles and must have followed the debate intently. Pepys thought that innovation could go too far and that sometimes Humphreys's anthems were nothing but instrumental music for the voice and the words, with their meaning, were lost.

This wasn't the only conflict that would have impinged on the Chapel pages. The appointment of Louis Grabu put the resident John Banister's nose out of joint and split the Private Music for a time into worrying factions. Banister had been one of the City musicians, the London waits, and had come to prominence in the Commonwealth. He had played in *The Siege of Rhodes*, that extraordinary seminal production from which all the composers and performers (except of course, Catherine Coleman, for whom no such opportunity existed) were taken into royal service at the Restoration, and, like Humphreys, he had been sent to France to study, principally how the violin band was managed.

Charles's passion for the fiddle and its exponents 'the fideldedies' is well documented during his exile by his attempts to engage violinists even when he had no money to pay them. The violin wasn't a new instrument to Britain, as Peter Holman's study *Four and Twenty Fiddlers* ably demonstrates, but, as North made clear in his musical memoirs, there was still an argument going on in Britain about the relative merits of the viol, considered a more serious and aristocratic instrument, and the violin, thought more 'brisk and airy', like the Prince who promoted its use. The amazing skill of the German performer Thomas Baltzar, who came to England in the mid-1650s, opened many people's ears to the instrument's potential and it rapidly gained in popularity, especially for dancing and in the teaching of the voice, gradually ousting the lute.

The King also disliked the fancy, or fantasy, the composition for viol ensemble held to be the most suitable form in which to express grief or loss. Part of this must have been due to his own restlessness, which Pepys observed on several occasions. If he wasn't himself dancing, he liked to beat time with his hand, even to the anthem in Chapel and often, North says, standing up. He had reinstituted public royal dining and this too had to be accompanied by music. Indeed, it's safe to say that Whitehall Palace was filled with the sounds of voice or instrument in some part of it all day and a great deal of the night, since there was both the Private Music and the Chapel Music, as well as other performers who might be brought in from outside or abroad. Anthems, symphonies, secular solos and dance music followed each other in private rooms and public places. The King's own favourites were the solo love song and the violin band.

On his return from France in 1662 John Banister was authorised to set up a select band of twelve violins chosen from the royal musicians, which was to accompany the King on his journey to Portsmouth to meet the new Queen, Catherine of Braganza, and then to develop this group for the royal entertainment. It replaced an earlier one in which Matthew Locke was involved, known to Pepys as 'Singleton's Musique'. The creation of this original group had caused friction among the musicians because it had been admitted to the Privy Chamber, where previously there had been only lutes and voices. In revenge, the other musicians had barred its new members from the practice room. Now it was the turn of this group to be superseded because the King was critical of its standard of performance.

The problem seems to have been that there was no one in direct charge of either the smaller Locke group or the twenty-four violins, and Charles clearly hoped that John Banister would be able to pull things together. However, either because of incompetence or a clash of temperaments, Banister was unable to get the musicians to practise and achieve the standard of ensemble playing that Lully had managed at the French court without causing deep resentment, to the point where some of them petitioned the Lord Chamberlain against him. Charles, no doubt disappointed, and disliking dissension as he did, was presented with a solution by the timely death of Nicholas Lanier, which enabled him to promote the French–Spaniard Louis Grabu.

Banister kept his place in the violins, which eventually passed to his son, but no other promotion came his way, and after being further petitioned against by his fellow musicians on charges of embezzling large sums of money due to them, he was forced to look outside the court for the exercise of his energy and talents, to the benefit of the developing commercial concert scene. Banister didn't give up easily, however; it may indeed have been a certain irascibility of temper that caused his downfall, for as late as May 1667 he was arrested for abusing Grabu and 'several of His Majesty's musicians'.

Locke, who also has a reputation of having been rather cantankerous, was probably not sorry to see him cut down to size. His closeness to the Purcell family, borne out by Henry Purcell's lament for him on his death, would have made the young chorister well aware of the conflicts not only at court, but also, more immediate in their effect on his own musical and temperamental development, among his musical elders and superiors. North describes the tensions and jealousies of the musicians who took part in the early concert programmes, and although he may have been exaggerating a little, it's easy to see how such disputes and jockeyings for position could arise in a group of artists dependent for life or death on royal and private patronage.

Cooke, unlike Banister and Locke, seems to have been of a more equable and cheerful disposition. The story of his dying of discontent at the promotion of his ex-pupil and son-in-law Pelham Humphreys is clearly apocryphal, since Humphreys's rise began in 1666, on his return from his travels, and Cooke didn't die until six years later. The many occasions on which he was required to be their executor testify to his fellow musicians' confidence in his ability and integrity. One of the last of these was Gregory Thorndall, who, judging from his rambling nuncupative will, had deteriorated badly in his last years and was living at some kind of charitable foundation in Water Eaton, Buckinghamshire. It was Henry Cooke's dismal task to go down and draw up the inventory of Thorndall's meagre possessions, among which were a theorbo lute and some music books 'of little value'. The taking up of a boy from a poor or tradesman's family didn't always lead to the financial rewards that would support the title 'Gentleman of the Chapel Royal'.

Playford wrote of Cooke in his *Introduction to the Skill of Musick* of 1662 that under him singing

> is come to that excellency and perfection there [in the Chapel] by the skill and furtherance of that Orpheus of our time Henry Cooke,

gent and master of the children of His Majesty's Chapel, whose compositions of anthems new used . . . and by him and other gentlemen most exquisitely performed to the Glory of God and honour of our nation . . . can compare with the most famous singers of Italy, both men and women.

In his outburst against Thomas Salmon's proposals for musical reform, the *Observations* of 1672, Matthew Locke gives a good picture of what a young professional musician was expected to have mastered by the end of his training: 'Once upon a time when I was a schoolboy, had got a smackering of the syntax, could sing my part, put three or four parts together in music and play a voluntary and service on the organ (perhaps well enough for the time) I . . . thought on nothing but setting up for myself.' In addition to these skills, which he acquired from Cooke, Gibbons and Blow, Purcell was taught the less romantic but always necessary craft of tuning and repairing the full range of keyboard and wind instruments by his godfather, John Hingestone.

From time to time, in the palace and in the Chapel, he would have been in the company of his uncle Thomas, who divided his energies between Whitehall and Somerset House, sometimes carrying letters from the King to the Queen Mother while she was in residence there in April 1669. In the late 1660s or early 1670s Henry was also joined in the palace by his brother Edward, who became 'Gentleman Usher assistant Daily Wayter', as his tombstone indicates, appointed first as an assistant without fee but confirmed in 1680 as 'in ordinary'. As early as 1673 he was in charge of the arrangements for the King's various moves and progresses and allotted a hundred marks from the Treasury to pay the bills incurred in this service. It isn't clear from the sparse records whom he was assisting. It's most likely that Thomas Purcell had a hand in this appointment, as he did in those of his own son, Francis, as groom of the Privy Chamber in 1673 and his assistant as under-housekeeper at Somerset House in 1674. There were now at least four members of the family in the royal household. Edward's post was one of great intimacy with the King, for the gentlemen ushers daily waiters were in constant attendance, especially during mealtimes, and it was they who were responsible, presumably at a royal nod, for saying who might enter the royal presence and regulating when the Private Music was to come in and play. The post was initially without fee, but carried many opportunities for 'gifts'. Pepys's many entries on such presents to himself make clear that the seventeenth-century ethic regarded these not as bribes, unless obviously so, but as acceptable gratuities.

The King's coffers had become even emptier following the first war with the Dutch, which had been both humiliating and expensive. By the end of the 1660s he was borrowing from his own servants, including Thomas Purcell and Henry Cooke, who alleged that the ragged Chapel pages were unfit to walk in the streets. According to a missing document, supposedly in the hand of Pelham Humphreys,[11] Henry Purcell composed an address of the children to the King and Captain Cooke for the King's birthday on 29 May 1670, setting out their condition, but it's not obvious from the account of this document in earlier biographies whether the 'address' was a literary or a musical composition. After the secret Treaty of Dover between Charles and Louis in the same year, and the second disastrous Dutch war, finances were to improve gradually. Ways of raising money were found through such devices as new wine duties and the sale of fee farm rents, but the memory of those hard times must have taught the choristers not to put their trust in princes as far as food and clothing went. Interestingly, Thomas Purcell wasn't among the musicians attending His Majesty on his lengthy trip to Dover. When in the following spring Charles was able to get away, as he liked to do, from London and spend two and a half months at Windsor, Thomas Purcell was with him the whole time. We know Blow was there too, but there's no list of the boys to say which of them stayed the full time and which were sent home after six days like half the Chapel men. Those attending were paid extra fees.

Thomas Purcell's accumulation of jobs continued. Even before the post of under-housekeeper at Somerset House was granted he had been made composer in ordinary for the violins, in conjunction with Pelham Humphreys, on the death in 1672 of George Hudson, another of the composers involved in *The Siege of Rhodes*' first production. Humphreys was a renowned Chapel composer and it's a little surprising that he was thought to need an assistant, but an examination of the records shows that Thomas very quickly took on the job of collecting and distributing the musicians' wages and being responsible for their practice. His function was administrative and there are no records of complaints against him from his colleagues to suggest that he abused his position or ruffled tempers, although the King had to issue an order to the musicians that he and Humphreys were to be obeyed in the matter of coming to practice.

In July 1672 Captain Henry Cooke made his will; he died on the 13th and was buried, like Henry Purcell senior, in the Abbey cloisters. A wealthy man, Cooke left houses at Hampton and in the City to his daughters, his Westminster lease and land in Kent to his wife, gold, diamond jewellery, furniture and nearly a thousand pounds in unpaid wages plus over three hundred pounds due to him as Gregory Thorndall's executor. To those of the gentlemen of the Chapel 'who shall be at my burial' he left ten shillings each.

His death marks the end of an era of which Thomas Purcell was now one of the few survivors. He was already Cooke's deputy in the Corporation of Music, and he at once took his place as marshal in what would be understood today as the forerunner of the Musicians' Union, but with Equity's power to control the right to work. Though the Westminster Corporation was in many ways unimportant in itself, being an institution whose days were numbered – it ceased to function at the end of the 1670s – Thomas Purcell's succession to the popular Cooke shows how he was regarded by his fellow musicians. His election may also have reflected their perception of him as someone who, because of his standing with the King, might be able to further the Corporation's chances of inclining the royal ear in their long-running battles with the rival City of London Corporation, and unlicensed teachers and performers.[12]

One or two equivocal entries in the state papers and a series of payments in the Treasury books – some are specified as money for the King's use, while others are given no purpose, but are quite distinct from his payments either as a musician or on behalf of his fellow musicians – suggest that Thomas Purcell had a dual role. Combined with his duties in the Chapel and Private Music as tenor and composer were functions, for the King's eyes and ears alone, which involved an intimacy with William Chiffinch, the King's closet keeper and confidant, who often provided cover for Charles's secret affairs of both an amorous and a political kind. A letter of January 1674 from Chiffinch to Secretary Williamson conveys Thomas Purcell's willingness to be of service to a man the upright Evelyn described as having wormed his way into Lord Arlington's confidence and 'the secret of affairs . . . by his subtlety, dexterity and insinuation'. Williamson was himself a good musician and seems to have taken a particular interest in the royal musicians' concerns. It's not too hard to see how, with their easy access everywhere, they could help the secret service which Arlington was responsible for.

In the early 1670s Thomas Purcell leased a large house on the south side of fashionable Pall Mall,[13] six doors from Nell Gwyn and with a garden backing on to St James's Park, where the King could be observed feeding the ducks, leaving his son Francis to carry out most of the duties at Somerset House since he now had to concentrate on his responsibility for the court musicians. His son Charles took up a scholarship place as a bishop's boy at Westminster School in 1672, while at about the same time his eldest son, Edward, married Temperance Wall, granddaughter of Moses Wall, former vicar of Mickleham in Surrey. There Edward, 'gent', as he's styled in local records, lived, presumably on his wife's inheritance.[14]

A letter of slightly later date, now in the Nanki Library in Tokyo, from Thomas Purcell to the Canterbury bass John Gostling speaks of 'my son Henry' and says 'my son is composing wherein you will be chiefly concerned'. This seems to imply and has been taken to mean that

Thomas assumed responsibility for, even 'adopted' Henry junior after Henry senior's death. If the letter is genuine, it raises several questions. Did Thomas assume responsibility for all his brother's children even though he had at least seven of his own? Or did he spot the talent in the five-year-old and single him out? Or is this another Henry, his own son or son-in-law? There's no evidence that Thomas did any more for Henry than his godfather, John Hingestone, or his father's friends Locke, Cooke and Gibbons.

Elizabeth Purcell sometimes found it hard to pay her poor rates and her highway rates, for which she was often still in arrears by the end of the year, as she was to the overseers of the poor in 1671. In 1676 she petitioned St Margaret's vestry for payment for lodging one Frances Crump. The vestry ordered the matter very carefully looked into, for Elizabeth Purcell wasn't one of their usual nurse-cum-landladies who cared for the poor, sick, elderly and orphaned of the parish at its expense, and there's no record of any money being paid to her. However, it does suggest that she took in lodgers to make ends meet, and that on one occasion the 'lodger' had been unable to pay, forcing Elizabeth Purcell to try to claim from the parish.

The term 'son' may refer to 'nephew', a word whose meaning was not yet firmly established. Practice in the naming of relationships was changing at this time. 'Son-in-law' and 'daughter-in-law' were more usually 'son' and 'daughter', and 'nephew' was often 'cousin'. Whatever the nature of the relationship of Henry to his uncle, his professional father-in-art was undoubtedly Matthew Locke, Purcell's true precursor in the sheer quantity and variety of his output, who was attached to the Savoy Palace (alias Somerset House) as the Queen's organist while yet retaining a foothold in Whitehall. Along with John Banister, Locke was providing the bulk of the music which accompanied and reinforced the plays staged in both the commercial and court productions of the 1660s and early 1670s, from simple songs to curtain music, act tunes (music played between the acts), dances and complete masques.

Purcell's apprenticeship was almost at an end. He would soon be on his own, out of the security and companionship of the choir, in competition for jobs and fame with those who had been his teachers and superiors. His friend Henry Hall left at the end of 1672 to continue his education with the new master of the choristers, Pelham Humphreys, still high in the royal favour. Henry Purcell had a further year during which his voice must have begun to break. In June 1673 he was made assistant to his godfather Hingestone 'in the place of keeper, mender, maker repairer and tuner of the regals, organs, virginals, flutes and recorders and all the kind of wind instruments whatsoever, in ordinary without fee, to his Majesty'. In the event of Hingestone's death or incapacity he was to come in ordinary 'with fee'.

Such arrangements were often made when the holder of a post was ill or old. Hingestone was to live another ten years. This looks like a special request from him to provide for his godson at the moment when the boy was about to be sent out into the world. It was valuable because it not only assured him of a future place and an income, but also allowed him to acquire an intimate knowledge of the workings of the full range of instruments for which he was to compose with such understanding, in particular the woodwind. Six months later came the warrant to provide 'the usual clothing for Henry Purcell late child of His Majesty's Chapel Royal, whose voice is changed and who is gone from the Chapel', together with a warrant to pay him thirty pounds a year.

He was judged mature enough to receive the money himself, unlike other ex-Chapel boys whose fee was paid to their mothers or the music masters who took them into their homes. He was sent home to Tothill Street to see how his voice would settle and whether there was any further use for him about the court or in the Abbey. It must have been a frightening moment when he left the Chapel and palace, wondering when and how he would return, except as Hingestone's assistant, unpaid.

· 3 ·

Sweeter Than Roses

A MISSING LETTER from Locke to Henry junior, which may be a Piltdown (that is, an elaborate fake, reported by W. H. Cummings, an early Purcell biographer, as being in the possession of the music historian E. F. Rimbault), provides, if it's genuine, an interesting illustration of their relationship in this crucial period between Purcell's leaving the Chapel and his first court appointment with fee.

Dear Harry,
Some of the gentlemen of His Majesty's Music will honour my poor lodgings with their company this evening, and I would have you come and join them. Bring with thee Harry, thy last anthem, and also the canon we tried over together at our last meeting. Thine in all kindness.

M. Locke
Savoy, March 16

The latest year for this letter is 1677. Locke was indeed living in lodgings in the parish of the Savoy, or St Mary Le Strand, as several documents, including probate, testify. The musicians' practice of getting together, rather as modern jazz players do, for rehearsal or impromptu music-making is mentioned frequently by Pepys.

It has been objected[1] that Locke, a Catholic, would have been unlikely to be trying over an Anglican anthem at a private gathering for pleasure, but Locke himself composed many anthems, some of which Henry Purcell transcribed,[2] and therefore couldn't have been opposed to it as a musical form. The further objection that the switch from the more colloquial 'you' in the letter to 'thee' and 'thy' suggests a forgery I think misses the joke that the writer was making about the language of anthems. The second part of the letter can be intoned like a psalm and this increases the likelihood of its authenticity, since a forger is unlikely to think up such an elaborate piece of play.

The very occasion is typical both of what can be assumed of Locke's circumstances at the time and of his character. Nicholas Staggins had been sent by Charles II to study opera in France and Italy. During his absence Locke assumed responsibility for the violins as acting master of the King's Music from February 1676. He was at the height of his reputation and powers. Although he seems to have had some difficulty at the Savoy with the Queen's other foreign musicians (particularly Giovanni Sebenico and Giovanni Battista Draghi who, according to Roger North, refused to let him play on the great organ and thus forced him to accompany the services on a chamber organ in the corner of the chapel) and although the decree against Catholics of 1673 would have kept him from coming into the King's presence, he more than compensated for these disabilities by his contributions to both the royal and public theatres. Dr Peter Holman identifies as many as eleven productions which Locke wrote music for, among them *The Tempest*, *Macbeth* and *The English Opera, or Psyche* by Thomas Shadwell, the playwright of the Protestant faction, produced at the Duke's theatre in Dorset Garden. Presumably both Shadwell and Locke agreed on the proud description 'The English Opera'.

Many of the royal musicians, including the Chapel boys, were seconded to or moonlighted in these commercial productions, and Henry Purcell no doubt took part in some of them as a singer until he left the Chapel Royal, and possibly afterwards as an instrumentalist. The Theatre Royal had preference in the use of royal musicians, but on at least one occasion, in what looks like a reference to *Psyche*, the King gave permission for Chapel boys to take part in a performance at the Duke's house,[3] and they also appeared in *The Tempest* in May 1674.

Purcell would still have been a member of the Chapel when the revival of the Davenant–Locke *Macbeth* took place in February 1673, 'drest in all its finery, as new cloaths, new scenes, machines, as flyings for the witches, with all the singing and dancing in it: the first composed by Mr Lock, the other by Mr Channell and Mr Joseph Priest . . . being in the nature of an opera', as Downes, the prompter, described it in *Roscius Anglicanus*. There's no record of Chapel musicians having had an official part in this, but by its nature it demanded a large cast of musicians and performers. It may well have provided Purcell's first meeting with Josias Priest, with whom he was later to work on many occasions.

In spite of his theatrical success, Locke's financial affairs show a high degree of disarray. He frequently had to commute his official salary to pay off debt and at his death owed large sums, amounting to several years' wages, to two London vintners, Mark Allinson and Jonah Mapleton. I can't be sure that this was money consumed in wine and not straightforward loans, but the evidence is enough to suggest that he enjoyed his musical evenings well oiled.

Purcell was in the uncomfortable position of waiting for dead men's shoes. The first that fell vacant were those of Pelham Humphreys, who died at only twenty-seven on 14 July 1674, but Purcell was too young for his posts; Robert Smith, a prolific composer, became musician in ordinary and Purcell's tutor, John Blow, replaced Humphreys as master of the children and composer in the Private Music. Smith died the following year. When Christopher Gibbons, another of Purcell's teachers, followed in 1676 leaving a place for the virginals, Purcell was still only seventeen.

He had to write himself into prominence if he was to be noticed in the jostling for royal favour. The letter from Locke suggests that he had already begun to do this with sacred music. Pepys makes it clear that the Chapel boys of Blow's and Humphreys's generation were already composing anthems before their voices broke.

No work by Purcell is known to exist from before his leaving the Chapel, but in the earliest autograph, which is in the Fitzwilliam

Museum, the table at the front of the book is dated 13 September 1673. It lists four anthems by Pelham Humphreys, three by Blow and four by Locke, all Purcell's immediate masters. A little over halfway through the list Blow becomes Doctor instead of Mister, which gives a date of 1677. The first anthems are copied in a very neat school hand using the open form of 'e'. This changes in the third anthem to 'ℯ'. Then in copying Pelham Humphreys's *Lift up your heads* the writing becomes more mature and uneven. The ascription to 'Dr Blow' follows for the next anthem, *Cry aloud*, and the 'e' alters again, back to the first form, two anthems by Locke later. The book is then reversed and a new series begins using the 'ℯ', which occurs in the first anthem by Purcell himself, *Save me, O God*, followed immediately by Child's *Sing we merrily* with an open 'e'. This means that *Save me, O God* must belong to around 1677.

The place he had been waiting for came, suddenly and tragically, in 1677 with the death of Matthew Locke, who had no time to make a will or set his affairs in order, though he may have been able to put in a word for his protégé. Certainly Purcell must have shown enough promise for him to be made 'composer in ordinary with fee for the violins' on what may well be his eighteenth birthday, 10 September, the other date which appears on the Fitzwilliam manuscript with the addition of the words 'God bless Mr Henry Purcell. 1682'.

In May the following year there appeared a collection of *New Ayres*, edited by John Banister and Thomas Low, containing six songs attributed to a Henry Purcell, several of which have passed, though with much heart-searching, into the Purcell canon. The next year John Playford brought out his second book of *Choice Ayres*, in which there appear several more songs with the same attribution, including one which undoubtedly belongs to Purcell: the elegy on the death of Matthew Locke.

'Sweet tyranness', from the earlier volume, is generally attributed to Henry Purcell senior, if only on the grounds that at its first known publication in 1667[4] Henry junior was between seven and eight. His father would have been very much in the public memory when the collection was put together, possibly even in late 1666. Three of these songs have words 'made by Mr Charles Webbe', which might help in dating if there weren't several possible candidates of that name, none of whom seems to have published another line of verse. However, I'm prepared to say that on both textual and musical grounds, by which I mean the sheer sound and feel of the pieces, this group is all by Henry Purcell senior. A comparison of these texts with those known to be the earliest by Henry junior shows the first set to be Cavalier verse (dilute Carew or Herrick), while the second, for all their faults, are unmistakably post-Restoration.

John Banister, who died in 1679, was the elder Purcell's contemporary and had composed some of the music for *The Siege of Rhodes*. It's perfectly possible that he had the originals of these songs or could have been given them to publish by Elizabeth Purcell. In the whole book of *New Ayres* there are a great many by William Lawes, who had been dead for over thirty years, including the famous setting of Thomas Carew's 'Ask me no more where Jove bestows'. The second-largest contribution is by Abraham Coates, a member of the Chapel of Charles I, who seems to have spent some time at one of the German courts, judging by his rare setting of a couple of German texts. At the other end of the scale are one song apiece by John Blow, Michael Wise and Isaac Blackwell, four by William Turner and two by James Hart, both of whom feature strongly in the Playford collection, which claims, in the address to the reader, that the songs are all post the first book of 1673, and the work of His Majesty's musicians.

New Ayres may well be a collection of some of the songs given at Banister's concerts, which were advertised in the *London Gazette* as beginning in December 1672, when he took a room in Whitefriars near the George Tavern and presented music at four o'clock every afternoon. Newly published they may be, but most of them aren't new in the sense in which Banister intended. The texts in the Playford Purcell group are quite different. While the Banister songs are concerned with the traditional Cavalier theme of the constant but disappointed lover, the later collection offers a drinking song, a seduction, an argument for sex and a song in the female voice. The language of all these is rougher and brisker, more colloquial and less formally romantic and courtly than the earlier songs. They are designed to catch the attention with their boldness, with an adolescent desire to shock.

Since the pox or the plague of inconstancy reigns
In most of the women of the town,
What ridiculous fop would trouble his brains
To make the lewd devils lay down.

I resolve against cringing and whining
In a lover's intrigue so unfit,
'Tis like saying grace without dining
And betrays more affection than wit.

Ian Spink in *English Song: Dowland to Purcell* points up the difference between the settings in the first and second group, and listening to them supports his analysis. Musically, the Banister songs are simple and linear by comparison with the developing richness of the Playford group, which culminates in the elegy for 'My Friend Mr Matthew Locke' that ends the whole collection, as if Playford had hung on until the last minute in order to include it. The title states that Locke died in August 1677. The latest datable pieces in the collection are, following the dates in *The London Stage*, from Aphra Behn's *Sir Patient Fancy* and Shadwell's *Timon*, both belonging to January 1678. It looks as if Purcell composed his elegy about this time.

Where was it performed? The most likely place is at a music meeting, perhaps one of Banister's on St Cecilia's Day, which, after a break, were resumed in November 1678 at new premises, to be known as the Musick School, in Essex Buildings in the Strand. The time of performance was a little later too: five o'clock. Jeremiah Clarke's lament for Purcell was performed in the theatre, but it's a much larger-scale work requiring greater forces. Locke was probably buried in St Mary Le Strand, but the records are missing for this period. He left no will and his wife was either unable or unwilling to administer his estate, which was done by their daughter Mary.

Purcell's elegy is part of a tradition of which the most plangent example is surely Byrd's lament for Tallis. By comparison, William Gregory's elegy for Pelham Humphreys, to a text by Thomas Flatman, fails to move. Locke had set one of Flatman's elegies for the Earl of Sandwich, which had appeared in the 1673 Playford *Choice Ayres*. No author has been found for the elegy for Locke, which sounds very much as if written by Purcell himself, perhaps with some advice from Henry Hall or another; it certainly speaks in Purcell's own persona as the representative of Locke's fellow musicians. It follows the form of such early anthems of his as *O Lord, rebuke me not*: grave recitative breaks into a triple-time chorus. The opening, straight into grief, is extremely moving, recalling Weekles's *When David heard*.

What hope remains for us now he is gone
He that knew all the power of numbers, flown
Alas too soon.

Later the elegy celebrates Locke's power to cure the fear of death or even hold it up, but the sense here is slightly adrift and it's not clear whether it's his own death or that of others that his 'mystic touches' were sovereign against. This obscurity reinforces my feeling that Purcell was the author, for the dedication of his 1683 *Sonatas* shows a similar syntactical confusion; neither is surprising in so young a writer whose skill was music.

This kind of song, the free-standing recitative, or *arioso* – one that Purcell was to develop to exquisite perfection – was in many ways the most characteristic musical mode of the period, one which depended for its effect on a marriage of both English and Continental idioms. It's the musical equivalent of the Pindaric ode, to which it was often married. On the Continental side it's easy to trace it in Monteverdi's longer madrigals, for example *Il combattimento di Tancredi e Clorinda*, and a fragment from Monteverdi exists in Purcell's hand. *Arianna's Lament* is another near relative. On the English side the anthem is the musical parent, together with Henry Lawes. But it's the development of the ode, arguably the least accessible form for a modern audience, and principally Cowley's ode, that gives the recitative its literary fostering.

Abraham Cowley, whose name is barely known even to most students of poetry today, was the most influential poet of the generation between Donne and Dryden. His achievement was to produce a form, the Pindaric ode, which was capable of expressing at length any sustained exploration of religious and political themes which could include a full range of emotions: passion, adulation and lamentation. It could be and was adapted to the elegy, the pastoral, the welcome song, and was conceived by Cowley as a burst of free-wheeling passion which in some ways foreshadows modern, free, cadenced verse. Kings could be praised, God implored, a child's death mourned, a mistress yearned after. The elegy for Locke is the first of Purcell's almost infinite variations in this quintessentially English baroque form to be published. Its nature was meditative, not dramatic, an important element in any consideration of the failure to develop a native tradition of opera.

At last Purcell was entitled to call himself truly one of His Majesty's musicians and, in theory at least, be paid for it. But the political upheavals of the late 1670s, with plot and counterplot and the alternating exiles of the Dukes of York and Monmouth, must have made the future still seem very unsure. All the same, he was to commemorate the date of his official appointment five years later with 'God Bless Mr Henry Purcell' scribbled on the manuscript (now in the Fitzwilliam Museum) in which he continued to keep a record of his anthems.

If I'm right about the authorship of the Banister songs, it must have been disconcerting for him to have his father's work in print as by 'Henry Purcell'. His contemporary Alphonso Marsh also had the same problem in relation to his composer father, appearing in collections as junior to his father's senior. Purcell would have been anxious to appear in print as unmistakably himself. The songs in the Playford collection other than the Locke elegy don't appear to be theatre pieces, but rather court songs. Straight after his appointment as composer for the violins he must have been involved in providing the kind of royal diversion which appears in the collections of D'Urfey's poems, songs sung before the King, particularly during his long summer retreats to Windsor and Epsom. There was music to be written for the Chapel and to amuse the King both while he dined publicly and in his private moments.

A list of services transcribed into the Chapel Royal books from 1670 to 1676 shows Purcell's immediate forerunners in composition. Significantly, there's only one by Locke, but several each by Blow, Michael Wise, Pelham Humphreys and William Turner of the younger generation. At the first Christmas after Purcell's appointment he would have been present and probably taken part when the French players performed at the Theatre Royal on a stage modified for the occasion by Christopher Wren.[5]

He had kept up his father's connection with the Abbey by tuning the organ every year from 1675 and sometimes copying out music for the organ. Then in 1679 John Blow resigned as organist and Purcell took his place at a salary of ten pounds a year plus a housing allowance of eight. Much has been made of Blow's unselfishness in giving up this post to his pupil, but Purcell was by now in the royal employ and Blow, in addition to his other tasks as master of the children and composer for the virginals, was trying, together with Nicholas Staggins, back from his study tour of France and Italy, to set up an 'academy' for composing and performing operas. Relieved of his post as Abbey organist, Blow was free to spend the summers with the King at Windsor and Newmarket. An Abbey entry for the year 1681–2 shows a payment for writing 'Mr Purcell's service and anthems'. His early anthems were obviously written for both the Chapel Royal and the Abbey, presumably the 'brisk and airy' with ritornellos and symphonies for the former to occupy the King, and the more traditional for St Peter's, which enabled him to keep a grasp on both the Continental and English modes.

By this time Daniel had joined him in the royal service as a Chapel boy, first appearing in the accounts in 1678. There were therefore at least five members of the Purcell family dependent on Charles II's bounty and shaky accounting. Henry was receiving one shilling and eight pence a day and a yearly livery of sixteen pounds two shillings and sixpence: roughly forty-six pounds. His total income from official sources was around sixty-five pounds, and he would also be paid for playing for special occasions, teaching and composing. The money he was earning would have been especially welcome, since the records show that the thirty pounds a year he had been awarded on leaving the Chapel had never been paid. He was still living at his mother's in Tothill Street; his sister would have been there as well, unless she was away at school.

At about the same time his cousin Charles, now fifteen, left Westminster School. He must have gone to sea very soon after, for five years later the King gave him a commission as captain of the sloop the *George*, on which he died in 1686. The fact that he had made his will at home in June 1682 suggests that this was when he first went to sea after his majority was reached. His place at school was taken by a Henry Purcell. It has been assumed that it was the composer who became a bishop's boy or 'Lord's Scholar', an award given under a benevolent scheme of the sometime bishop of Lincoln, John Williams, for the education of two boys from his own diocese and two from his native Wales. I believe that this Henry Purcell was not the composer, but a boy from the Welsh–Shropshire branch of the family, perhaps Richard's son Henry, who was christened in Wortham on the borders in 1670.[6] It seems to me very unlikely that the composer would have had either the time or the inclination for full-time schooling at this point, particularly since the 'Henrici Pursell' entry continues until 1680, by which time he had provided the extensive music for Nat Lee's *Theodosius*. According to John Downes's account in *Roscius Anglicanus*, this was 'the first he e'er composed for the stage'. It must have been staged before April when the court left London, for it was their presence and 'especially the ladies by their daily charming presence' that 'gave it great encouragement'.

As I said earlier, his godfather Hingestone's will also makes it extremely likely that there was another Henry Purcell, not 'the son of Elizabeth', in the vicinity, with whom there might have been confusion. Hingestone, living nearby in St Anne's Lane and in constant contact with the small world of court and church, would know about such another Henry Purcell, Westminster scholar, particularly since at the time of his death the Purcells were also living in the same street. That Purcell had a mourning ring from Richard Busby, the headmaster of Westminster School, has been thought to indicate a close relationship between them, but Busby's will makes clear that the money to buy the ring was left to Purcell as organist; in the same sentence he leaves money to the chaunter, petty canons and master of the choristers for 'the like use'.

Even supposing the composer did become a nominal Westminster boy, he would have been far too busy to take part in the strenuous curriculum that gave the school its academic status. In 1680 he began the second extant of the series of scorebooks, in which he was to keep fair copies of his music after first composing on loose sheets, with the heading 'The Works of Henry Purcell Anno Dom 1680'.[7] The front of the book contains a dozen anthems written up to this point, then there's a gap and the volume has to be reversed to start again with 'Here beginneth the 3 part Fantazia's'. There are two undated fantasias and then there is a second group, of which the first is dated 10 June 1680 and the final one 24 February 1683.

The anthems are all for voices to a ground without symphonies or ritornellos. Following Thomas Tudway's comments quoted earlier, it can be argued that these were therefore either for the Abbey or for days on which the King wasn't present in the Chapel Royal. Textually they fall into three groups: straight 'King James' biblical texts, metrical paraphrases and Latin texts. The first is a paraphrase, *Plunged in the confines of despair*.

George Sandys's metrical paraphrases, first published before the rebellion in 1638, had been reissued in 1678. Sandys was the son of an archbishop of Canterbury, Edwin Sandys. The intense political activity of the late 1670s stimulated its religious counterpart, and this republication can be read as part of that process. The centrality of the Church of England – now seen not just as the state church, but as a valid vehicle for religious expression and experience in its own right – was reaffirmed in the face of the extreme claims of both Roman Catholicism and those forms of Protestantism which can be conveniently grouped under the term 'Puritan', although they were in no sense homogeneous, and which depended for their appeal and doctrine more on individual communion and inspiration.

The death of Matthew Locke inevitably created a gap in Purcell's life, which I suggest was filled by 'a bass from Canterbury', John Gostling. The letter from Thomas Purcell to Gostling while he was still in Canterbury in February 1679, waiting for the royal summons which came in the same month, thanks to a little nudging from Thomas Purcell, shows an already established intimacy between the two families which was to be continued after Henry Purcell's death, and even after Gostling's in 1733, by his son William's preservation of Purcell manuscripts. Both Gostling and his brother Isaac were ordained priests of the Church of England. However their friendship had begun, Thomas's letter suggests that Henry, if indeed it is him, was already composing with Gostling in mind.

Gostling was older than Purcell. Born in 1650 in East Malling in Kent, the son of a mercer, he was sent to school in Rochester and admitted to St John's, Cambridge, in 1668. By 1676 he was married and held the curacy of Littleborne; he was a minor canon of Canterbury Cathedral, where his children continued to be baptised, rather implying that he lived a peripatetic life after his summons to the Chapel Royal and that his wife, Elizabeth, remained in Canterbury. Their first child, John, died very soon after his birth in 1676. The second, Elizabeth, was born in 1678, and it may have been she who constituted the 'occasions and ties where you are' which had to be complied with before he could come to London. There was also the matter of finding a locum for Littleborne, who had to be paid. But the royal summons wasn't to be disobeyed when it came: 'His Majesty having occasion of your service you are immediately upon receipt of this to dispose yourself to come to court.' So keen was Charles to have John Gostling that he paid him fifty pounds a year from the royal bounty to cover this expense. Charles certainly enjoyed his company and took him along on journeys by land and water to provide music and general good humour.

Thomas Purcell's letter, as well as containing the reference to 'my son Henry', is full of domestic references to mutual friends and family. It ends with the curious sentence: 'F faut and E lamy are preparing for you.' Coincidentally, in a list of services and anthems copied for the Chapel Royal up to 1680 Michael Wise's creeds appear in these two signatures. However, the reference may simply be a family joke: for example, two of Thomas Purcell's children, Francis and Elizabeth, might have been called by these terms as nicknames or, since Michael Wise himself was a countertenor, it may be a musical joke on Gostling's bass voice.

The relationship with Gostling, together with the sequence of 1680 anthems and his appointment as organist to the Abbey, reinforces the impression of Purcell at this period as a convinced member of the Anglican Church. A list of scores he copied from around 1678, now in the Fitzwilliam Museum, shows which musicians influenced these early anthems, among them several Tudor composers of established reputation: Orlando Gibbons, Tallis, Byrd and Tomkins, as well as Purcell's immediate predecessors and contemporaries, Locke, Blow and Humphreys.

The anthems and the 1680 fantasias seem, from the ink and their position in the scorebook, to be contemporary. Sandys's texts express a mood of almost romantic gloom:

Ah few and full of sorrow are the days
Of men from women sprung.
He like an empty shadow glides away
And all his life is but a winter's day.

The King had been seriously ill in 1679, which may account for the general tone of despondence; the political situation alone was grounds enough for gloom. 'O, I'm sick, I'm sick, O, I'm sick of life' begins one anthem two thirds of the way through the sequence. These metrical forms in particular allow Purcell to develop his dramatic use of word-painting.

The Latin texts form a layer of three in the middle of the English anthems. It has sometimes been thought that his use of Latin words has some biographical significance, but I think this is a misreading. All the composers set such texts, and their audiences, from Pepys to Oliver Cromwell, appreciated them. From the composer's point of view it was a way of laying claim to an international hearing not limited by the use of English, but in the frenetic politicking of the late 1670s which saw papist priests under every bed it could have been open to misinterpretation. On the other hand an anthem like *Jehovah, quam multi sunt hostes mei* ('Lord, how many are my enemies'), which clearly refers to the King in one of his mythological incarnations that included King David, Pan and Caesar, made such an embodiment easier simply because it was in Latin.

Nothing could have been more unequivocally English than Purcell's interest in the fancy or fantasia, especially since the King was known to dislike them. The reverse of the 1680 scorebook is laid out to suggest that Purcell intended to compose even more elaborate pieces of up to eight parts. Those that exist must have been written with specific performers in mind, perhaps on commission. They seem to be a last act of homage to Matthew Locke, or even to John Hingestone, both of whom had written fancies. Purcell possessed a copy of Locke's, for the transcriber of those in the British Museum has added a note that they have been examined against 'Mr Purcell's score'.[8]

Purcell doesn't specify the instruments, which may be viols or violins, but it's not, I think, unreasonable to connect his fantasias with a possible performance by the North household. John Jenkins, who was recognised as the great protagonist of the fancy, especially for viols, had been a protégé of Sir Francis North. According to Roger North, Purcell certainly performed his post-1683 sonatas at the Lord Keeper's house on more than one occasion, himself directing from the harpsichord.[9] Bearing in mind Sir Francis's fondness for music, skill in performance and the group of musicians he liked to retain, I believe it highly probable that, although Roger North mentions only the sonatas as being those works whose performance he was part of, the earlier pieces could also have been for a North *ad hoc* consort.

In 1680 the King was away at Windsor from April to September and then at Newmarket until October, that is, all the summer in which Purcell was busy with the four-part fantasias, completing nine brilliant pieces between 10 June and 31 August, as well as another two in three parts of presumably earlier date (copied out before them). The notes seem to jump off the page, giving an impression of energy and precision. The notation of the anthems, where the music has to be fitted to the words, is more spaced out, but even so there's a feeling of music being poured on to the page. If Purcell had gone with the court for the summer, it's difficult to see how he could have found the time for such a strenuous burst of composition, particularly in a form the King despised.

He was also writing the first of what was to be a series of welcome songs and odes spanning three reigns. Charles much preferred his country gentleman's summer life and had to be coaxed and mollified on his return to a city he found hostile. *Welcome, viceregent* by an anonymous scholarly author sugars the pill with flattery. The treble duet is delightful.

When the summer in his glory,
Was delightful, warm and gay,

All was but a winter's storm
While our sovereign was away.

No real clues to the conditions of composition and rehearsal of these odes exist. Was there competition among authors and composers for the privilege, and how was the winner chosen? From the number that Purcell composed over the next few years it looks as if this was part of his job as royal composer; he seems to have had an arrangement whereby Blow as the senior composed the important odes for New Year's Day and the King's birthday, which was celebrated at Windsor, while Purcell wrote the autumn welcomes. This year the King returned on 9 September. The ode requires the full forces of chorus, instruments, especially for the opening symphony, and at least four soloists. If it was to be ready to greet Charles on his re-entry to London, Purcell must have come back himself in time to rehearse such a complicated piece. However, there's no specific mention of a payment for his riding charges to Windsor, and I think it more likely that he stayed behind at least part of the time. By the end of the year he had tried his hand at all the forms he was to work in: anthems, theatre music and songs, odes, instrumental works and keyboard music. And to crown the year the songs from *Theodosius* were included in the new volume of *Choice Ayres* Playford had put together by 2 November, by which time Purcell was certainly in love and probably married.

· 4 ·

Thrice Happy

HIS WIFE WAS Frances, daughter of Amy and John Baptist Pieters. Her father had died in 1675, and it's from the inventory made of the family's house and its contents that so much can be known about Frances's background although neither a will nor probate record has survived.[1] The family lived in a large new house in Thames Street, one of the first parts of the city to be gutted by the Great Fire, between Coldharbour and Red Bull Alley, and up against the remains of All Hallows the Less and its churchyard.

Frances's father was a Flemish immigrant. He had been born in Ghent in 1622 and baptised at the Roman Catholic church of St Michiels Noord.[2] Whether this was a piece of diplomatic conformity in difficult times on the part of his father, Josse, and mother, Cecilia van Wademont, it's impossible to say, but certainly by 1663, when he was naturalised by Act of Parliament,[3] John Baptist Pieters, as he still spelt his name, was a conforming Anglican and able to produce the necessary sacrament certificate for denization. Frances's mother may also have been a Flemish immigrant.

There's no trace of the family in the records of All Hallows the Great and Less before the record of his death, and just one mention in a rates payment of about the same time, when the house is rated the highest in the area; it shows up clearly on Ogilby's map of 1676. Close by were the halls of the Vintners', Dyers' and Fishmongers' companies and the Still Yard. The streets on either side led down to the river and the New Key.

There were a great many rooms in the house; seventeen are listed, richly furnished with Spanish leather or turkey-work chairs, Spanish tables, pictures and tapestries. The count of linen included twenty dozen napkins, five dozen towels and thirty-six tablecloths. Room number eleven contained a hundred skins of gilt leather. There were two cellars and two vaults full of wine, including eighteen hogsheads of claret, malmsey, Rhenish and canary. The ready money account listed a large sum for wines sold 'since the death of the deceased'. There were also twenty dozen plates, fifteen chamber-pots, jewellery, plate and rings, including presumably the diamond ring 'which was my father's', bequeathed by John Baptist Peters junior to his son.

Obviously the house was a kind of tavern, but just for the sale of wine and food: there were only beds and pairs of sheets enough for the family. The gilt leather skins may have been to repair the many chairs and tables or for sale, since the house straddled both the vintners' and leather merchants' area. The poll tax shows that by 1678 Amy was living there with two unmarried daughters, a married daughter and her husband, three apprentices and two servants, Ann Glaspe and Ann Humersome. Earlier that year the marriage of Amy Peters, about twenty, and John Howlett, soapmaker, had taken place under licence with the consent of her mother, Amy, widow.[4]

John Howlett was the 'boy next door', son of Thomas, citizen, soapmaker and leather-seller of the Three Arrows, Thames Street, a rich wily merchant described in the state papers among eminent Nonconformists; he led a group petitioning to import potash for soapmaking. Amy junior had done what was expected, marrying within her social group. Frances's marriage must have been at the least worrying to her mother, and possibly opposed. Purcell was of the court, his future unreliable, dependent on a king who feared and disliked London's Whig merchants, except for the aldermen and the bankers whom he felt he could trust and on whom he relied for loans. On both sides the marriage could have been deemed unsuitable, and it must therefore have been a love match. The lack of any record of the wedding suggests that it may have been clandestine.

The Howletts had connections in Surrey, in Kew and Richmond, where a daughter, Frances, was born to John and Amy in 1680. Their first child, John, was baptised at All Hallows the Great in 1679; their third, Amy, there in August 1681, less than a month after the birth and death of Henry and Frances Purcell's first child, Henry, baptised on 9 July and buried on the 18th in All Hallows the Less. Frances, as was common practice in this period, had had her first child at her old home. Perhaps it wasn't the best choice: 'Mrs Pieters maid' also died at the beginning of the month, which may indicate the presence of sickness in the house.

For their first child to be born and survive for even a week in those days, the marriage must have taken place at least seven months before, by January 1681, if the child was conceived within wedlock. It seems unlikely, given the family's wealth and position in a part of the community that was much more strict in its codes than the court, that Frances would have allowed herself to be seduced before marriage. The safest bet is that they were married in the autumn on or after Purcell's twenty-first birthday (which, as I have suggested, may have fallen on 10 September). John Gostling could have performed a private ceremony.

Wherever and however Henry and Frances met, music must have played a part. Their lives were too different for them not to have come together through its agency. Frances may have been at a school, for instance Mrs Playford's, wife of Purcell's music publisher, or even at Josias Priest's in Leicester Fields, where Purcell gave lessons; they might have met at a music meeting, where flirtations often took place. Aphra Behn has described it graphically in *To Lysander at the Musick Meeting*:

It was too much ye Gods to see and hear
Receiving wounds both from the eye and ear
. . . .

Had I but gorg'd and fed my greedy eyes
Perhaps you'd pleas'd no further than surprise
. . . .
At least, so quick the conquest had not been;
You storm'd without and harmony within
Nor cou'd I listen to the sound alone,
But I alas must look – and was undone
. . . .
Beauty and music must the soul disown
Since harmony like fire to wax does fit
The softened heart impressions to admit:
As the brisk sounds of war the courage move
Music prepares and warms the soul to love.

They could also have met at a ball, perhaps an elaborate formal affair or simply a dance in the modern sense. Playford's book of instructions and tunes called *The English Dancing Master* had been appearing since the Commonwealth. Even Puritan parents regarded dancing as, at least, a healthy exercise, but also as an opportunity for their children to show off their social graces, which reflected the parents' status and attracted eligible marriage partners. The Playford dances were ideally suited to private homes or the schools of the dancing masters, as Melusine Wood has pointed out.[5] The dance for two to four couples could easily be fitted into a squarish room, while galleries and halls were ideal for the 'longways for as many as will'. Once the basic steps and movements had been mastered, the instructions enabled the dancers to apply them to any suitable music. The music itself might be that of the older, boisterous country dance, such as Sellenger's Round, or a new theatre air of a more graceful and courtly style.

The movements were closely related to those of the morris dance. 'Up a double and back' and 'the hey' come directly from there, while the energetic caper of the morris is replaced by the set to right and left more suitable for mixed social dancing. The people of the court danced the

French dances, branles and corantos, which Pepys found so boring, but they also enjoyed the Playford dances – or at least the younger among them did, especially the Duke of Monmouth, who in his various exiles was to be found teaching English country dancing to the ladies of foreign courts.

The other possibility is that Purcell was visiting Frances's mother's house, either to eat and drink himself or to supply the customers with music. Pepys's descriptions of such occasions usually contain a reference to music-making. Fish seems to have been one of the dishes served in the Pieters' house for there are two or three fish kettles mentioned in the inventory and the house was conveniently near the Thames. Perhaps Amy Pieters didn't oppose her daughter's marriage, but saw it as an opportunity for a little social climbing. Her son, John Baptist, was training for the law, which was already a step away from his father's occupation.

Frances was close to her family, and at least two of the Purcell children were called after them. John Baptist, her brother, was Henry Purcell's attorney and witnessed his will, and Frances's own will was witnessed by her sister, Amy Howlett, with whom she was then living in Richmond. There are no musical instruments in the Pieters' inventory, presumably because they weren't part of the business, but girls from such a wealthy bourgeois family would undoubtedly have been taught, like Susanna Perwich, to dance, sing and play. Although they might not have been allowed to go to the theatre, music meetings were more socially acceptable. John Banister died in 1679, but Thomas Britton, a coal merchant with a passion for music, had started a new series of concerts and Purcell's music figures in the list of his music books sold after his death.[6]

The young cynicism of the 1679 *Choice Ayres* had been replaced by passion. There's no other feasible explanation of the marriage. The loss of their first child in the summer of 1681 must have been a bitter blow to the young parents. 'Few and full of sorrow' had his days been indeed. At that time, the court was away at Windsor, but it's likely that Purcell would have spent at least some of July in London. Apart from any other consideration, he had to set up a new home. Elizabeth Purcell gave up the house in Tothill Street during 1680 and seems to have moved eventually into the house Henry took in St Anne's Lane, where Frances had joined him by 1682.[7]

As composer he had again to supply the welcome song for the King's return to London, though I'm inclined to think this was performed before the baby's birth and death, in March 1681, when the King came back after dissolving the parliament he had convened at Oxford. The reference to the Thames by its Oxford name in the first line, 'Swifter, Isis, swifter flow', would have been understood by every listener. When followed in the fourth stanza by the lines

Though causeless jealousy
May by the factions be broached,
Your Augusta will never be
From your kinder arms debauched

and taken with the reference to the spring, the song best fits this occasion. The duet, a form in which he excelled from the beginning, with its fresh and lyrical writing is particularly lively. There are opportunities for Gostling to show off his bass against a descant recorder, and the sprightly ritornellos which Charles II so enjoyed. The opening symphony after a stately introduction echoes the ringing of joyful bells and leads directly into the tenor solo, followed by a chorus that drops right down in imitation of 'dead low waters'. If his first welcome song of the year before can be said to be a little tentative in the vocal writing,[8] this second is entirely confident and accomplished. Charles must have been encouraged by its expression of cheerfulness and optimism, and he no doubt beat time as he listened. His subjects were yearning for spring in both senses, for Evelyn wrote in his diary that the weather was sharp and cold, and snow was lying; 'the whole nation [was] in a great ferment'.

During the summer Purcell wrote a full service for the Abbey, such a task chiming well with what must have been his emotions at the time.

Perhaps Frances's own life was in danger. It was a worrying time after a woman had given birth in the seventeenth century, and thousands of women didn't survive the ordeal. Frances had charmed him in spite of competition from actresses and singers, court ladies, the acceptable daughters of friends and fellow musicians. There's no portrait of her, but it seems safe to assume that she was attractive and talented to have engaged Purcell's passion and imagination.

In his *History of the Science and Practice of Music*, Sir John Hawkins presents Frances Purcell in a poor light. Hawkins was born in 1719. His book wasn't published until 1776, but it was the work of a lifetime and drew on many other written and oral contemporary accounts. The matter in it that concerns Purcell came mainly from two sources: Thomas Tudway's letter to his son, mentioned earlier, and William Gostling, John Gostling's son, who was not born until the year after Purcell's death. One of the strictures repeated by Hawkins against Frances Purcell, however, comes from Humphrey Wanley, antiquary and librarian, born in 1672, twenty-three when Purcell died and thirty-three at Frances's death. He was thus in a position to have known, if not them, then the gossip about them and their marriage. Wanley's chief source appears to be his close friend the musician Bernard-Martin Berenclow, the son of a German physician and Katherine Lanier, a member of the family of court musicians. Berenclow certainly knew Purcell, since he contributed to the second book of *Harmonia Sacra* along with Purcell in 1693, and shared his interest in Alessandro Stradella and other Italian composers whose works he collected.

The Gostling material must represent opinions and anecdotes current in the family at least until the death of John in 1733 and passed on by William Gostling to John Hawkins. Though these opinions may have become tainted by time and in their passage from one to the other, they are unlikely to be either a complete reversal of the truth or not to contain a residue of it, and they are all there is. A close examination of this material in the light of a knowledge of John Baptist Pieters's occupation and therefore Frances's upbringing makes the picture of their life together more plausible.

The Gostling family's allegation is that Frances killed her husband by ordering the servants to bolt the doors if he was out after midnight, drinking with his fellow musicians. Heated with wine, he allegedly caught the cold which caused his death. Hawkins's attitude to this story is revealing. On the one hand Purcell had to seem perfect to posterity. The new puritanism of the late eighteenth century couldn't have it suggested that England's greatest composer had a human face, that he might have been in temperance's eyes a drunk; on the other hand drinking was a male prerogative, the man was master and it was wrong of his wife to deny him his pleasure and to lock him out. The story reflects what must have been the view in the Gostling family that Frances was repressive, lacking in understanding and unloving. Hawkins's comment that Purcell loved 'mirth and good fellowship, of which he seems to have been very fond', must also come from this source.

Frances had grown up in a house filled night after night with revellers smoking, drinking and singing bawdy catches. Perhaps she had hoped to escape through marriage to a young gentleman of the Chapel Royal, only to find that part of the musicianly ethos was the music-making both in taverns and for courtly and private patrons; often, as is clear from Pepys's accounts, it went on until late into the night, and a great deal of wine was drunk. It would hardly be surprising if she showed her disapproval and tried to counter such behaviour. She could also have thought it damaging to Purcell's not perhaps robust health.

Pepys's wife found his constant absences and late nights very hard to put up with and persuaded him to let her have a maid-companion to offset her loneliness. In his case, of course, being out on his own gave him the chance of extra-marital sexual encounters, but, interestingly, these mostly took place during the day. Nights were given over to drinking and music. While I don't believe that Purcell was unfaithful, I'm sure he was often absent. Obviously it wasn't the custom to take the wives along to these sessions; apart from any other consideration, the words of the glees and catches wouldn't have been thought at all proper for women to hear unless they were prostitutes or actresses.

Wanley has a further allegation, or innuendo rather, which is much more serious because of its imputation of sexual irregularity. In telling the story of the Italian composer Stradella's assassination by his mistress's former lover, Wanley claims, according to Hawkins, that when Purcell heard the story 'and he was informed jealousy was the motive for it he lamented [Stradella's] fate exceedingly; and in regards of his great merit as a musician said he could have forgiven him any injury in that kind, which those who remember how lovingly Mr Purcell lived with his wife or rather what a loving wife she proved to him may understand without further explication'. Wanley gives the year of Stradella's assassination as 1670, which makes a nonsense of his own story since the actual date of Stradella's death in Genoa was February 1682. This fits perfectly with the account of Purcell's reaction to it, a reaction which presents Purcell as sexually correct in approving of passion. In Hawkins, Stradella is to be forgiven his affairs only because of his quality as a musician. Looked at again, however, in Wanley's Harleian catalogue itself, it seems that Hawkins has inserted two clauses not in the original. Wanley doesn't mention jealousy, but just says 'upon that account'. Nor does he mention Stradella's 'great merit as a musician', only that Purcell said 'he could have forgiven him any injury in that kind', meaning presumably running away for love. The sardonic comment that follows about the nature of Purcell's own marriage seems merely tacked on to vilify Frances and to suggest that she was in some way unvirtuous and, again, unloving. Since this first appears as a note during Wanley's cataloguing of the Harley manuscripts from 1708 onwards, he was repeating still current gossip about someone only just dead whose children and other relations were very much alive. I therefore infer that it wasn't just Frances's family who might have disapproved of the marriage. Significantly, while preserving much of his friend's music, Gostling made no documented effort to cooperate with Frances Purcell in her various publications after Purcell's death.

Henry, his brother Edward and Gostling took the oaths of the Test Act together at Michaelmas 1681, swearing loyalty to the King, the established church and abjuring the doctrine of transubstantiation.[9] It's interesting to see the three of them together in this way and a testimony to their closeness. Edward signed as 'Gentleman Usher, Daily Waiter', the elegance of his signature contrasting with Henry's rather wayward hand.

Whatever the Gostling family or indeed Purcell's mother and brothers thought of his marriage, the most important view apart from his own was the King's, on whom he depended not only for his chief livelihood, but also for the opportunity to exercise his talent to the full. Charles cannot have been pleased by Frances's background, but if she was pretty would have forgiven Purcell an imprudent marriage out of his general liking for women. The length of time before they moved into their house in St Anne's Lane certainly suggests a hiccup of some kind, either that her health wasn't good or that there was resistance from some quarter to be overcome.

It must have helped at court that the songs from Purcell's *Theodosius* (1680) had been so popular that one, 'Hail to the myrtle shade', had been taken up and turned round as 'Hail to the Knight of the Post', a satire on Titus Oates and the Popish Plot, which the King had never believed in but had been forced to take seriously by public anti-Catholic paranoia. However, Purcell's next theatrical involvement in the autumn of 1681 was less fortunate, for the play was banned and taken off after only two nights. It was *The Sicilian Usurper*, Nahum Tate's version of *Richard II*, a play always liable to be forbidden in times of civil unrest because of its support for a usurper and the murder of the rightful king.

Staging it at a time when, although Charles was politically in the ascendance, there was a great deal of unrest and both dukes were again in exile, shows a lack of sensitivity on Tate's part. It was only too easy to see James of York as Richard and James of Monmouth as Bolingbroke.

Given his strongly Protestant sympathies, it's surprising that Tate was so successful and it says something about either Charles's indolence or his willingness to make an exception for artists.

Purcell had already learned the invaluable rule for any creator that nothing is to be wasted, and the song 'Retired from any mortal's sight' turns up in December 1681 in Tate's next shot, a version of *Coriolanus*. These productions are particularly important as the beginning of a long and creative relationship between author and composer, rivalled only by those of Dryden and D'Urfey with Purcell. Shortly before *Coriolanus* came the first known of his many collaborations with Tom D'Urfey, King's favourite and court wit, in *Sir Barnaby Whigg*, for which Purcell wrote his first sea-song, 'Blow, Boreas, Blow'. (The knowledge that two of his brothers and a cousin were at sea, where two of them were to die, adds resonance to his compositions in this genre.) Purcell's ability to work with authors from both sides of the political spectrum caused Hawkins to comment wonderingly on his political ambiguity.

Music may be neutral, but in the case of vocal music the text inevitably carries meaning, particularly in the propaganda hothouse of seventeenth-century politics. Love and death were safer themes. Charles himself had to walk a tightrope. Unable to express his own latent Catholicism and finding his brother's inability to compromise an embarrassment, he took to hearing prayers ostentatiously twice a day, at least while the court was at Whitehall. He continued to spend as little time there as possible, putting in a brief appearance in September between Windsor and Newmarket, and only returning reluctantly after the racing was over in October for what he regarded as six months' hard labour.

The references to Augusta in the first two welcome odes, and the fact that it's London who speaks as the King's lover welcoming him home, imply they were performed at a specific occasion, such as when the Mayor and aldermen came to kiss the King's hand on his return to London and reassure him of their fealty, or the feasts of the Honourable Artillery Company, which usually took place in the autumn. The texts suggest commissions external to the court while employing the court's musical facilities even so. By the time of the next such ode the following year the King was in the full flush of his campaign to control the City, which culminated in the issue of a *quo warranto* writ against London's Charter in 1682 on charges of levying tolls without royal licence and making seditious comments in a petition to the King earlier in the year. The viewpoint of this ode, *The summer's absence*, is quite different.

How far did Purcell acquiesce in or support the texts he was setting? This is a vital question to which, in default of any words from him, there can't be a definitive answer. But the question is, it seems to me, a valid subject for speculation. His first loyalty was to the King – that much is clear from the dedication of the *Sonatas* in 1683. A large part of his family was in the royal employ. A descent into anarchy was not a situation in which the arts could flourish. The nature of his vocal composition insisted that he pay attention to the words, using all his skill to reinforce their meaning with his setting.

Critics have frequently poured scorn on the texts, both anonymous and by lesser poets than Dryden and Congreve, that he was 'forced' to set, calling them the work of 'hacks'. This is to misunderstand their essence, or rather to apply anachronistic standards to the evaluation of these works because their purpose was political and since the Romantic Movement it's been received opinion that polemical writing must always be inferior to lyrical. A true appreciation of what Purcell was doing in a large part of his output depends on an ability to set this preconception aside and empathise with the circumstances in which the compositions were made, and the emotions behind them. Anything else is to reduce the composer to an automaton, ready to produce music for words to which he was indifferent, by rule of thumb. I don't believe that anyone as passionate about his art as Purcell could have worked so brilliantly under such cynical conditions. Nor was any of the monarchs for whom he wrote a Hitler or a Stalin, figures who have formed our modern view of collaborationist composers, authors and artists.

By the beginning of January 1682 the Purcells were in their new home and Frances was pregnant again, less than six months after losing their first child. Her sister, Amy Howlett, had also lost a child, Amy, her second, in October, but undeterred their brother, John Baptist Peters, married Martha Ellis at All Hallows, London Wall, in January. No doubt there were the usual festivities at which all the family must have been present, with feasting and music after the ceremony and the bedding of the bride and groom.

Thomas Purcell surrendered his post as groom of the robes in January too. He was obviously ill and the previous May had appointed his son Matthew as his attorney to receive his salary and arrears. Prepared for death, he had made his will in June; he rallied, though not enough to continue with his duties. His son Francis became second groom with a fee in the place of Gilbert Spencer, who moved up into Thomas's job.

The end of 1681 and the beginning of 1682 had seen a great deal of musical activity at court. In November a 'great play' was performed for the Queen's birthday, after which several of the musicians had their wages docked for non-attendance. Then in December the Russian ambassador was given an audience and a fortnight later the Moroccan ambassador was also received, both in the Banqueting House. Each brought presents, and the Moroccans were entertained with a great banquet later in the month at the Duchess of Portsmouth's 'glorious apartments at Whitehall where was a great banquet of sweetmeats and music'. Evelyn gives us the full flavour of such an occasion, describing the diners seated at a long table: 'a lady between two Moors and amongst these were the King's natural children, namely Lady Lichfield and Essex, the Duchess of Portsmouth, Nelly etc., concubines and cattle of that sort, as splendid as jewels and excess of bravery could make them'.

By the end of February Charles felt he had the political situation sufficiently under control to send for the Duke of York, who returned from Scotland on 27 March. A welcome ode by Purcell, *What shall be done on behalf of the man?*, celebrates the event. The words make it quite clear that the Duke came back at Charles's behest, whereas his and

Monmouth's earlier return from exile had been unauthorised. James's first visit in March was to Newmarket, where the court was enjoying the races and from where he returned to London with Charles on 8 April, to be greeted by the ringing of bells and bonfires. Purcell's ode belongs either to this occasion or to the feast given in the Duke's honour by the Honourable Artillery Company at Merchant Taylors' Hall on 20 April, which Narcissus Luttrell reported in his *Brief Historical Relation of State Affairs* as 'a very noble entertainment' with which the Duke was 'very well satisfied'.

Charles, however, wasn't inclined to linger in London, where he was forced to live in the Duke's apartments at Whitehall while his own were being rebuilt, and by 22 April the court was off again to Windsor for the summer. With it went a large body of musicians, including Daniel Purcell, still a child of the Chapel, although he must by now have been at least seventeen, and their brother Edward as the groom responsible for the King's removes. Thomas was too sick to go.

The King himself was ill in May, but recovered and returned briefly to London in June. The City was in tumult over the election of the sheriffs, for which both the party favourable to the court and the City Whigs put up candidates. The press abounded 'with all manner of libells. It has been the endeavour of late of some persons to run things up to a strange height, creating feuds and differences,' Luttrell reported; 'now no other names are known but Whig and Tory, church papist, tantivy, fanatick etc.' The weather too was 'strange and unseasonable', with incessant rain, 'so that most fruits are little worth and commodities considerably risen'. The King went again to Windsor, but was forced to come back to London to settle the matter of the election of the City sheriffs, which continued to drag on; the Whig candidates obtained huge majorities in every poll. So great was the heat of all kinds generated at Guildhall during the July attempt at elections that several people fell ill and died.

The whole summer was spent toing and froing over the business of the sheriffs, but Charles found time to visit the races at Winchester, where he had conceived the idea of building an English Versailles, far from the dangers and troubles of London. In July Purcell received a fresh appointment as organist of the Chapel Royal in the place of Edward Lowe, who seems to have spent much of the latter part of his life in Oxford. Henry now held two posts for the organ as well as one as composer and, what was to be the most lucrative of all, the assistantship to John Hingestone. At the beginning of August his uncle Thomas finally died and was buried in the Abbey cloisters near his brother and fellow musicians. Perhaps his own burial chant was sung at the service, which was possibly less spectacular than might have been expected since most of the royal musicians were out of town. Henry's and Frances's second son was born and baptised in the Abbey on 9 August, and named John Baptista after his maternal grandfather and uncle. The court came back to London a month later. On 30 September Charles set off again for Newmarket for hawking and racing. Altogether the court had been officially away from London for 181 days that year, as the payments for riding charges to the musicians show, even though Charles had been forced to break up his stay with lightning visits to London.[10] Purcell now had to prepare a welcome ode against the King's eventual return. He must also have worked on his volume of three-part sonatas during this year, as well as composing anthems and songs, many of which would have had their first performance at Windsor rather than Whitehall since, although he probably wasn't there full-time, it was close enough to London for him to take part in some of the musical events and to try out a new song. Sometime between his appointment in 1677 and 1682 he was among the group who stayed all summer in Windsor, but the payment for this is in a mopping-up list of arrears in May 1682, and no specific date is attached to it.[11] The most likely year would seem to be 1679 before he took over the post as Abbey organist from John Blow.

The King came back to London for the winter on 21 October. The protracted business of the City elections, which had been further prolonged by the election of a new lord mayor, was at last resolved with a great deal of fudging and riotous assembly by the end of October. The choice of sheriffs and of Sir William Pritchard as lord mayor was acceptable to the King, who, it was remarked nevertheless, didn't dine at Guildhall this year. The King's return was an occasion for pageantry, and the Lord Mayor and the City fathers turned out in full dress to welcome him back. Thomas Jordon's 1684 Lord Mayor's Show, which was entitled *London's Royal Triumph* and ends in its published form with 'A Welcome Home to the King and the Duke upon their return from Newmarket October 23 and passing through the city. Bells ring and bonfires blaze, high huzzas sounded, the trimmers in a maze and the Whigs confounded', gives some idea of the spectacular nature of the official royal returns. Purcell's official ode was presumably sung after the royal progress as the King re-entered the Palace of Whitehall. Dated 21 October in the autograph, 'on the King's Majesty's return from Newmarket', it reflects that summer's political troubles. There's no mention of a welcoming Augusta, only an unspecified 'we'.

The summer's absence unconcerned we bear
Since you Great Sir more charming fair appear,
Scattering the mists of faction with our fear.

The words, not surprisingly, castigate the rebellious, support the succession of the Duke of York and tilt at Monmouth's illegitimacy. Charles's efforts at peacemaking abroad are hailed along with Britannia's dominion over the seas and her growing empire. Yet for all the attempts at celebration and the repeated 'Happy, happy' of the trio section, the music is somehow plaintive, reaching after joy and falling back into wistful discords and modulations until its final resolution on a plangent dissonance which seems more like an abandonment than a conclusion.

Four days earlier John Baptista Purcell, just two months old, had been buried in the Abbey. Some people assume that in an age when the deaths of small children were so common they were less felt. Maria Charlotte, the daughter of the Duke and Duchess of York, was born a week after John Baptista and died ten days before 'to the great grief of their Royal Highnesses'. James, who had been at Newmarket when she became ill, took post to get to St James's the same night that the news reached him. It's hard to believe that Henry and Frances Purcell would have felt their own loss any less. They had been married only two years and had buried two children.

• 5 •

Hail, Bright Cecilia

AFTER THE CEREMONIES for the King's return the annual autumn season continued with the Lord Mayor's Show. It began at seven in the morning with the Mayor's progress by barge to Westminster and then the return to Guildhall, passing various pageants, where speeches were made and, after a final salvo by the Honourable Artillery Company, the Lord Mayor entered the hall to dine. The King's trumpeters, fifes and drummers were part of the procession and the royal musicians took part in the feast. The show of 1681 had been particularly splendid: the King and Queen and Prince Rupert, as well as the Archbishop of Canterbury, the London bishops, the judges, the Privy Council, the ambassadors and all their ladies, had been present. For it Tom D'Urfey wrote the words of the song 'All hail to Great Caesar', which was 'sung before the King and Queen'; he doesn't give the composer's name, so perhaps he wrote the music himself as he sometimes did.[1]

There were usually several songs during dinner and instrumental music. A bill of 1674 mentions that twenty-four of the King's Music and twelve trumpeters were all provided with green bows for the occasion, and a resolution of the organising committee makes provision for those members of the City Music who were not the King's servants to share in whatever payments were made, presumably benevolent donations from the satisfied company.[2] The feast was provided by the livery company the new lord mayor belonged to. The pageants and entertainments were usually devised and composed by Thomas Jordon, gent, and published by John and Henry Playford.

Preparations in the City normally took several days, but 1682 was different. Because of the confusion and uncertainty surrounding the elections, there had been no time to prepare elaborate pageants and masques. Sir William Pritchard had only been elected on 25 October and sworn in at Whitehall on the 28th; the show followed two days later. The version of the festivities published by T. Burnel makes no mention of Thomas Jordon, nor does it use his rhymed description of the assembly and progress as in the accounts for the year before and the two succeeding years. Jordon gave each show a title, such as *London's Glory* or *The Triumphs of London*, whereas Burnel's is simply *The Lord Mayor's Show*.

It was essential, after all the court party's machinations of the previous months to ensure the election of their candidates and to ensure that London's government was one favourable to the King, that there should be some celebration of their victory, however hastily the show was put together and in spite of the King's absence. As if in compensation, the turn-out of royal trumpets was the biggest ever: sixteen of the King's and twenty of the Duke of York's. Instead of the usual performances there are 'several new loyal songs and catches'. The first is 'London is changed and the Times are turn'd', 'a song made upon the election', whose composer is not given. Then, while the Lord Mayor is at dinner, he is entertained with some loyal songs, such as 'Let the traytors plot on til at last they're undone'.

The chorus of this song is pro-Charles but anti-Pope, which seems like a sop to the City:

And he that dares hope to change King for Pope
Let him die while Caesar lives long.

This song wasn't new. It had appeared in the 1681 book of *Choice Ayres*, attributed to Thomas Farmer. The second song is also in praise of Charles, but takes a more middle course politically:

let both the Whigs and Jesuitical train
Be silenced in darkness while Caesar does reign.

This song may indeed have been new words to an existing tune, perhaps by Purcell. The third, unequivocally billed as 'this new song which is set to an excellent tune by Mr Purcell', is specifically pro-James and is a drinking catch: 'Since the Duke is return'd we'll slight all the Whigs'. No other composer is named in the proceedings. They conclude with the drinking of healths to all and sundry – 'King, Queen, Duke, etc.' – and with the singing of loyal catches, which may also be by Purcell, given that he wrote a great many such tunes to every kind of theme.

Here's a health to the King, down let it roll,
There goes ocean, ships and all.
Drawer make haste and quickly provide
A fresh supply to maintain this tide.

A second catch follows: 'Come here's to the man that lives quiet'.

According to Luttrell's diary account, 'several of the nobility were present' and one of the new disputed sheriffs was Dudley North. He had been a merchant in Turkey and was the brother of the Lord Keeper, Sir Francis, at whose house Purcell played the sonatas he was working on at this time. There's no mention of King's musicians apart from the trumpeters, fifes and drummers, and performance of the songs is attributed to 'one of the City Musick'. It's likely, though, that some of them were present, probably Purcell himself. His involvement with court politics is evident in his willingness to compose a new song for such an occasion, presumably with at least royal approval, and in support of James. Those who commissioned it and those who published it must have been well aware that his name would add lustre to the event and that he had the facility to turn out something worthwhile at very short notice.

The last of the fantasias is dated February 1683, so either Purcell was writing them in conjunction with the sonatas he was to publish in June or they were produced in a burst immediately afterwards. Musically the whole sequence is continuous and continuously brilliant. What strikes the listener is their amazing modernity. It seems as if it would be possible to jump from Purcell to the twentieth century without the intervening period of classicism, which, by contrast with the inventiveness and freedom of Purcell's instrumental work, can seem almost formal and repetitive. Purcell believed that there was a difference between the fantasias and the sonatas, and that in the latter he was following Italian models. To mark this change he abandoned English terms such as 'slow' and 'quick', and replaced them with Italian: 'adagio', 'grave', 'vivace', 'allegro' and 'largo'. For those who didn't speak Italian, he explained their meaning in the preface to the printed version.

Court and, in particular, royal influence must be at work in this shift. The King's preferences can also be seen in the songs Purcell was composing at this time, but I believe the process was encouraged by his apprehension that he had a rival in Pietro Reggio.

Reggio, an Italian who had been in the service of Queen Christina of Sweden, had come to England by 1664. He rapidly made a name for himself, being known to both Pepys and Evelyn, and finally settled in Oxford. He became the darling of the poets, including Flatman and Shadwell, who addressed laudatory verses to him, in effect saying, as Dryden was to do, that native British composers were a long way behind their Italian contemporaries in the setting of verse. Reggio published *The Art of Singing* in 1678 and compiled an unpublished collection of Italian songs by such composers as Carissimi, Cavalli and himself, which was no doubt circulated in manuscript. In 1680 he brought out a volume of English songs to verses mainly by Abraham Cowley and dedicated it to the King. Meanwhile in 1679 Purcell's publishers, Playford and Godbid, published a volume of pieces collected by the castrato Girolamo Pignani, which was dedicated to the Duke of Norfolk and called *Scolta di canzonette Italiane*. It contained songs by Stradella,

Carissimi and others, including several Italian musicians resident in England: Albrici, Draghi, Matteis and Pignani.

The marriage of the Duke of York to an Italian, Mary, daughter of the Duke of Modena, in 1673 had encouraged the expansion of the Italian musical style in England at the expense of the French, especially since she had taken over the upbringing of the two princesses, her stepdaughters Mary and Anne, around whom much of the musical activity of the 1670s was centred. Purcell was full of admiration for the music of the Italians and, according to a Hawkins story from Berenclow, Mary's musicians were also impressed by him and Blow.[3] It must have been partly owing to her influence that the Italian opera which Evelyn described as 'the first I ever saw here' was staged in 1674.

Nevertheless, Reggio's publication of English songs was unfavourably commented on by John Playford in the introduction to his third book of *Choice Ayres* (1681). After lamenting the long sickness that had caused the collection to appear later than he had intended, Playford goes on to describe those who have contributed to the third book as 'ingenious authors who are men that understand to make English words speak their true and genuine sense both in good humour and ayre which can never be performed by either Italian or French they not understanding the proprieties of our speech'. He then mentions Reggio's collection, referring to it as a book 'of English songs by an Italian master who has lived here in England many years', and says Reggio is 'much to blame for disparaging and undervaluing most of the best English masters and professors of music'. Playford further castigates 'the vanity of some of our English gentry to admire that in a foreigner which they either slight or take little notice of in one of their own nation' since 'the same rules in this science' are 'generally used all over Europe'. Evelyn would certainly have fallen into this category: he not only chose foreign masters for his beloved daughter Mary, but constantly praises music that he has heard, predominantly by Italian musicians.

The third *Choice Ayres* has seven songs by Purcell. The next, of 1683, includes some of his finest. Playford continues his complaint in his new preface. A critic had publicly declared that there were only three good songs in the last book, 'the rest being worse than common ballads sung about the streets by foot boys and link boys'. Several of Purcell's songs which should have been available for these two volumes weren't published until much later. 'Haste, haste, gentle Charon', a song in a long tradition of Charon dialogues,[4] and 'Hark, Damon, hark what musicks this' may have been thought over-elaborate for the amateur performer. They are part of a sequence of a dozen songs that were written between October 1682 and July 1683 and copied by Purcell into the scorebook of anthems and welcome songs he was currently using.[5] Those setting words by Cowley were to appear in *Harmonia Sacra* in 1688; perhaps they were felt too melancholy for *Choice Ayres*. One of them, 'How pleasant is this flowery plain', is a little cantata clearly designed to please the King in its variety – it offers airs and recitatives, solos and duets after an opening symphony for flutes – as well as in its use of the pastoral setting so beloved of Charles the country gentleman.

Strangely, the songs which do appear in the *Choice Ayres* of 1683, including the brilliant 'Bess of Bedlam' and the moving and uneasy recitative of sex warfare 'Sleep, Adam, sleep', are not in the vocal manuscript for this date. This may mean that the songs and odes in this manuscript were specifically written for the King while the others were for more public occasions, such as the music meetings. The two main theatre companies which had existed as rivals since the Restoration, the King's and the Duke's, had been amalgamated under the actor-manager Thomas Betterton in 1682 and they had hardly begun to play again before the great frost of 1684 made public life extremely difficult. Playford noted that it had closed the presses for more than ten weeks. Purcell's theatrical career, which seemed to have begun with great promise in the early 1680s, had to wait in the wings for the next stage of its development.

It's hard to imagine Charles enjoying such a piece as Taylor's 'Let the night perish' (*Job's Curse*), which shows Purcell already having developed the recitative song to perfection. Much more to Charles's taste must have been the setting of Cowley's 'She loves and she confesses too'. Reggio had already produced a version of this and Purcell even used Reggio's bass line, as if to show how easily he could outstrip him.

Sometime not later than March 1683 a performance took place which was to affect Purcell's work profoundly and lead to the writing of his most popular production, *Dido and Aeneas*: his friend and master John Blow's *Venus and Adonis*. The earliest score of this is to be found in a manuscript copied for Gilbert Dolben and dated 1681/2.[6] This date is, in theory, open to two interpretations: either the collection was written early in 1682, by modern dating, or it spans the period April 1681 to March 1683 (since in 'old style' the year ran from Easter to Easter, simplified as from April to March). It's a composite manuscript, with many songs by 'Dr Blow', William Turner, Matthew Locke and James Hart, whose name appears on the cover along with the attribution 'Mr Dolbin's book'. The first song is Purcell's welcome ode for the King's return from Windsor in 1680, which sets a date for the book's beginning. The last songs before Blow's 'masque' which can be dated fairly precisely are Purcell's 'Haste, haste, gentle Charon' and 'Hark Damon' both of which in his own autograph are after October 1682.[7]

The owner of the manuscript, Gilbert Dolben, was a steward of the Musical Society to whom Purcell was to dedicate his ode for St Cecilia's Day, *Welcome to all the pleasures*, when it was published in 1684. The other stewards include William Bridgeman Esq., Dr Nicholas Staggins, as might be expected, and Francis Forcer, a fellow composer and contributor to the theatre and the anthologies who had no court appointment. The Musical Society is a shadowy organisation. Piecing together various hints in Roger North, it seems to have been a group of 'gentlemen' who met originally to play, and took upon themselves the organisation of the first St Cecilia's Day ceremonies. Several of them, including North, were from the Inns of Court. Gilbert Dolben was the son of John Dolben, the hero of Marston Moor and dean of Westminster who had led his choristers against the Great Fire and this year had become archbishop of York. Gilbert had also attended Westminster School and was currently at the Inner Temple. William Bridgeman, a son of Richard Bridgeman of Amsterdam and a graduate of Queen's College, Oxford, was to become a member of parliament, secretary to the Admiralty and clerk of the Privy Council.

Also in the group were Sir Roger L'Estrange and Sir William Waldegrave, according to North: 'a pair of virtuosos and our chief connoisseurs at that time'. It was they who had taken it upon themselves to persuade the Neapolitan composer Nicola Matteis to be less proud and stand less upon his dignity as a professional musician by pointing out 'how much it would be for his interest to comply with the genius of the English nation, who declined those who stood upon high terms and were most obliging to such as were compliant and familiar'.[8] Matteis had dared to suggest that people should be quiet while he was playing.

North includes Bridgeman among those who talked him round so that 'he came to little meetings and did just what they would have him'. Most of the members seem to have been violinists, the 'sort of gentlemen . . . who used to meet weekly or oftener sometimes at private chambers and not seldom at taverns'. They eventually hired a room at the Castle Tavern in Fleet Street under the auspices of John Cressett, also of the Inner Temple, but when word of the excellence of their music got about and 'divers ladies and gentlemen desired to be admitted', the taverner began to charge for the best seats and the gentlemanly amateurs gradually dropped away because of the overcrowding and loss of privacy. 'The masters observing such a *penchant* after musick agreed with the taverner and held on the meeting till the crowds were too great for the place' and they built a concert hall in York Buildings. The list of stewards of the Musical Society suggests there was an interim period between the first private meetings and their takeover by the professional musicians, after which a gentlemanliness still pervades the proceedings. By 1685 meetings were being held at the 'Dancing School' in York

Buildings, presumably before the concert room was built. Dolben's manuscript could be of works performed at these gatherings. It raises the question of whether the first or at least an early performance of Blow's *Venus and Adonis* took place not at court but at one of the Inns of Court in the royal presence – for example at Gray's Inn on 2 February 1683, when the royal family, court and the nobility were entertained at a masque with a ball and a banquet.[9]

The 'gentlemen' who constituted the Musical Society were the most likely performers of and subscribers to Purcell's *Sonatas*. The pavane and chaconne which succeeded the four-part fantasias (the last of which is dated February 1683) are just the sort of dances that formed part of the Inns of Court revels, usually the post revels of general dancing, and there are instructions by a master of the Inner Temple for pavanes and alemains.[10] These were the Tudor dances. In Purcell's time they would have been based on French models as danced at court and by the nobility, and incorporated into theatre productions. By the early eighteenth-century revels the young lawyers and their guests were dancing minuets before the country dances, both of which could have been to tunes by Purcell. *Venus and Adonis* includes a saraband and a gavotte for the Graces, very suitable for court ladies such as the maids of honour. There were also lavish Christmas celebrations. In 1681, a particularly festive year, huge quantities of drink were consumed and over fifty pounds was spent on music, in addition to the two days' payments for drums and trumpets; sweetmeats were bought for Nell Gwyn.[11]

In Blow's masque Venus was played by another of Charles's 'stage misses', Moll Davies, whom Pepys had so much admired in her professional days, and Cupid by their daughter, Lady Mary Tudor. Technically this makes it a masque. Adonis' fellow huntsmen would have provided suitable roles for young gentlemen. There's nothing in the stage directions to suggest any need for more than the simplest staging: no flyings or trapdoors, just a simple curtain which opens to disclose the actors already in position. All these aspects would have made it eminently suitable for transfer to Josias Priest's school for young gentlewomen in Chelsea in 1684 and imply that if its first performance was at court, it was probably at Windsor rather than Whitehall, where the theatre was more elaborate.

The text has an educational flavour in the schooling of the young cupids, who might have been sung originally by the Chapel Royal children, or by Charles's and James's even more royal children. It could also have provided an Inn joke for young scholars if it was performed as part of a revel. *Venus and Adonis* is essentially a comedy until the moment of Venus' grief over Adonis' death, when the longing 'Ah' of the second act becomes the 'Ah' of lamentation. Its tone, apart from that moment, is quite different from *Dido and Aeneas*, which is tragic throughout.

Blow composed a powerful lament at about this time which was to become one of his most popular works. In the subject-matter of the text and in its intensity 'Go, perjured man' anticipates Dido's rejection of Aeneas. According to Hawkins, it was composed in response to the King's request that Blow should do something after the style of Carissimi's 'Dite o cieli'. Blow's song appears both in the Dolben manuscript and in the *Choice Ayres* of 1683. The anecdote shows the extent of Charles's influence on music and musicians.

Purcell's admiration for Blow was unstinting, and they constantly responded to each other's musical output. Sometimes Purcell produced an innovation, such as his elegy on Locke, which Blow emulated in his lament for the death of the Earl of Rochester; sometimes the traffic went the other way, as in the case of *Venus and Adonis* and *Dido and Aeneas*. Blow's achievement was to produce a chamber opera descended from the masque and therefore to lay the ground for Purcell's later work, while strangely not building on it himself. Having seen what could be done, the ambitious young composer was no doubt anxious to try his hand at a form which was so acceptable to their royal patron and to push it further at the earliest opportunity.

The country continued in a state of political and religious tumult. Laws against dissent were rigorously enforced. Sacrament certificates were drawn up to be presented to the magistrates as a sign of conformity. Henry Purcell, Moses Snow, Robert Tanner and John Goodwin took communion together at St Margaret's, Westminster, on 4 February 1683 and acted as each other's witnesses. The certificates, countersigned by the minister and the churchwarden, were presented in court on 16 April. Snow and Tanner were both members of the Abbey choir, and Snow and Goodwin were Chapel musicians.[12] It seems, from records in the Greater London Record Office, that people usually went in little groups to provide witnesses for one another.

Early in March the court set out for the racing at Newmarket, intending to stay until the end of the month, but on 22 March a fire broke out, caused by a groom smoking in one of the stables, and half the town was burned down. The racing was spoilt and Charles and James returned to London four days early, foiling a Whig plot to kidnap or murder them on their journey back. Immediately investigations were begun. Charles went nowhere without a guard. The conspirators of the Rye House Plot, as it was dubbed, proposed to put the Duke of Monmouth on the throne, and although he protested his innocence of any intention to murder his father, Charles was bitterly wounded. Many leading Whigs fled abroad, others were imprisoned and tried. Among the lesser players involved, including some who turned King's evidence and provided the chief witnesses, was, according to Luttrell, Samuel Shepheard, a wine merchant and one of Frances Purcell's father's two chief suppliers.[13]

Charles retreated to Windsor in the middle of April and in May plans began to be made for the marriage of Princess Anne to Prince George of Denmark, giving Purcell time to compose an ode for the occasion. Meanwhile he gave notice in the *London Gazette* that the *Sonatas* would be available to subscribers on 11 June at the reduced price of ten shillings for the set. A second notice appeared on time saying that the sets could be collected from his house in St Anne's Lane. He had given up his earlier intention of leaving their distribution to the three London booksellers, Playford, Hall and Carr, and decided to hand them over himself, perhaps so he could further explain the care he had put into the work and receive the subscribers' praise in person. In his dedication to the King he said that he owed everything to Charles's patronage: 'They are the immediate results of your majesty's royal favour and benignity to me (which have made me what I am)'. It was his first solo publication and put him ahead of Blow and Matteis, whom North singles out as having been responsible for the penetration of the English musical scene by Italian musicians.

Given his involvement with the 'gentlemen' players of the Musical Society, who would have shared Roger North's view that professional musicians were getting above themselves, it's unthinkable that Purcell would have been allowed to publish a spurious coat of arms below his portrait. Any such unfounded pretension would have been pounced on by satirists, and actively discouraged, if not sneered at, by his gentlemanly friends. There was, however, a degree of gentrification in the act, and it may have been encouraged by Frances. Her family assumed a coat of arms to which they were not entitled, though they may have had a right to one in Flanders and merely translated it into the English equivalent. They aren't the only family of immigrant Pieters to assume arms.[14] Frances's insignia are coupled with Purcell's on the Abbey monument, and the remaining fragment of sealing wax on Purcell's will shows the top of the Peters arms from the impression of the seal of her brother, John Baptist.

The partbooks of the *Sonatas*, beautiful objects in themselves, were produced for a limited, discerning audience, so that some remained unsold at his death. They show Purcell at twenty-four staking a claim on contemporary society and on posterity. The preface says that the author 'has faithfully endeavour'd a just imitation of the most fav'd Italian masters, principally to bring the seriousness and gravity of that sort of music into vogue and reputation among our countrymen, whose humour, 'tis time now should begin to loathe the levity and balladry of our neighbours'. The Latinate ending to it, 'Vale', suggests, as does the whole tone of the piece, a young lawyer's hand in the drafting. Purcell's own voice comes through most strongly in the sentence in which he laments his lack of Italian, but justifies himself on the grounds of 'the unhappiness of his education which cannot justly be accounted his fault', and in the practical comment that the books would have been printed much sooner 'but that he has now thought it fit to cause the whole thoroughbass to be engraven'. This was Lord Keeper North's part, which he told Evelyn he had been trained from childhood to sightread. Purcell must have felt that with this publication 'Henry Purcell, composer in ordinary to His Majesty, and organist of his Chapel Royal', as he's described on the title page, had indeed arrived and, whatever ritual modest disclaimers there are in the preface, he could now be ranked among his great predecessors. In the reversed end of his Fitzwilliam manuscript he inserts his own anthems among those not only of his contemporaries but also of the acknowledged masters, his forerunners Tallis, Gibbons and Byrd. Several of his works from this manuscript turn up in another compilation in the Fitzwilliam,[15] one of works for the Chapel Royal. Its very ornate tables of contents are dated 1683, and within the text this is made precise by the attribution of Blow's anthem *Hear my voice* to 18 July.

No other collection gives a better impression of the sheer quantity and quality of the Chapel Royal music or the methods of performance which, as Dr Peter Holman has pointed out, were polyphonic and three-dimensional. Small groups of musicians were situated in different places in the singing loft above and the choir below and on opposite sides of the church, a device Monteverdi used in his works for St Mark's, Venice. The effect was dramatic as well as lyrical; the perfect training for secular theatre could be had in providing Chapel music, from the dancing symphonies and ritornellos to sustained recitative, such as Blow's 'Christ is risen' for Easter Day. In spite of his secret change of religion Charles the pragmatist, unlike his brother, James, had no intention of endangering his position by withdrawing himself from the public worship of the royal chapel which supported the state and the monarchy, and in his continued favour towards its music and individual musicians he presided over one of the greatest periods of English composition. The music seems to come echoing off the pages.

Purcell's anthems in this great collection include the early *Save me, O God*, *By the Waters of Babylon*, *I will sing unto the Lord*, *Lord, who can tell*, *Let God arise*, *Blessed be the Lord my strength*, *O Lord our governor*, *Blessed is he whose unrighteousness*, *Hear me, O Lord, and that soon*, *Bow down thine ear*, *Man that is born of a woman*, *Thou knowest, Lord, the secrets*, *I was glad* and *My beloved spake*, encompassing the full range of emotions and their musical expression. The collection also contains several parts of his B minor service for morning and evening prayer, together with the *Benedicite*, *Cantate*, *Deus miseretur* and the accompanying anthem *O God, thou art my god*, which were copied for Westminster Abbey too.[16]

At the same time he continued to produce secular songs, among them a new clutch for the fifth volume of *Choice Ayres*, which John Playford registered with the Stationers' Company in June 1683. Some of them are light airs to entertain the King, like the two 'serenading songs' in his manuscript scorebook for this period. 'In Cloris all soft charms agree' and 'A thousand several ways I tried' from the Playford volume are typical examples, but one song in the fifth book, 'Through mournful shades and melancholy groves', is a complex despair song that picks up from Blow's 'Go, perjured man' and Purcell's own 'Bess of Bedlam' in the previous book.

Prince George arrived at Whitehall on 19 July. Evelyn saw him there at dinner, and again on the 25th, the night before the wedding: 'He had the Danish countenance, blonde of few words, spoke French but ill, seemed somewhat heavy, but reported to be valiant, and indeed he had bravely rescued and brought off his brother, the King of Denmark, in a battle against the Swedes.' As a younger son, he had no country to take his wife to and Anne set up her own household at court, where she was to be an important Protestant counterpoise in the next reign.

Purcell had had over a month in which to compose his welcome ode, *From hardy climes*, and it's one of his most consistently successful. The text implies that it was performed before the marriage. A work for the wedding itself would surely have taken the form of an epithalamium for both of them, rather than a welcome for Prince George. The long instrumental passages between the verses are most interesting. Their strangely dance-like rhythms suggest that perhaps this and other works were performed rather than simply played, that they were in fact more in the nature of the French *ballets de cour* or *opéra-ballets* than cantatas; in particular, the two ritornellos bracketing the delightful tenor solo 'The sparrow and the gentle dove' call out to be danced to.

The wedding over, the court set off again for Windsor and remained there until the end of August, when it moved on to Winchester for a month, the 'seat of his autumnal diversions' of racing and hunting; the King inspected the progress of his new Versailles, which had been made even more desirable by the discovery of the assassination plot.[17] This year the visit to Newmarket, which was being rebuilt by public subscription, lasted only twelve days. Purcell was ready with a new ode to welcome Charles on his return to London: *Fly, bold rebellion*. If there had sometimes been hesitancies in the earlier odes, those of 1683 show a fully matured skill. Purcell could handle all text with complete confidence in his ability to find a musical correlative for the words and their meaning. This ode is unashamedly and precisely polemical, calling on the citizens whose ancient rights the King had just set aside to 'Come then, change your notes, disloyal crowd'. It supports arbitrary monarchical government and gloats over those who have been executed or have fled. The gentlest moments are reserved for a lilting alto solo over a ground bass, one of Purcell's favourite techniques. He admitted in his revision of *An Introduction to the Skill of Musick* that he always found it easy to compose using a ground.

To modern ears and even some moderate contemporary ones, as Luttrell and Evelyn both make clear, the text is extreme in its views and their expression. But from the standpoint of a court employee whose family had served the Stuarts for many years, the maintenance of the monarchy was the prime consideration, and the murder of a king, the worst imaginable act, carrying with it all the resonances of '41 is come again to endanger the continuity of the musical establishment that provided Purcell's lifeblood. This time there's no mention of James, Duke of York, and the succession. Charles (Pan, Caesar, King David) is alone and all. 'Be welcome then, Great Sir, to constant vows.'

Less than ten days after the court came back Elizabeth Blow died at the age of thirty, giving birth to the Blows' fifth child. She was buried in the Abbey cloisters the following day, 13 October, attended no doubt by many of the musicians, including her father, Edward Braddock, a gentleman of the Chapel. He had a house in the Sanctuary next door to the Blows, and was to outlive everyone except Gostling. Blow never married again. He was said to be rather haughty and cold in his demeanour, but this loss after nine years of marriage can't have helped. The night before had been the annual feast in honour of the new lord mayor; this year the King's approved appointee, Sir Henry Tulse, had been elected. Thomas Jordon was ready with *The Triumphs of London*, but the two songs he prints have no composer's name and are studiedly apolitical.

Purcell meanwhile was composing a further two odes to complete the year's astonishing output, for the Feast of St Cecilia, patroness of music, on 22 November. No earlier reference to this celebration has been found, although Purcell's rubrics both in his autograph scorebook and in the printed publication of the music suggest that it had been going for some time: 'What day is commemorated yearly by all musicians', says the score of the Latin ode he set, and 'whose memory is annually honoured by a public feast made on that day by the masters and lovers of music as well in England as in foreign parts' is the heading of the printed song.

According to the warder's accounts of the Stationers' Company, this first recorded celebration[18] wasn't held at Stationers' Hall, and no venue is indicated on Purcell's printed text or in the journals. The hall was first used for the St Cecilia's Day Feast in 1684, when it is listed as 'the Musick Feast'. John Playford, as music publisher and a member of the company, must have been instrumental in fixing on this site, which was used with one or two breaks until the end of the century at least.

The Latin text *Laudate Ceciliam* must be by one of the 'gentlemen' of the Musical Society. The English words, *Welcome to all the pleasures*, are by Christopher Fishburn, who wrote music as well as verse, and contributed several songs to the 1684 edition of *Choice Ayres*. It seems as if Purcell intended to publish both songs, since he speaks of 'musical compositions', but changed his mind and transferred a copy of the Latin one to his scorebook. Perhaps it was felt there was less interest among the amateur market in something exclusively for lower male voices, or perhaps the great frost affected this publication too. The piece is strong and vigorous, reminiscent of some choruses in Monteverdi's *Vespers*.

The English song, after a rather wistful opening, moves into a mood of unalloyed pleasure, and delight in its subject.

> *Hail to this happy place, this musical assembly,*
> *That seems to be the arc of universal harmony.*

This is followed by one of Purcell's most beautiful alto lyrics, 'Here the deities approve'. These things are very much a matter of personal taste, but it seems to me that a composer who could produce this fine sustained melody and its ritornello was already capable of Dido's lament. It's as though the chance to write an apologia for his art and his own practice has freed the music, after the constraints of so much political writing, and the greater formalities of the Latin text, in which he appears to be rather straining to impress. *Welcome to all the pleasures* is unflaggingly brilliant, but also shows great freshness and tenderness in the setting of words that link his preferred themes of music and love.

Purcell's connection with the gentlemen was further strengthened during this year by the so-called Battle of the Organs described at length by his old schoolfellow Thomas Tudway. After a fire in the

Middle Temple in early 1679 much rebuilding had to be undertaken. Roger North had chambers in the Temple and in 1683 was elected treasurer for the coming year. As part of the refurbishment a new organ was ordered; two foreign organ builders, 'Father' Bernard Smith and the younger Renatus Harris, were to compete for the commission.

Smith had been in England since the early 1670s when he installed a new organ for the King in Windsor, for which he was paid under a contract with Thomas Purcell. He was also employed on occasion by John Hingestone to repair, set up and tune the royal instruments. Not surprisingly, Smith chose Blow and Purcell to demonstrate his instrument while Harris chose Giovanni Battista Draghi of the Queen's chapel. The competition was already under way by October; the Inner Temple Records show that by then payments had been made for 'a treat for Dr Blow and the other masters of music when they come about the organ'. North came to believe that the whole affair had been a mistake and that the two men had been almost ruined by a process which dragged on for several years. It was finally resolved in 1688 when Judge Jeffreys awarded the contract to Smith.

Just before the St Cecilia's Feast of 1683 Frances's brother, John Baptist, and his wife Martha, celebrated the birth of their first child, named after her mother.[19] There were to be at least ten more, among them a Frances and a Henry. A fortnight later John Hingestone died and was buried in the chapel of St Margaret's, Westminster, leaving Dr William Child as the senior survivor among the musicians. It was a sickly time: the smallpox was 'very prevalent and mortal', the Thames froze before Christmas and the court was in mourning for the King of Portugal, the Queen's brother.

At once Purcell was confirmed as his godfather's replacement as tuner and repairer of the King's instruments at a salary of sixty pounds a year. He had powers to take up the materials, including 'metals, wire, timber, strings and feathers', and the workmen he needed from anywhere in the kingdom; he could hire 'land and water carriages, work and storehouses'. He needed all the money he could get. Daniel at last left the Chapel about this time and there's no record of any payment for his further tuition. Inevitably it would have fallen to his elder brother to fit him for a career in music.

· 6 ·

Sighs and Tears

THE FROST DIDN'T go away, but continued until February. The Thames became a fair of streets of booths and entertainers, where coaches came and went on the ice. The sea froze too, so no ships could get in, food became scarce and dear and there was no news from abroad. The country was cut off and the poor were unable to follow their usual trades; the thousands of coal fires turned the air into a thick smog that choked the lungs. The King was particularly concerned for the poor, frozen and starving, and took the lead in setting up contributions for their relief. Plants, animals and fish all died, as did the deer in the parks. Houses burned down because there was no water to put out the fires. Even in April Evelyn reported that there was hardly any sign of spring. On the 5th the court, eager to leave the stinking city, set out for Windsor, where Prince George and the Dukes of Somerset and Westmorland were installed as knights of the garter with elaborate ceremony.

In February Frances Purcell's brother-in-law, John Howlett, and his son John both died, leaving her sister Amy a widow still living in their mother's house. There are no extant rate books for All Hallows the Great and Less for the period after 1681, but the family had left by the time of the 1690 poll tax. Perhaps this double death was an effect of the bitter winter. It must have been a time of sadness for Frances on her sister's behalf, with only Mary remaining of Amy and John Howlett's several children.

Compared with that of the previous year, Purcell's output seems small for him, although for anyone else it would be more than enough. Between the St Cecilia ode of 1683 and the song to welcome back Charles in the autumn of 1684 there are a mere four songs in his autograph scorebook. There were undoubtedly anthems and also the five songs in the first book of *The Theater of Music* (early 1685), the first anthology by John Playford's son Henry, whose preface thanks Blow and Purcell for their assistance.

Early in spring 1683 Blow and Nicholas Staggins had petitioned Charles for a licence to set up 'an Academy or Opera of musick for performing or causing to be performed therein their musicall compositions'. The King referred the petition to Sunderland, the lord chamberlain, for his advice, and nothing more seems to have been heard of it. Not that Charles had lost his interest in opera. If anything it had grown. A few months later he sent the manager of the newly united theatre company, Thomas Betterton, to Paris to try to bring back the French opera. This was clearly an impossibility, as Louis XIV was unlikely to give permission, but Betterton did manage to persuade Louis Grabu, who had returned to Paris sometime after 1673 when he had lost his job because of his Catholicism, along with several other musicians, to come to London. The more relaxed times made it possible for him to return to the country, although not to an official post.

There was no love lost between Grabu and Staggins, who had been appointed in his place as master of the King's Music. Charles's referral of the Blow–Staggins petition to Sunderland was, I believe, a deliberate piece of procrastination and a way of avoiding the kind of confrontation which he so disliked. A licence for an academy would effectively have given the pair an operatic closed shop, where only their works were to be performed. Charles, who wanted to keep his options open, showed a preference for foreign opera, which he'd been brought up with in exile, over the most recent native works: Staggins's *Calisto* and Blow's *Venus and Adonis*. He shared this preference with his poet laureate, John Dryden, who was still contemptuous of British composers.

On Grabu's return he and Dryden set out to produce an opera for the King. It was to become the ill-fated *Albion and Albanius*, though it was some time before the actual form and subject were decided on. Dryden says in his preface to the published edition that *Albion* was 'originally intended as a prologue to a play of the nature of *The Tempest*', but that he had then added two acts more and made it a play, or rather an opera, in its own right. Referring again to the Shadwell–Locke *Tempest* and not, I think, to his own earlier adaptation with music by John Banister, Dryden notes that the English were pleased with it and with 'some pieces that followed which were neither much better written nor so well composed as this'. He obviously means the works of Blow and Staggins, 'the English musicians and their scholars' who 'make a party maliciously to deny' Grabu.

Where did Purcell stand in all this? On the one hand he had an intense and recently expressed admiration for the Italians, whom Dryden specifically praises in his preface to *Albion and Albanius*: 'Whoever undertakes the writing of an opera is obliged to imitate the design of the Italians.' In further praising Grabu, Dryden goes on: 'the knowledge of Latin and Italian poets which he possesses, besides his skill in music and his being acquainted with the performances of the French opera, adding to these the good sense with which he was born, have raised him to a degree above any man who shall pretend to be his rival on stage'. Further, 'the most eminent in the land', that is, the King, 'has himself attended the rehearsals' and publicly pronounced that 'the composition and chorus were more just and more beautiful than any he had heard in England'.

Purcell's natural loyalty was to his teacher Blow, if not to Staggins. Blow and Purcell were constantly coupled together, particularly in the prefaces to the anthologies which the Playford family produced, and therefore in the public mind; in John Playford's will they are described as his 'dear friends'. Purcell would also have remembered his old master Locke's defence of the 'English opera' *Psyche*, which was effectively a defence of the right of English musicians to be considered capable of compositions in the operatic form. What Staggins and Blow had been proposing in their petition, however, was a potential monopoly that would have excluded not just foreign composers but aspiring young British ones as well.

As a move in this operatic struggle, Blow's 'masque', as it's called both in the British Library and in the Westminster Abbey scores, *Venus and Adonis* was given another performance in 1684 at the Priests' boarding-school for girls in Chelsea. This strongly suggests that Josias Priest had been responsible for the original choreography. The school, in a large house next door to the Chelsea home of the Bertie family, earls of Abingdon and Lindsey, had been in business since the 1670s, when it was run by two musicians, Thomas Lowe and Jeffrey Banister. The Priests took it over in 1680 and it became the school most sought-after by the nobility and gentry. For the Priests this performance, which allowed their scholars to display themselves in parts originally taken by members of the court, was a splendid advertising occasion. Typical of the pupils was Molly Verney, who was very happy there from the early 1680s until the end of the decade.[1] Among other accomplishments, they learned to dance gracefully and to japan, which was an extra; such skills were thought to make a girl 'considerable and lovely in the sight of God and man'. The audience of rich and influential parents made any production there more than just a school performance, and the Priests may have been after Lady Mary Tudor, the King's natural daughter who had played the original Cupid, and might have already spent some time at the school, simply repeating her role on this occasion.

The librettist for *Venus and Adonis* is unknown, although Aphra Behn has a dialogue that could easily be a cast-off from it. For his opera Grabu had the Poet Laureate, Dryden himself. *Albion and Albanius* is a very strange piece indeed, since it's a naked allegorical rendering of recent events, in particular Charles's triumph over the Whigs; Albion is Charles and James, Duke of York, is represented by his brother Albanius. It followed on from Dryden's other great political allegory of this period, *Absalom and Achitophel*, whose symbols are taken from scripture and not from rather doubtful history. So popular had the first part of this been that the public had demanded a sequel. Dryden, having agreed, found himself too caught up with other work and involved in a bitter controversy with the poet Shadwell, the subject of his *Macflecknoe* (one of the harshest satires ever propagated by one poet against another), because of Shadwell's vituperative attack on *Absalom*. The two had once been friends and collaborators, but the fierce political conflicts of the late seventies and early eighties had split them into the chief propagandists for the Tory and Whig factions. Dryden passed the commission to Nahum Tate and the resulting sequel, to which Dryden contributed some two hundred lines, was published in 1682.

For Tate to be asked to help out not simply the Poet Laureate, but the acknowledged contemporary master of their craft was a great accolade, though it was of little consequence to Dryden, who in any case was always inclined to be generous to younger writers. Tate had jumped to the defence of *Absalom and Achitophel* when it was attacked by Shadwell. Dryden was showing his gratitude, and also his critical approval of Tate as a writer.

Tate is such an important figure in Purcell's life, a friend to the end of it and after to his brother Daniel, that he merits more attention than he's previously been given. Seven years older than Purcell, he was the son of an Irish clergyman (the name should properly be spelt Teate), and had taken his degree at Dublin University in 1672. He published his first book of poems in 1677 and his play *Brutus of Alba* was produced the following year. Tate and Purcell had met by 1681, the year of *The Sicilian Usurper* fiasco.

As an Irish Anglican and a Tory who had written a poem congratulating the Duke of York on his escape from the wreck of the *Gloucester*, Nahum Tate is a strange mixture. Later in life and for the next two hundred years he was to be known chiefly for his and Nicholas Brady's metrical translation of the Psalms, as well as the hymn 'As pants the hart'. The popular Christmas carol 'Whilst shepherds watched their flocks by night' is also attributed to him. Highly intelligent, he was of a solemn, perhaps morose cast of mind. Before his birth his family had suffered the sacking of their Irish home, when his mother and the elder children had been treated with appalling brutality, as a result of which three of them died. The usual clutch of jolly drinking songs is absent from his work. He took love seriously. Even if it does not reflect an actual event, the remorseful poem beginning 'Chains, straw and darkness', written after he'd beaten his mistress, shows a temperament which contemplates the darker side of passion and manifests itself in Dido's death. Tate appealed to the part of Purcell's own nature that produced not only her lament but the intense settings of George Herbert's and Cowley's more anguished cries which he was occupied with from the early 1680s.

In his preface to his play of *Brutus of Alba* produced in 1678 Tate writes: 'I had begun and finisht it under the names of Dido and Aeneas but was wrought by advice of some friends to transform it into the dress it now wears.' This raises the questions of why his friends should have given such advice and why he should have accepted it. One answer is that, with only one volume of juvenilia to his credit, it would have seemed too cheeky to be laying poetic hands on one of the great legends of the age; another perhaps that he knew that what was regarded as the definitive version of Book IV of Virgil's *Aeneid* in which the story was enshrined, the one by Sackville and Waller, was being reissued. By 1684, however, he was in a very different position as one whom Dryden had trailed the edge of his mantle over and, as he says in his prologue to the farce *A Duke and No Duke*, he had also had 'the good fortune to divert his majesty' with this when it was produced in 1684.

Whose idea it was that they should collaborate in an opera can't now be known. Purcell would have been anxious to attempt the form and Tate to openly claim the subject he had reluctantly overlain with the story of Brutus. They must have hoped either for a royal commission or at least a command performance, as *Venus and Adonis* had received, and Purcell undoubtedly knew of the King's desire for such a work. They must also have known of the *Albion and Albanius* project, especially by the time it reached rehearsal stage. Purcell might have been involved in these as harpsichordist, and Tate's close association with Dryden would have kept him informed of progress. Grabu's work must have been seen by the King in the autumn and early winter of 1684–5 at the lodgings of his patron Louise de Kéroualle (the King's mistress and Duchess of Portsmouth), which Evelyn describes as the most sumptuous in Whitehall. The libretto, except for the final amendments, would have been finished in early 1684 to allow time for Grabu to write the music, Priest (who, I take it, was responsible for the dances) to devise and rehearse them and the designs for settings to be 'put forward' (as Dryden said they were) by Betterton. The elaborate nature of the designs implies the piece was ultimately intended for the public theatre, unlike *Venus and Adonis*. Once he'd finished with the libretto, as he thought, Dryden turned to his first version of *King Arthur*. A letter from him to his publisher Jacob Tonson, dated from internal evidence to summer 1684, refers to both 'the opera' not yet finished, which sounds like the first *King Arthur*, and 'the singing opera'. With regard to the latter he says, 'I desire to know whether the Duke's House are making clothes and putting things in readiness', which suggests it is *Albion and Albanius*.[2]

Meanwhile Tate had a second collection of poems in the press. Two of them show that his mind was running along the lines of his previous play, though rhyme, which had been missing from *Brutus of Alba*, is added. These are *Beldam's Song* ('Appear my kib walkin'), and a song for sailors, *The Hurricane* ('What cheer my mates, luff ho'). Already in *Brutus of Alba* Tate had departed from the Virgilian original to introduce the elements which are still there in the libretto of *Dido and Aeneas*, principally the sorceress, the hunt and the storm. If they were there from the beginning and weren't an afterthought, these changes had probably also influenced his friends' advice in 1678 'to transform it', in case he was criticised for tampering with something that had the status of literature's Holy Writ. He had also turned the story completely around by shifting the focus and the audience's sympathy from Brutus-

Aeneas to the Queen-Dido. In his version the sorceress is an external force for evil, not Dido's fiction of an old witch's rites to cover up her intended suicide. So far does this reversal go that in both play and libretto the Queen dies of a broken heart rather than killing herself as Virgil has her do.

Tate's heroine-oriented version must have particularly appealed to Purcell, since in this it resembled *Venus and Adonis* rather than *Albion and Albanius*, whose protagonists are male. The whole shape of Purcell's work and the musical forces employed suggest a private rather than a public performance, a chamber opera for the King. It was therefore, like its forerunner, eminently suitable for a school production, although I don't think it was intended for the latter when Tate and Purcell first conceived the project.

Musically and historically, everything points to an earlier date for the composition of *Dido and Aeneas* than its first known performance at Josias Priest's school in 1689.[3] I also believe, for reasons which I'll discuss later, that neither the prologue nor the epilogue belongs to the original opera, but were written for the school production. *Dido and Aeneas* is quite unlike the semi-operas which immediately followed it – *Dioclesian* in 1690, *King Arthur* the following year and *The Fairy Queen* the next – not least because *Dido* is a genuine opera in which the text is completely set to music, as in *Venus and Adonis*. Tate and Purcell expected a high standard of both singing and acting from the same performers, which was the usual theatrical arrangement in the early 1680s. By the end of the decade the roles of actor and singer were undertaken by two different performers, and the dramatic structure had divided into spoken text with musical interludes. The great days of such dancing and singing actors as Henry Harris, Nell Gwyn and Moll Davies belong to the earlier years.

The actress who, I feel, would have been capable of performing Dido was Charlotte Butler. During this period she had left the stage and was pursuing a musical career, appearing not only at court, but at public concerts:

to save her tott'ring fame
At music club she strives to get a name.[4]

In the same letter to Tonson quoted earlier Dryden was trying to get her for Octavia in a revival of *All for Love*.

Instrumentally the music which most resembles that of *Dido and Aeneas* is the welcome ode for Charles's return in the autumn of this year, 1684, to words by Thomas Flatman, *From those serene and rapturous joys*; the symphony to the ode and the overture to the opera are particularly similar. The King had come back from Winchester on 25 September. On 4 October the court set out for Newmarket, but it returned to Whitehall on the 23rd.

The ode begins by celebrating the country life which the King loved. He was intending to enjoy it for six months every summer by removing the whole court to Winchester, where the new palace was now rising like Carthage beside the sea. According to Wren's drawings, the central cupola was to be visible from passing ships. The building was designed to have two wings – one for the King with his chapel and one for the Queen with hers – and four storeys, of which the third alone had sixty rooms. There were to be water gardens for the King's beloved ducks, a park, terraces, galleries and a new road to the town for royal progresses and access to the port of Southampton.[5]

The King had spent the month of September inspecting the building work. The main parts except the cupola were roofed but not leaded by the end of the year. There were marble columns sent by the Duke of Tuscany, and the brickwork, in the same style as Wren's remodelling of Hampton Court, was particularly fine. In the eighteenth century the huge building was capable of housing six thousand French prisoners of war. Many of the nobility had built grand houses in the town in anticipation of the annual royal residency, and the Bishop of Winchester had employed Wren to rebuild the episcopal palace. No artist appears in Wren's palace accounts as having been commissioned, but it would surely have been Antonio Verrio, the most sought-after of the day, who the year before had illustrated Dido's pyre on the walls of Montagu House.[6]

The opening of the new palace would have been attended with an elaborate ceremony which must have included music, and I believe Tate and Purcell had this kind of occasion in mind; perhaps there was even a hint from the King that such a composition might find royal favour. The ode which he heard on his return to Whitehall in October is arguably the finest of Purcell's early ones and contains every musical ingredient necessary for *Dido and Aeneas* other than its laments, which are closer to the *arioso* recitatives for religious texts Purcell was writing at this time. Tate's new volume of poems was published in 1684. He was also putting together a collection which contained not only poems by himself, but John Oldham's St Cecilia ode for that year, set by Blow, and a *Pindaric on Musick* by John Wilson. Tate was passionate about music, saying in his verse epigraph to Henry Playford's fourth book of *The Theater of Music*, licensed in October 1686:

What charms alas can our dead rimes impart
Without the inspiring great musician's art.

Did Dryden know what his two younger rivals were up to? Unless they deliberately kept it a secret, it would have been unusual for him not to know, although he was in the country for much of 1684, nursing his son who was ill. I think there's a hint that he knew something had been going on in his preface to *Albion and Albanius*. From his words quoted earlier about what pieces the English had been able to hear and approve, it can probably be assumed that there had been no production of *Dido and Aeneas* before Dryden's publication of *Albion and Albanius*. I don't believe that he would have written contemptuously of Tate's and Purcell's work if he had heard it, or if it had been produced without his hearing, since at this stage he and Tate were on very good terms.

I think he knew of the work and that it was in his mind when he hedged his bets in his criticism of British composers by saying that if anyone arose to equal Grabu in composing opera, he would change his opinion and be pleased 'for the sake of old England', a rain check he was to call in with his praise of Purcell in the preface to *King Arthur*. The two comments are worth setting side by side:

> When any of our countrymen excel him [Grabu] I shall be glad . . . to be shown my error. *Albion and Albanius*

> There is nothing better than what I intended but the musick, which has since arrived to a greater perfection in England than ever formerly, especially passing through the artful hands of Mr Purcel. *King Arthur*

In 1684 St Cecilia's Feast was held at Stationers' Hall for the first time and, in addition to Blow's ode, the friends of music might have heard Purcell's undated ode *Raise, raise the voice*, with its extraordinarily complex string writing and soprano solos. I'm inclined to date it to this year because it doesn't appear in the scorebook, which seems to contain works there was no immediate intention to publish. An announcement in the *London Gazette* early in 1685 says that both Blow's and Purcell's odes are to be published, although only Blow's eventually appeared. Perhaps the soprano solos were for the French boy Evelyn heard on 29 January, 'so famed for his voice, singing at Lord Rochester's'. The next evening, at the home of the newly released Catholic Lord Howard of Wardour, who had been in the Tower since Titus Oates's plot and celebrated his freedom with a dinner 'for a world of people of quality', there were performances by Evelyn's daughter Mary and the Catholic musicians Samuel Pordage and Giovanni Battista Draghi of the Queen's chapel.

The French boy was present again the following day, singing love songs before the King and the Duke while twenty courtiers played at basset in the glorious long gallery. The Duchess of Mazarin (who had introduced the game and brought her own croupier from France) was there with the other 'concubines', as Evelyn calls them in his unforgettable description: the King 'toying with' Portsmouth and

Cleveland, a heap of gold shining on the gaming table, Gostling there to sing, and perhaps Purcell to accompany the singers on the lute or harpsichord.

Ten of the royal musicians had been ordered to practise for a ball to be given before the King in the Theatre Royal. The phrase 'given before the King' and the fact that it was to be at the theatre in Whitehall suggest that what was intended was more of a ballet than a ball, reflecting the great popularity at court of dance as an art form, as well as the importance of the numerous dances in *Albion and Albanius* and *Dido and Aeneas*. A great ball had followed the magnificent fireworks for the Queen's birthday the previous November, but on that occasion 'the young ladies and gallants danced in the great hall'.

At eight in the morning three days after the scene in the long gallery, as he was being shaved preparatory to visiting Portsmouth's apartments (where she was used to receiving him and several of the court in her loose morning robe while her maids were combing her hair), Charles, who had been complaining of pains in his chest and stomach, fell down in a fit. Fortunately, there was a surgeon present who bled him, and he seemed to recover. He was a little better the next day and again on 4 February, but in the evening he grew worse. The Anglican bishops present gave him absolution and urged him to take communion, but he said there was time enough. The Duke of York requested everyone to stand a little way off so that he could speak to his brother privately, and then asked him if he should send for a Catholic priest. 'For God's sake, brother, do, and lose no time,' Charles answered. The rest were sent away except for Louis, Earl of Feversham, and the Earl of Bath. Father Huddleston, who had helped to save the King's life after the battle of Worcester, was brought in up the backstairs to administer the sacraments. Charles lingered until the following morning and died just before noon, having consigned the care of the kingdom, and of his mistresses, to James.

· 7 ·

Caesar's Godlike Sway

THE NATION'S POETS burst into a paroxysm of grief. Over sixty elegies and lamentations were published. If Charles had had his vices, like frequent non-payment for artistic and other services, at least he had loved and encouraged all the arts. At once a difficulty arose over his burial. Because of his last-minute conversion, or acknowledgement of his latent Catholicism, there could be no Anglican state funeral. A committee was appointed to oversee the post-mortem, embalming and official mourning. The full funeral regalia were laid on, as for the death of James I. There were mourning clothes for the kettledrummers, fifes and trumpeters, but no mention in the royal accounts of any for the Chapel Royal musicians. The King was buried quietly at night on 14 February in the Abbey with everyone present. The officers of his household broke their white staves over the grave as was the custom.

James was proclaimed king and all appointments were confirmed for the time being, but the new broom was already beginning to sweep. The Duchess of Portsmouth retired to the French ambassador's, but was barred from leaving the country until she had paid her debts and returned some of the royal jewels; the Duke of Richmond was sacked from his job as master of the horse; the new King put away his own mistress, the daughter of Sir Charles Sedley. All work was stopped on the new palace at Winchester. 'The whole court was changed into a more solemn and moral behaviour.' Retrenchment was to be the new policy.

In his first speech to the Privy Council James had promised to defend and support the Church of England. The day after the funeral, however, he publicly attended mass in his own chapel while Dr Tenison, archbishop of Canterbury, preached in the Chapel Royal to an empty chair. Significantly Purcell, who could have had the pick of the poetic outpourings to set, chose an anonymous text whose first lines express the worries of the Anglican Church:

If prayers and tears
The shields the Church of England only bears,
In some exigence of state,
Could those have warded off the blows of Fate,
We had not fallen, had not sunk so low;
Under the grievous heavy weight,
The pressures of this day's sad overthrow.

Nevertheless, he was among the earliest to sign the oath of allegiance on 1 June, 247th out of a roll of almost 700; his friends Blow and Gostling were numbers 507 and 572, while fellow musician Thomas Farmer was 409th.[1]

King Arthur was laid aside, together, I believe, with *Dido and Aeneas*. Hawkins tells a story of another work that Charles didn't live to hear, *They that go down to the sea in ships*, an anthem said by Gostling to have been composed to verses selected by him after a near-fatal incident at sea. According to Hawkins, Charles had commissioned a new yacht to be called *Fubbs* after the Duchess of Portsmouth because, like her, it was broad in the beam. Soon after it was launched the King and the Duke, with, as usual, Gostling along to sing bass to the King's competent tenor, sailed the new ship down the Thames to the Kent coast. By the time they reached the North Foreland a violent storm had blown up and it was all hands, including the royal ones, to the ropes. They managed to make land, but the deep impression of the horrors of the deep received by Gostling caused him to give Purcell an appropriate text to set.

This story shows some discrepancy with the dates of actual events, although I'm inclined to believe that the incident did take place. The *Fubbs* was built at Greenwich dockyard and launched in August 1682. James records in a letter to his niece Charlotte Lichfield on 15 September that the King is 'very pleased with his new yacht the *Fubbs*, she out sailing all the old ones', but in a letter of July he described an incident when he and the King sailed down to the North Foreland 'in his yachts . . . we had bad weather and some little accidents'. This ties in nicely with the story of sailing down river and round the Kent coast, but if, as Hawkins says, the King didn't live to hear the anthem, then Purcell took two years to write it, which seems an unusually long time for one who worked so quickly. It must be that when he was remembering the story over thirty years later Gostling either conflated two voyages or placed the incident much closer to the launch than it really was. The connection with the sea and the desire to compose something for those that go down to the sea in ships is entirely appropriate, since Purcell had two brothers, Charles and Joseph, at sea, although when they first became sailors is hard to trace. There are few records that mention assistants until they become fully fledged officers – in the case of Purcell's brothers, warrant officers as purser and surgeon. In his diary the naval surgeon James Young records that he was apprenticed at as young as eleven for eight years, and set sail at once for Newfoundland in 1658, so Purcell's brothers may have been already at sea when the anthem was composed.

There's some mystery about Edward's movements for the last year before the King's death. His final appearance as an assistant gentleman usher daily waiter is on 9 July 1683, when he was either upgraded or left the royal service.[2] For some time Edward had been on full pay, as his successor pointed out in an aggrieved petition. What's certain is that he either didn't wish or wasn't asked to become James's body servant after ten years of serving his brother: five days after Charles's funeral in 1685 he was given or bought himself a commission as lieutenant in the Queen Consort's regiment of foot. I'm inclined to think that, if he left the royal service in July 1683, he joined the band of English gentlemen going as volunteers that month to aid the Habsburg Emperor against the Turks who were besieging Vienna. Such an adventure would have given Edward a taste for the military life. Nahum Tate published a satirical poem on the English volunteers and their eagerness to rush off and fight. Aphra Behn's piece in the popular form of a Scotch lament was more sympathetic.

Edward was the head of the family and later, after Henry's death, was still Joseph's protector, invoking his own patron, Sir George Rooke, to speak for him in finding a new post.[3] If he went abroad for a time, Henry would have missed his support, for it's clear from their taking the oaths of the Test Act together and from Edward's later care for his niece, Henry's daughter, that they were as close as Frances Purcell was to her family.

The Purcells moved again, to a house in Bowling Alley East, early in 1685; according to the rate books, they were there before Easter, when the new financial year began. The King's death must have been as great a shock to Purcell as to the whole nation, and it inevitably brought uncertainty to his future, although he had always been a supporter of James. The next task after the funeral was to plan the coronation. For this, James had to submit himself to the full Anglican service, omitting only the communion and taking care to have himself anointed with holy oil by his own priests beforehand.

Apart from his other duties in the run-up to the ceremony, Purcell was responsible for setting up a second organ in the Abbey and removing it afterwards, for which he was later paid a special sum that was also to serve as settlement for unspecified services in the Chapel Royal from 25 March, presumably also to do with his job as organ keeper. The coronation was magnificently organised and sumptuous in its ceremony. In the interest of economy, the new monarch did not spend the previous night at the Tower as was customary and the state procession the following morning was left out. Mary slept at St James's Palace, her favourite, and James at Whitehall. In the morning, after an elaborate robing, they met at Westminster. A full pictorial record was published after the event by the Garter King of Arms, Francis Sandford, so it's possible to know exactly who and where everyone was on that St George's Day.

Purcell walked with the basses, and his anthems opened and closed the ceremony in the Abbey: *I was glad*, which he'd already written, began the proceedings and a new composition, *My heart is inditing*, ended the day with a brilliant shower of music. Afterwards the King and Queen, along with many of the nobility, went to Westminster Hall to a banquet consisting of hundreds of dishes, among them pistachio cream, blancmange and mangoes, as well as cold puffin and hot cabbage pudding. The choir wasn't present, but from a rather cramped gallery the violins played music which Sandford doesn't specify, but there was probably some by Purcell and perhaps Staggins, who was later paid for writing out a work for forty parts, including trumpets. Everyone was so exhausted that the fireworks had to be put off until the next day. There had been no fewer than nine anthems to be sat through in heavy coronation robes: two by William Turner, a fine countertenor, three by Blow, one by the eldest member of the Chapel Royal, William Child, and one by Henry Lawes, *Zadok the priest*. Purcell's were in pride of place. Oddly, one of the rubrics in the margin calls him organist of Westminster, while another has him at St Margaret's. The fireworks next daywere followed by a ball at Whitehall, which might have been the occasion for the performance of Purcell's *Coronation Pastoral*. Three days later the playhouse reopened.

James now set about rationalising several institutions, including the navy, and the chaotic affairs of the royal servants, among them the musicians. He was determined to make a plan for paying off the arrears due to them, to establish fixed wages and to cut back on the perks, such as riding charges, claimed when they accompanied the royal household on their summer progresses. New riding charges were set at three shillings a day when the musicians didn't lodge 'in the House' and reduced to one shilling and sixpence after the first week when they did.

Fees for the Private Music were also set. Nicholas Staggins was reappointed master at two hundred pounds a year and Henry Brockwell was confirmed as keeper of the instruments. There were to be thirty-three musicians, including three new basses to replace those who had died. All were to be paid a uniform forty pounds a year, quarterly. Blow, Gostling and Purcell were listed, Blow as composer and Purcell as 'harpsicall'.

Purcell still had his job in charge of the organs and other instruments, and his position at the Abbey was unaffected. Soon three chapels were operating in the royal household, and a smaller one at Somerset House, where the Queen Dowager Catherine took up permanent residence. There was the old Chapel Royal, whose members remained roughly the same, James's new Catholic chapel and Mary of Modena's Italian chapel. The private musicians were distributed according to their religious persuasion. There were ten 'Gregorians' in James's new chapel, a master, 'Signior' Fede, Grandi and Sansoni, John Abell and Pordage, both, according to Evelyn, fine singers, a mysterious Mr Anatean, and nine instrumentalists. Mary of Modena's chapel employed the Sachelli, senior and junior, the Ronchi, Ruga and Galli, all Italians, and four others more difficult to give a nationality to from their names alone. There was also an Italian flautist in the Private Music: Francesco Morieno. Giovanni Battista Draghi transferred from Somerset House to James's chapel as organist later in the reign. The Italian influence was very strong. Staggins was appointed in March, before the coronation. Then sixteen trumpeters and their sergeant, Gervase Price, were admitted, but it wasn't until August that the list of the Private Music was drawn up.

The two books of *The Theater of Music* published in this first year of James's reign, one before and one after the coronation, contain thirteen songs by Purcell. Only one, Cowley's *The Rich Rival*, which was written before Charles's death, appears in the autograph score. Several other songs were composed in this period, according to the scorebook, but weren't published until much later, bringing the total for the year to about twenty before the long welcome ode for James's return from Windsor on 6 October.

Purcell isn't in the list of those who accompanied the court on its summer progress. During its four days at Winchester Evelyn visited Charles's abandoned Versailles and remarked that James seemed to have no intention of finishing it. Perhaps it was too far to the west, or too close to where Monmouth had landed in the spring, blighting the public performance of *Albion and Albanius*. It had finally reached the stage, after some necessary rewriting, on the day Monmouth raised his standard at Lyme.

The opera ran for only six nights, not enough to recoup the money spent on its lavish scenery and sets. The rebellion was blamed for its failure, but there was also a lampoon going the rounds suggesting Grabu's music was the real reason. Dryden's text must take some share of the blame; one of his least successful pieces of royal propaganda, it borders at times on the absurd and is given only a fake gloss by the defensive preface. The reason for its collapse probably lies between the quality of the piece and the consternation at Argyll's rebellion in Scotland and Monmouth's landing. Its time had passed with the King's death, unlike *King Arthur* and *Dido and Aeneas*, which were less creations of the moment. The public's attention was focused on real battles and defeats, not the scuffles at the hustings of the previous reign.

For the Purcells it was a doubly anxious time, since Edward's new regiment under its Cornish commander, Charles Trelawney, was sent against Monmouth's force and took part in the battle of Sedgemoor. The country, apart from the Nonconformist west, stood firmly by James and the established succession, but there will always be a question as to whether Monmouth could have succeeded in winning the crown if he had won the battle and not been deserted by his own horse. When news of his defeat came, it was accompanied by the death toll: 'above eight thousand', Evelyn recorded, 'the King's but two thousand seven hundred. The slain were most of them Mendip-miners, who did great exertion with their tools, and sold their lives very dearly.'

James had no real option but to have both Argyll and Monmouth executed. Evelyn, expressing the majority Anglican view, feared 'an inundation of fanatics and men of impious principles . . . universal disorder, cruelty, injustice, rapine, sacrilege and confusion, an unavoidable civil war, and misery without end'.

Purcell's autumn ode, with its extraordinary solo tenor opening, echoes these fears. In the autograph it's headed 'Being the first song performed to King James the Second', that is, the first welcome song.

Why, why are all the Muses mute?
Why sleeps the viol and the lute?
Why hangs untun'd the idle lyre?
Awake, 'tis Caesar does inspire
And animates the vocal choir.

The music is very close to Dido's lament. A beautiful symphony follows as the instruments awake indeed. The text goes on to praise strong monarchical government in 'Caesar's godlike sway', seducing the listeners with a charming xenophobic alto solo, 'Britain thou now art great'. The late rebellion makes its appearance with the bass, and the writing here anticipates later solos for this voice by Purcell. This dissolves into a duet for soprano voices and a ritornello ushering in a celebration of James's mildness:

let unenvied blessings flow,
On his obedient world below.

For the resolution Purcell returns to the tenor, whose flowing dance tune is taken up in the ritornello and then by the chorus. There are strong echoes of the finale of *Dido and Aeneas* in its dying fall.

His fame and the world together shall die,
Shall vanish together away.

All in all it's one of Purcell's longest and most inventive odes. Pepys was present at its evening performance and described it as 'a mighty musique entertainment for welcoming home the King and Queen'. Like all the welcome songs, it ends rather than finishes, raising questions about what happened next in the elaborate ceremony of welcoming the King back to his capital and chief residence. Eight days later they were celebrating again for his birthday with 'public demonstrations of joy, as ringing of bells, showe of bonfires etc.'. There was also 'a solemn ball at court with before it instruments and voices',[4] so it's possible that Purcell's ode was performed again then, or perhaps his anti-Monmouth song with words by Tom D'Urfey, 'The grass-hopper and the fly' (subtitled 'an allegory'), which was published the following year in the third book of *The Theater of Music*.

For Purcell and the gentlemen of the old Chapel Royal these were strange times. They no longer accompanied the King on his summer progress unless they were also such members of the Private Music as had been commanded to attend. The new Catholic chapel went instead, as well as Mary of Modena's largely Italian musicians. The rest were left behind to service a chapel from which the heart had been removed. Princess Anne, in a letter to her sister, Mary, in Holland in early 1687, describes the bizarre business it had become: 'ever since the late King died I have sat in the closet that was his in the chapel and there the great choir stands just as if the King were to come hither and I sit on a stool on the left hand and the Bishop of Rochester who is clerk of the closet is on the other side.'[5]

Purcell and the other Protestant Chapel musicians continued to compose anthems. After the magnificent *My heart is inditing* for the coronation Purcell's autograph has *O sing unto the Lord*, *Praise the Lord, O Jerusalem*, *Praise the Lord, O my soul*, which a manuscript identified as having belonged to John Gostling dates to 1687, like the anthem for Christmas Day, *Behold, I bring you glad tidings*, and *Sing unto God*. Many were written with Gostling specifically in mind.

The diminished role of the old Chapel in royal affairs, and its concomitant estrangement from the seat of power, must have been difficult for an ambitious composer to accept. The pressure to consider conversion to Catholicism was very strong, and Dryden himself, the defender of the established church in *Religio Laici* of only three years before, was swept away by it, producing his Catholic apologia *The Hind and the Panther* in 1687. Even had he been drawn to convert to the Catholic Church, with all that would have meant in increased royal favour, Purcell's very close relationship with Blow, Gostling and Tate would have made it difficult for him, and he would have had to give up all his official posts in Abbey and Chapel. Yet the question was in the air for everyone who came into contact with James.

James's chapel came to be known as the Chapel Royal, while the old one was referred to officially as 'the chapel at Whitehall where her Royal Highness the Princess Anne of Denmark is present'. Affected by this change of status, the musicians began to neglect their duties and Staggins was reprimanded for not ordering them to attend. A year after the coronation Renatus Harris was commissioned to build a new organ in the refurbished King's chapel. By the end of the reign it was called the Chapel Royal in accounts, and a splendid new Catholic chapel seen by Evelyn had also been built at Windsor; its organ had been removed from Winchester and remodelled by Renatus Harris. The employment of Harris rather than the Blow–Purcell protégé Father Smith is significant. Significant too may be the failure to make any provision in the fiscal establishment to pay Purcell for his duties as organ tuner and repairer, both for the Chapel and the Private Music. By June 1687 he was driven to petition for payment and for a future settlement. He had gone on fulfilling his post and had already disbursed twenty pounds and ten shillings. The Bishop of Durham, fortunately a patron of Purcell and by then dean of the Chapel Royal, was asked to look into the matter and report on it.

The Catholic John Abell was now the favourite court performer, as frequent payments of bounty money to him show. The Protestant musicians must have felt themselves increasingly marginalised. Yet James was still their king and the Church of England taught passive obedience. Secular musical life at court continued unabated with frequent 'balls', especially at the maids of honour's lodgings, and command performances of plays with songs and act tunes. If the royal musicians took part in these, they must presumably have been doubling at the theatre. The French opera seems to have finally paid a visit in the new year, a fortnight after the festivities for the reception of the Venetian ambassadors 'with music, drums and kettledrums that sounded upon a whistle for every health'.

Princess Anne was a great dancer and play-goer. Indeed, she and Prince George were at the theatre on their wedding day, according to a letter from her father to his niece, and she took part in 'her play' while she was with James in Edinburgh in 1681. Five of the house party performed it three times; they 'did their parts very well and they were very well drest so that they made a very fine show and such a one as had not been seen in this country before'.[6] Her father also described her love of country dancing, and in the letter in which she speaks of her Chapel experience to Mary she writes enthusiastically of the new dance called the rigaudon brought over from France by the Earl of Rochester in the winter of 1686: it was 'very pretty' and had 'a great deal of jumping in it', which she thought had caused her to miscarry.

The first year of the new reign ended with the King firmly in control. The army had been recalled after the west was subdued. Now, instead of disbanding it as parliament expected, James insisted it was necessary that it be kept for the safety of the monarchy and the nation. Edward probably spent some time with his brother, for Evelyn notes that the troops were to be quartered in the towns, many of them in London. Among the officers of Edward's regiment, which was Mary of Modena's own, were the young John Churchill and a son of the notorious Percy Kirke, who had shown great cruelty against the Sedgemoor rebels.

Although he was no longer officially a composer to the Private Music, Purcell still divided the royal odes with Blow as they had done before, Blow continuing to write the ode for New Year's Day and Purcell the welcome home. He had inserted a complimentary song to James, 'How great are the blessings of government made', into Tate's new play,

Cuckold's Haven, which was produced in July 1685. The end of his first year and the next were the honeymoon period for James. He felt secure enough to bring back his Protestant mistress, Catherine Sedley, and to make her Countess of Dorchester, following his brother's practice of ennobling his mistresses. Evelyn saw the Queen's distress; she refused to eat or to speak to her husband or anyone else.

The lack of his salary of sixty pounds a year must have presented Purcell with financial problems. A letter to the Dean of Exeter in November of this year shows that he was already supplementing his income by taking pupils, and the move to the house in Bowling Alley East may have been for the greater accommodation needed because of this. Twenty pounds, the money for half a year's teaching and board for his pupil 'Mr Hodg', had been due in June, as well as seven pounds Purcell had had to spend on 'necessaries', clothes and materials for him. Nothing more is known for certain of this protégé of the Dean's who had caused the trouble, running up other debts with people 'so poor it were an act of charity as well as justice to pay 'em', though I suspect he was Robert Hodge, later organist in Dublin. The fluency and assertion of the drafting suggest Edward's helping hand in this letter.

Purcell no doubt had other, secular pupils to whom he taught the increasingly popular harpsichord. In addition, he kept up a continual flood of songs, many of which would have been performed at the rapidly growing number of music meetings. By October 1686, when the fourth book of *The Theater of Music* was licensed, he had contributed no fewer than fifteen songs to the final two volumes, with verses by authors including the 'matchless Orinda' (Katherine Philips), Sir George Etherege, Tom D'Urfey and Cowley. Although some of the songs had been written as much as eighteen months earlier, before Charles's death, many others, such as the powerful 'O solitude' by Philips, were new. Purcell and Blow had also had a hand in the editing, in an attempt to make sure that the music was playable by the largely amateur audience it was designed for. Purcell's songs cover the full range of musical forms, from the catch to the cantata, and a similarly wide spectrum of the emotions, from the joyous celebration of drink and sex to introspective meditation on death and nature. With every song Purcell seemed to refine and develop his mastery of vocal line and his ability to set verse that often sounds almost too angular and knotted to modern ears for musical expression at all. An exception from *The Theater of Music* for 1686, 'I saw fair Phyllis all alone when feathered rain came softly down', is a charming text of very high quality in its own right.

The publication of these anthologies had passed from John to Henry Playford, his son, after the final volume of the *Choice Ayres* series. In this year he died, quite suddenly and, as the elegy Nahum Tate wrote for him and Purcell set suggests, without time to have his will signed and witnessed. His widow advertised his printing press for sale in the *London Gazette* in May; his expressed desire to be buried either in the Temple Church or the parish church of St Paul's Cathedral, St Gregory's, wasn't carried out and his grave is unknown.[7] He had wanted Blow and Purcell to be present at his funeral. Purcell's tribute to his long-time friend and publisher is a sustained and moving recitative for tenor voice. Tate's words pay tribute to Playford's 'innocence and piety' as the publisher of the Psalms, and also to his goodness and friendliness, both shown in his relationships with his musicians, bearing out his character as described by Hawkins.

His death marked the end of an era which had started with the Lawes brothers. Purcell's music begins to show a change about this time, as does his handwriting, which reverts, probably under the influence of the popularity of 'the new round hand', to the backward 'e'. The change in his music, although more gradual, is more fundamental and, I believe, came about through the increased contact with Italy and Italian music of James II's reign.

Hawkins has a story, presumably from William Gostling, of how Blow's and Purcell's music first came to be known in Italy, and it dates to between 1686 and 1687, the time of the flamboyant embassy of the Earl of Castlemaine, Roger Palmer, to Pope Innocent IX in Rome. James had hoped for great things from this visit, which was extremely costly, but Castlemaine was given a chilly reception by the Pope and James was advised to proceed slowly in his attempts to reconvert England to Catholicism. Even James's chief representative at Rome, Cardinal Philip Howard, gave Palmer the same advice to carry home. On the second day after his first audience with the Pope he was entertained by Queen Christina of Sweden, and then again at the beginning of February 1687, with an operatic piece by Pasquini in honour of James II. The conductor was Corelli, who may also have visited Modena, and the court of Mary's brother, Francesco II.

Modena was enjoying a rich musical life under the elder Bononcini and Giovanni Battista Vitali, who had composed an oratorio in honour of James's victory over Monmouth, as well as many cantatas, dances, sonatas, anthems and another oratorio, *Il giano*.[8] Visitors from England to Italy brought back music which passed from hand to hand and was copied rather than printed. A manuscript in the British Museum[9] which belonged to Charles Morgan of Magdalen College and which contains many songs by Purcell dated between 1682 and 1687 also shows what Italian music was in circulation. Besides much by Carissimi, a great favourite in England, and the resident Pietro Reggio, there are songs by Rovetta, Marini, Cassati, Monfernato, Stradella, Gratiana, Silvestro and Sances, a daunting list for British composers to compete with.

According to Hawkins, one of the English travellers at this time was Ralph Battell, made a prebendary of Worcester by James's ecclesiastical commission in 1685. A High Churchman, urbane and cultivated, with a passion for music and a brilliant letter writer,[10] he was certainly in Venice in 1678, when he met Nicholas Staggins on his tour of the operas of France and Italy for Charles II. Staggins expressed the view that the music in Venice was 'mine arse', but that the scenery was 'pretty', though no better than in Paris. It's not surprising that he was so against Grabu. His views can't have been popular with Charles either and may have contributed to the failure of his and Blow's petition to be allowed to set up their own opera academy.

Whether or not he was part of Castlemaine's entourage, the story goes that Battell spent some time with the equally urbane and civilised Cardinal Howard, who had been out of England for ten years and was eager to have news of the state of English music. When Battell was about to return to England, Howard asked him to send him some English church music, particularly that of Blow and Purcell, which he had heard was very fine. Battell asked how he should send it and the Cardinal replied that he could send it in the Quaker William Penn's packet. This story has several marks of authenticity. Penn and the King spent much time together planning the Toleration Act, which would equally affect all Nonconformists, to the point where Penn was accused of being a secret Jesuit. There's every reason to suppose he corresponded with Howard about these delicate matters.

In a number of eulogies written to Blow and Purcell the fact that their music had reached Rome and been performed there is celebrated as evidence of their great achievement. It was the final triumph for an English composer, since Italy and its music were seen as the apex of the art. Purcell had already acknowledged its predominance in the preface to his sonatas. In this period of intense renewed communication with Italy and the elevation of so many Italian performers at court that influence increasingly permeates his vocal music too – not to the exclusion of his innate Englishness, which was audible to his contemporary Roger North and still is today, especially to foreign critics, but rather as a framework, like the armature of a sculpture. More and more the sound is baroque rather than late high Renaissance.

An account of Castlemaine's embassy was published in Italian soon after he had returned and kissed Their Majesties' hands at Windsor in August. It was Englished by its author, Michael Wright, one of Castlemaine's secretaries, who had been part of the entourage. This version has laudatory verses by Nahum Tate and no one else, and must therefore have been known to Purcell. His mouth would have watered at the descriptions not of the banquets, with their sculptured sweetmeats on groaning tables, but of the music.

Queen Christina's entertainment, which should perhaps be styled a cantata, employed 5 soloists, 100 voices in the choir and 150 instrumentalists under Corelli's direction – in other words, a full-scale orchestra of a size unheard of in England. The performers were placed on a rising tier of benches at one end of the great audience chamber. Once again the theme was James's triumph over Monmouth and the whole performance was presented 'for several days together'.

Not to be outdone, Cardinal Pamphilio presented a tragedy sung in recitative, the story of Dympna, the Irish saint, on a stage beautifully set out with proper scenes, and Cardinal Barberini provided a musical entertainment of 'an excellent composition of vocal and instrumental music', after which there was a two-hour dinner with more music. Music figured at the Clementine College, where the ambassador was entertained with a prelude and chorus, followed by young men vaulting and fencing in between dancing: a French minuet, a 'high dance', a saraband and several figure dances of six and eight with a concluding symphony. It's to be hoped that Castlemaine enjoyed music.

What emerges from this account, apart from the glittering picture of tables heaped with food and gold plate, is the prominence of music as a manifestation of civilisation. In spite of the splendour of Castlemaine's train, especially the coaches and liveries, the English appear uncouth. He had made a mistake in not taking English musicians with him. If Hawkins's story does belong to this period, it gives an added meaning to Cardinal Howard's request for the English church music of Blow and Purcell in the light of his advice to the King to tread slowly and warily in matters of religion. Howard took every opportunity to meet English visitors to Rome of whatever religious persuasion and he was continually in attendance during the ambassador's long visit. Castlemaine failed to make any cultural presentation in response to those he was shown because James's and Mary's preference was for all things Italian. Purcell's answer to this was to incorporate what he could learn from Italian composers into his own music. He must have longed for their opportunities to write for such massive forces.

Tate's verses in praise of 'great Caesar' and the embassy exemplify the position of Anglicans at this time. Most of them were alarmed by James's move towards toleration, seeing it as a way to bring in Catholicism. The emblem of Britannia on her knee to 'the Church' described in Michael Wright's account must have been disturbing. It had been left out of the report of Castlemaine's audience with the Pope in the *London Gazette*, the language of which so closely resembles the printed book version that Michael Wright must have written it. Obviously it was felt that this part might inflame public opinion if it appeared in such a prominent place as the *Gazette*. Unless Tate was toying with conversion at this stage, and there's no other evidence for this, his eulogy must portray the unswerving loyalty of James's Church of England subjects, in spite of their worries about the promotion of Catholics and the standing army that now camped every year on Hounslow Heath.

The subtle changes in Purcell's music make themselves heard in the two later Jamesian welcome odes, of 1686 and 1687. The sound is round, dancing and very lyrical for the first of these, *Ye tuneful Muses*, and particularly tender when the words introduce Mary into the picture with another lovely alto solo. In 1686 the court returned from Windsor on 1 October. Eighteen musicians had accompanied it on its summer travels, but Gostling, who had been used to go everywhere the King, and indeed James, while still a duke, went, wasn't among them. As an ordained priest of the Anglican Church he was unacceptable to the increasingly single-minded James and his court circle. His place was taken by the new basses Balthazar Reading and Solomon Eagles.

Purcell must have used Gostling in the ode, along with the countertenor William Turner, who wasn't part of the Windsor group either. Meanwhile Blow and Purcell had been overseeing the building of a new organ at St Katherine Cree in London by Bernard Smith. Purcell, who played the finished organ in September and pronounced judgement on it, was one of the four musicians who, along with a group of parishioners, heard the four candidates compete for the position of organist. The winner in what seems to have been a fair and anonymous contest turned out to be Moses Snow, Purcell's friend and colleague from the Abbey, who was now regularly publishing new songs in the anthologies. After the judging they all went to the Crown Tavern for refreshments.

A growing number of catches and glees by Purcell were appearing in the songbooks and in private collections. Some of them are drinking catches, others were bawdy enough for a later age to feel it had to bowdlerise them. It's unthinkable that he could have been writing dozens of these without taking part in the activity they were designed for.

'Would you know how we meet o'er our jolly full bowls' is typical of the drinking songs, while 'Young John the gardener' is an example of those based on sexual innuendo. The practice of men coming together at taverns and coffee-houses to sing was becoming more popular all the time and was seen as an essential part of the musical fabric. By the end of the century Henry Playford had evolved a scheme for a national federation of music clubs based on the taverns and all singing the same sets of catches, published in his second book of *The Pleasant Musical Companion*, with printed standing rules for an enterprise that was to be 'beneficial to the publick in forwarding a commendable society'.

The King's birthday on 14 October was celebrated with a muster and march of the guards in Hyde Park, and at the ball and music at night the ladies appeared particularly fine to Evelyn. He was less impressed by 'the music of the Italians' in December when he went to James's sumptuous chapel, newly opened to the public. A few weeks later he heard the Italian castrato Grossi, usually known as Siface or Ciffaccio, sing there and had to admit it was 'indeed very rare and with great skill'. Siface didn't stay long in England; Purcell wrote an instrumental piece, *Sefauchi's Farewell*, when he left in June the following year.[11] Evelyn heard him sing again at Pepys's home and was once more forced to praise 'his holding out and delicateness in extending and loosing a note with incomparable softness and sweetness'. Siface also played the harpsichord 'rarely well', but Evelyn found him proud and coy, 'a mere wanton effeminate child'.

For the birthday ball there are accounts of the beer and wine drunk and the bread eaten. There was a similar provision a week later for 'the music playing among the scenes' at a play and in December for another play and a ball, after which Blow's New Year's ode was performed at night by the light of white wax candles. The country was holding its breath while the court danced, but for the Purcells the most important news was that Frances was pregnant again.

· 8 ·

Harmonia Sacra

LIKE THE NEW King and Queen, the Purcells were still without living children, in their case after six years of marriage. Whether there had been other Purcell children among the hundreds of unnamed 'abortives' and 'cryssomes', or 'still born', who appear pathetically in the registers of St Margaret's, Westminster, no one can say, but they had now been without even the birth of a named child since John Baptista four years before. It's clear from his tone when writing for the 'young practitioner', his support for a boy singer in one of Hawkins's stories and his instructions to Frances about his children's education (mentioned in her will) that Purcell was fond of children and young people. This continued childlessness must have been painful to them both and put a strain on their marriage.

What was now the Princess of Denmark's chapel at Whitehall was steadily becoming a focus for the Anglican backlash against the inroads made by Catholicism on state and church. A series of preachers spoke out there to large congregations, in support of the established religion and against the proposals to abolish the Test Acts. Foremost among them was the saintly Dr Ken, bishop of Bath and Wells, who was an eloquent and fearless preacher. Inevitably Anne and, by association, the Chapel musicians found themselves in a difficult and at the very best equivocal position. Anne grew frightened that her father would make an attempt to convert her. She advised her sister, Mary, not to come to England in case, as the next and Protestant heir, her life should be in danger. She also began to hate Mary of Modena, who had always tried to be a good stepmother, feeling that she was responsible for the pressure she, her father and the country were under. Increasingly her letters reflect someone on the edge of hysteria, kept sane by her stolid but boring husband George, even though she admitted that the King was more likely to 'use fair means rather than force'. It's possible that she exaggerated the danger, but since she and George had lost their only two daughters in February within four days of each other, it's not surprising that Anne's psychological state was shaky and fearful.

What was going on was a struggle for supremacy between two powerful factions: the old Catholic landed aristocracy, who had been dispossessed from power by the Reformation and supported an absolutist monarch on the French model, and the newer Whig Protestant party, whose wealth was based on trade and who looked to parliament as the ultimate authority. In this conflict, with a king not much younger than his recently dead brother and a Protestant heir over the water, the Catholics felt impelled to hurry matters on while praying for a Catholic heir. This bitter struggle must have been particularly disturbing to those, like Purcell, who were in the King's service yet still Protestant, and in the service of the established church as well.

The court divided for the summer progress, Anne and George going to Richmond while James went to Windsor. No doubt Anne was glad to be out of the city, where every church she visited was thronged with people expecting an inflammatory sermon. The King had at last given permission for George to make a visit to his native Denmark, but without his wife. She had hoped to use the opportunity to confer with her sister, but she was forbidden to leave the country.

Early in April James published his declaration for liberty of conscience. At the same time one of the masters of Magdalen College, Oxford, died. The King's ecclesiastical commission sent instructions that the college should choose a Mr Farmer, reputed to be a Catholic priest, to fill the post. Instead the fellows chose Dr Hough, chaplain to the Duke of Ormonde, precipitating a long-drawn-out and complex struggle for control of the universities. From a modern standpoint the Church of England's determination to maintain its monopoly over people's minds and education seems hard to defend, but it has to be remembered that another Catholic monarch, Louis XIV, had just revoked the act of toleration known as the Edict of Nantes. Thousands of Huguenot refugees were fleeing to Britain and other Protestant countries from murder and pillage as well as civil and religious oppression. Though James wrote to Louis condemning his action, many people in Britain began to fear that in the course of time he might behave in the same way, especially since it looked as if a parliament would never be called again after a series of prorogations. The dissenters, of course, welcomed liberty of conscience, and many loyal addresses were presented to the King, congratulating and thanking him for the new freedoms.

It is against this background of conflicting loyalties that Purcell's many anthems for the last years of James's short reign have to be set, for example *Sing unto God*, written for John Gostling in 1687, which can be read in its choice of text as a piece of Protestant apologia to accompany one of the more rousing sermons. The work is for small forces over an organ ground; it has none of the earlier string ritornellos, but simply a powerful bass solo punctuated by the choir, leading to the final chaste 'Amen'. There's no mention of kings, only of a very Puritan God who alone has power over Israel.

> *He will give strength and power to his people*
> *Blessed be God.*

Other anthems from this period in the Gostling manuscript are *Praise the Lord, O my soul* and *Thy way, O God, is holy*. The musicologist Charles Burney's father remembered how the crowds used to flock to hear any new anthem by Purcell at the end of his life, and his music must have added to the drawing power of the preacher at this time too.

The Purcells' son Henry was born in June and christened in their parish church of St Margaret's on the 9th. The following day Purcell put in the plea for payment as organ tuner which was passed to the Bishop of Durham, one of the ecclesiastical commissioners. In his final bill Purcell claimed that by the beginning of 1688 the organ was so out of repair that it would cost forty pounds 'to cleanse, tune and put it in order' and twenty pounds a year 'to keep it so'.[1] He also claimed for the loan of a harpsichord, portage and tuning, and for four songs at four pounds a song, 'for three practices and performance to the King', which gives an insight into how much rehearsal there was for each court performance.

The decision to compile and publish a volume of sacred songs which was taken by Henry Playford, Blow and Purcell sometime before early November 1687, when the collection was licensed, has to be seen as part of the religious conflict that intensified during this year and culminated in James's re-establishment of his chapel on even more elaborate and costly lines in March 1688. The anthology, *Harmonia Sacra*, contains hymns by Pelham Humphreys and Matthew Locke, representing the older generation of composers, and by Purcell, Blow and William Turner for their contemporaries. Some of Purcell's contributions, and indeed Blow's, date back to much earlier, but others appear to be new, or at least aren't included in the earlier scorebooks.

Playford's introduction is very skilful in that it treads a fine line between not criticising recent developments and making it clear that this is a book of Protestant devotional music: 'the words are penned by such persons as are, and have been, very eminent both for learning and piety; and indeed he that reads them as he ought, will soon find his affections warmed, as with a coal from the altar and feel the breathings of divine love from every line'. Purcell is specifically identified as the editor. 'Here therefore the musical and devout cannot want matter both to exercise their skill and heighten their devotion.' In case anyone should still miss the point, the book was dedicated to Bishop Ken, the Church of England's eloquent apologist who was soon to find himself in the Tower.

The emotional drive behind many of Purcell's meditations may have been the death of his son Henry after only three months of life, three months that must have given his parents hope that this time their child would survive.

How long, how long, great God, must I
Immur'd in this dark prison lie

are the first lines of a poem expressing a longing for death in the certainty of being linked with God, which had just been republished in June of 1687. The author, John Norris, was at this time a fellow of All Souls, later to be known as the last of the Platonists, and rector of George Herbert's old parish of Bemerton near Salisbury. In his introduction he castigates modern poetry and music. 'From grave majestic solemn strains . . . 'tis now for the most part dwindled down to light frothy stuff consisting either of mad extravagant rants, or slight witticisms and little amorous conceits, fit only for a tavern entertainment.' *Harmonia Sacra* sets out to prove him wrong by its very existence and by Purcell's composition to Norris's own words.

A final ironic touch is given to the collection by the closing piece, 'Upon a quiet conscience close thine eyes', Purcell's setting of words attributed to James's father, 'Charles I of blessed memory', who had been, although High Church, a convinced Anglican. 'Let the night perish' by Jeremy Taylor and 'With sick and famished eyes' by George Herbert both belong to 1683. Purcell was taking the opportunity to get some of his more serious earlier work that hadn't found its way into the 'light frothy' anthologies into print.

Not only was the collection very popular, judging by the number of reprints, it also enhanced the reputations of those involved with it, doing exactly what Playford had claimed in his introduction – that is, providing the more thoughtful with serious compositions to complement the many light anthologies. The first *Banquet of Music* and *Harmonia Sacra* were entered in the Stationers' Register on the same day, 6 December.

After receiving back the Castlemaine embassy in August, the King and Queen had gone their separate ways, Mary to take the waters at Bath in the hope of conceiving, and James on a progress through the West Country to receive more expressions of loyalty and support for his proposals for liberty of conscience. He joined her in Bath at the beginning of September. She must have conceived at once, for Luttrell writes of her being two months pregnant in late November, when she was afraid of miscarrying and was let blood. James returned to Windsor on 17 September and Mary joined him there at the beginning of October.

On 11 October the whole court went back to London in the evening, to be welcomed by the last of Purcell's Jamesian odes, *Sound the trumpet, beat the drum*, arguably the best and most innovative of them, with its startling opening after the symphony, in which alto and bass imitate trumpets and drums. The soloists weren't Gostling and Turner but John Abell and John Bowman. Abell was at Windsor with the King until the court returned, so either he or Purcell must have made the journey to and from London to rehearse.

The centrepiece of the ode is a stately chaconne, once again raising the question of whether the odes were accompanied by dancing. In the text much is made of both Caesar and Urania, as Mary takes her place prominently beside James. This is the most Italianate of Purcell's odes so far. The shake is used a great deal more than in the preceding years, though it appears in the printed version of the song which comes immediately before the ode in the scorebook, 'This poet sings the Trojan wars', or 'Anacreon's Defeat', to words by Cowley. Published in the first *Banquet of Music*, which was licensed in November, it has an instruction after the title that all the notes marked with an asterisk 'are to be sung as demi-quavers'. It was a technique that Abell certainly could have perfected during his Italian visit.

The next evening Anne and George, who had been reunited at Hampton Court after his visit to Denmark, also returned to Whitehall, where, within less than a fortnight, she miscarried an unnamed son whose burial entry in the Abbey register immediately follows that of 'Henry Purcell, a child'. The King's and Queen's birthdays were celebrated jointly with a ball, though bonfires were forbidden. James realised that a general moratorium on them; even for his own birthday, made it easier to forbid them on the two most popular Protestant festivals due in November, those of Guy Fawkes and of Queen Elizabeth's accession.

The Lord Mayor's Feast took place a fortnight later. The King and Queen and Prince George, as well as the newly received papal nuncio, Count D'Ada, were present at the usual banquet. The new lord mayor was Sir John Peake, whom Evelyn describes as an Anabaptist, proof of how far advanced James's policy was of uniting the dissenters from both wings against the established church. Luttrell noted that nine hundred of the 'violent tories' had been removed from the livery companies and the City's Court of Assistants. The show, however, 'was splendid and the entertainment great'. There was at least one song, but no music obviously by Purcell, although he must have been among the performers.

The next important musical event was the St Cecilia's Day celebrations. So politicised had even music become that both the writer of this year's ode, John Dryden, and the composer Giovanni Battista Draghi were Catholics. The Musical Society, because many of its members were from the Inns of Court, reflected James's policy of encouraging the appointment of Catholic lawyers and those favourable to himself, as does its choice of composer Draghi, who was now organist of James's Chapel Royal. It can't be a coincidence that this year the Inner Temple entertained Count D'Ada, Father Edward Petre and the Duke of Berwick, James's natural son, during the twelve days of Christmas. On the day of St Cecilia's Feast the Catholic John Abell entered a petition for a patent which would give him the monopoly of all music publishing, vocal and instrumental, religious and secular.[2]

For Christmas at Anne's chapel Purcell composed a new anthem, *Behold, I bring you good tidings*, which complements the music on the passion in *Harmonia Sacra*, a lamenting treble solo, 'The earth trembled'. The Christmas music was another great opportunity for

Gostling's full range; sprightly choruses and rich string writing are interspersed. The instruction to Staggins in late October to ensure that the violins attended at the chapel now that Anne was back suggests that those anthems with only an organ or other continuo accompaniment of this period belong to the summer months when she was away. The anthem ends with a delightful 'Alleluia' followed by a proto-Handelian 'Glory to God. Amen.'

Purcell was simultaneously composing an anthem for another birth. The Queen's pregnancy was announced to the nation, and prayers preceded by an anthem were ordered to be read in all Anglican churches, on 15 January 1688 in London and for ten miles around, and on the 29th in the rest of the kingdom. Once again the power of music was understood and invoked. Purcell's *Blessed are they that fear the Lord* failed, however, to sway the congregation even in as near a church to Whitehall as St James's, Piccadilly, where Purcell's aunt (Thomas's widow, Katherine), his cousins Matthew and Katherine, and others of the family worshipped. The Earl of Clevedon, who was there, wrote in his diary that few people brought the paper of prayers with them and that it 'was strange to see how the Queen's great belly is ridiculed as if scarce any body believed it to be true. God help us.'

The pace of change now quickened. Catholic chapels and schools opened up all over the country, but especially in London. Purges of civic life replaced any who objected to the removal of the Test Acts and penal laws with people sympathetic to the new order, and particularly Catholics, of course. The affairs of Magdalen College came to a head with the dismissal by the ecclesiastical commission of all the fellows. The Lord Mayor was given permission to abandon the Book of Common Prayer in Guildhall Chapel and put in 'a fanatic parson'. Edward Purcell's regiment was ordered to get ready to go to Ireland to support the new Catholic governor, the Earl of Tyrconnel.

In February 1688 the anniversary of the death of Charles II was commemorated in James's chapel, followed two days later by music for James's accession and a play at night. This is thought to have been a revival of *The Double Marriage* by Fletcher and Massinger, with act tunes by Purcell.[3] James had now decided that in order to carry through his policy of toleration it was necessary to call a new parliament, but he had to be sure that it would contain enough of the right members to pass the legislation. His method of attempting to achieve this was meanwhile to rule by warrant, appointing lieutenants, deputies and sheriffs who would ensure that those who were elected were amenable to his wishes.

A trial set of instructions for packing the parliament had been sent to the Duke of Newcastle at the end of October 1687. The deputies and justices of the peace were to be called in and asked whether, if they were elected, they would support the legislation for taking off the penal laws and the tests, whether they would help in electing members willing to do so and whether they would support the declaration for liberty of conscience and live 'friendly with those of all persuasions as subjects of the same Prince and good Christians ought to do'.

Again the terms seem acceptable to modern ears, but the duty laid on the lieutenants of the counties to report back to the King what everyone had said, so that those who didn't agree could be replaced by others who did, is a clear negation of democracy. What had happened to the old Chapel Royal, which had gradually but effectively been demoted, had been the forerunner of what was to happen throughout the country. James was now able to appoint his chaplain of the Chapels Royal at Whitehall and St James's, and therefore a Catholic, to be archdeacon of Canterbury, then York and finally bishop of Bristol.[4] If the impending revolution hadn't intervened, the result would have been the gradual takeover of the Church of England. Those who didn't agree would have become simply another Protestant sect, as many at the time realised,[5] and the course of history would have been completely changed.

Logically, if the King was the head of the established church and the King was a Catholic, the church would follow. Whatever the political or moral arguments, the effect on the tradition of English music, as instituted by Queen Elizabeth and re-established by Charles II, with its educational structure of choirs and choir schools for the training of professional musicians and the performance of their music, was devastating. They were being squeezed between two pincers: one the radical Protestant who disliked any religious music other than a simple psalm, and the other the Catholic who looked abroad for music and musical tradition.

The Bishop of Durham approved Purcell's bill for repairs and songs on 18 February 1688 and an order was made on the Treasury to pay him fifty-six pounds. In April Princess Anne lost the baby she, like Frances Purcell, had conceived close to the death of her last child.

Her son, had she had one, would have been third in line to the throne, displacing Mary's husband, William. Mary of Modena's pregnancy was now, of course, the focus of everyone's attention, Catholic and Protestant alike. There had been several alarms when it was feared the Queen would miscarry. The Purcells too must have been anxious as the summer approached. Fortunately, they now had as neighbour the apothecary William Eccles,[6] who would later attend Purcell in his illness and witness his will. Perhaps in desperation at the trend of affairs at Whitehall, Purcell now turned again to the stage, and to a Protestant poet who had also lost favour in the changing times, Tom D'Urfey. The play *A Fool's Preferment*, or *Three Dukes of Dunstable* as it was more often known, was acted in April at Dorset Garden and published in May 'with all the songs and notes to 'em excellently composed by Mr Henry Purcell', including two of his most popular: 'I'll sail upon the dog star' and 'I sighed and I pined'. The singer was Will Mountfort, a skilful comedian who had a fine voice. The old prompter Downes doesn't mention the play in his *Roscius Anglicanus*, but it was later said in a satire against D'Urfey that the scene about the card game of basset had given 'offence to a Great Lady', perhaps Princess Anne or the Duchess of Mazarin (who had introduced the game to this country), and that in terms of box office it had 'failed'.

Henry's and Frances's first daughter, Frances, was born at the end of May and baptised in the Abbey on the 30th and two days later in the parish church of St Margaret's. The two baptisms raise the question of whether the second was a way of affirming their Protestantism. Many Catholics regarded Westminster Abbey as neutral ground; a baptism there could have been construed as outside the Church of England, whereas one in the parish church could not. Now the period of fearful watching began, to see if this child too would succumb after only a few weeks or months.

The King had commanded that his proclamation for liberty of conscience should be read in all churches and chapels in London on 20 May. Westminster Abbey and the chapel at Whitehall had both complied, but seven bishops, led by Archbishop Sancroft of Canterbury and including Ken, the dedicatee of *Harmonia Sacra*, had petitioned the King to be excused from 'the reading of it to the several congregations within their dioceses'. Their grounds for the petition struck right at the heart of James's course of action. The bishops objected not because of the idea of toleration but because it was being advanced by the King's own assumption of a dispensing power rather than by parliament. If accepted, this would mean that any law in the land could be set aside as the King thought fit. They saw the reading of the declaration as an illegal act that they would be made party to. James's reaction was to dismiss them in a rage, commanding them to obey him at their peril.

Evelyn was in the chapel at Whitehall when one of the choir, who usually read the lesson, read out the declaration. He noted that it 'was almost universally forborne throughout all London'. On 8 June the bishops were summoned before the Council and, after refusing to give bail to appear at the King's Bench, they were sent by barge to the Tower. 'At their going into the barge and at their landing, thousands of people knelt down and had their lordships blessings, and acclamations on the water and prayers for their deliverance.' Never had the Church of England been so popular. Two days later the Queen went into unexpected labour and quickly gave birth to a son.

After her miscarriage Anne had gone to Bath to drink the waters and so missed the birth. Rumours at once began to circulate that the baby was a substitute, brought in, some later said, in a warming-pan. Anne, who hadn't been convinced by the Queen's pregnancy because she had never been allowed to feel her belly and the Queen had been careful, out of modesty, not to be seen removing her smock, was forced at last to accept the child as genuine, having carefully questioned the midwife, Mrs Dawson, as she wrote to her sister, Mary. There was a day of thanksgiving in London and for ten miles about on 17 June, for which an anthem by Blow (dated the 19th in the Gostling manuscript), *O Lord, thou art my God*, seems to fit.

The bishops were tried on the 29th and acquitted. The hall was full of people who shouted with joy for half an hour, so that no business could go on, and the King's solicitor was hissed. As the bishops left, thousands lined the streets and knelt for a blessing. At night the bells rang and forbidden bonfires and candles were lit. Meanwhile the young Prince had been ill of the gripes and Anne wrote to Mary that if his health didn't improve, he might soon be 'an angel in Heaven'. Her bitterness is understandable. The order had gone out displacing Mary and Anne with the new baby in the order of prayers for the royal family, and she had lost so many children of her own.

In celebration of the birth John Abell, who aspired to be not only performer, composer and publisher but impresario as well, staged a water show that's a precursor of those Handel was to compose for and looks like an attempt to produce an entertainment approaching the scale of those Castlemaine's embassy had been treated to in Rome. A richly decorated barge moored in front of the palace and illuminated by torches was the theatre for 130 vocal and instrumental performers, which must have included all the available musicians from the three chapels and the Private Music, described as 'The Royal Band'. The music was by Innocenzo Fede, master of James's chapel, who may have been French in spite of his Italian name[7] or, like Grabu, of mixed descent.

The members of the audience were in barges and boats lit by flambeaux. At the end they gave three shouts and everyone, including the musicians, adjourned to John Abell's house, where the entertainment went on till three in the morning; there was music and the constant sounding of trumpets following the custom when healths were drunk. It was no wonder if Frances Purcell objected to certain aspects of a musician's life. She had been left at home with a three-week-old baby, since women had to be churched after childbirth before resuming normal social life. The Queen didn't dine in public until nearly a month after the birth of the Prince.

The affair of the bishops might have ended, but that of Magdalen College continued. The fellows had finally accepted as president James's second nominee, Samuel Parker, bishop of Oxford, whom Evelyn called a 'violent, passionate, haughty man'. A High Churchman, he was an apologist for the doctrine of transubstantiation. Parker died in March and on the 28th James sent his warrant to the college to admit Bonaventure Gifford, one of his long-time chaplains and now Catholic bishop of Madauras, to the job. The year before James had forbidden the college to make any appointments. Now at the beginning of June he wrote to Gifford lifting the embargo and encouraging him to appoint fellows and masters to lectureships 'and all other places which shall be vacant'. Gifford proceeded to choose Daniel Purcell as organist.

Daniel's first salary (paid at Easter 1689) is short by three pounds and seven shillings, showing that he was admitted a month or two after Easter 1688. A satirical, punning letter to him late in his life describes his religion as 'in alt', that is, 'high'. He hadn't been made a gentleman of the Chapel Royal when his voice changed, as might have been expected for Purcell's brother, which suggests either that his voice was not good enough or that he had some other disability. If he had been a convinced Catholic, he would surely have been found some post by James. It looks as though he was 'high' enough to give promise of conversion but not for the Catholic chapel, where Draghi was organist. It may be that there was simply no job for him, but there could be another reason for his appointment by Gifford.

Gifford was a member of the Staffordshire family who had helped to rescue Charles II after Worcester and intermarried with the Staffordshire–Berkshire Catholic Purcells.[8] A Francis Purcell, who may be from a separate Irish branch or a relative of Gifford and possibly, distantly, of Henry and Daniel Purcell, was now sacristan in Queen Mary's chapel. Such a connection would be a strong reason for Gifford's appointment of Daniel. Whatever the reason, it removed him from the family home in Bowling Alley East at about the time the baby Frances entered it. Daniel had begun contributing songs for the anthologies with *The Banquet of Music*. Now he had his first salaried job, at forty pounds a year, and moved out of his brother's shadow to Oxford, where he began to make a life of his own.

The birth of the baby Prince gave a new turn to the simmering conflict. If he lived, there was no hope of a Protestant succession and nothing to deter James. Within a week, on the day of Abell's water show, a group of nobles, including the Bishop of London, wrote to William of Orange asking him to intervene. James's army was at its annual camp for exercises on Hounslow Heath, and the King and Queen dined there on St James's Day. He was continuing to build up the army. Thomas's son Matthew Purcell was one of his new recruits in July, as an ensign in the Prince of Denmark's regiment.

August was spent in issuing new charters to the corporations giving James the right to appoint officials he approved of. The King refused to believe warnings, because they came from France, that William was gathering forces for an invasion. It was as if the court was unable to admit that there was any discontent, in spite of the joyful public reaction to the release of the bishops. An order from the Lord Chamberlain that the musicians of the Private Music 'should attend the Queen Majesty's maids of honour to play whensoever they shall be sent to at the hours of dancing, at such hours and such a number of them as they shall desire' gives the impression of a strange blindness when the country was on the brink of civil war and invasion.

It may have been partly out of a sense of relief that the baby Prince who had suffered on a dry diet of powdered currants, recommended by the doctors, and in the heat of the city, to the point where he seemed to be sinking, had begun to thrive after being taken to Richmond for fresh air and found a healthy wetnurse, a tile-maker's wife, whose milk undoubtedly saved his life.

Anne took the opportunity of the King's pleasure in the baby and her absence with George at Tunbridge Wells to have her own chapel at Whitehall 'fitted up and beautifyed'. Purcell has two anthems in the Gostling manuscript with 1688 as their date: *O sing unto the Lord a new song* and *The Lord is king*. Anne usually attended prayers once or twice a day while she was in residence. This year the court's summer absence was short, lasting from the end of July to 20 September, and even that was broken for the King and Queen by the visit to the camp.

There was no welcome ode from Purcell to greet the royal family's return. Anne and George came back first, on the 17th, and the Queen and Prince on the 20th. Two days later the Lord Mayor and sheriffs 'attended their majesties to congratulate them on their safe return to the town'. James seems to have come back on the 18th, when Evelyn found the court 'in the utmost consternation on report of the Prince of Orange's landing which put Whitehall into so panic a fear that I could hardly believe it possible to find such a change'.

The autograph scorebook is confused at the point where, if Purcell had written one, a new welcome song could be expected to be entered. Instead there's *The Resurrection* 'out of Cowley', published in *Harmonia Sacra*, Part II, of 1693, followed by a Latin song, 'Crucie, crucie in his flamis' (Tormented in these flames). The next piece is dated the following year. The absence of an ode implies that the court returned much earlier than expected and that Purcell usually composed the odes very shortly before its re-entrance to the city in October.

James's reaction to the invasion was a U-turn. As a result of the issuing of new charters and putting out of the old officials the country had lost those it was used to obey and, in particular, those who had always been responsible for calling up the militia and in many cases providing it with horses, weapons and supplies. The King was forced to countermand all the warrants that had been sent out, including those for the summoning of parliament. The employment of Catholics in responsible civilian and military positions was stopped, and Anglican Tories were brought back into their old positions. The immediate effect on musicians was an order for the sergeant trumpeter, Purcell's friend Matthias Shore, who had only just taken over the job on the death of Gervase Price, to impress trumpeters from the city and town waits all over the country for the army and the fleet. Prayers were also commanded to be said in all the churches 'during this time of public apprehension'.

The City of London was given back its Charter and the bishops who had so recently been in the Tower were received by the King; in return they offered him their support and advice. Bonaventure Gifford was removed from Magdalen College and replaced with the candidate the fellows had chosen at first, Dr Hough. The Purcells must have been anxious that Daniel would lose his so recently acquired job, but he survived, which also indicates that although 'high' he wasn't a professed Catholic.

The panic was a little premature. William had been kept from sailing by contrary winds and didn't land until 5 November. It was a signal for the mob to begin attacking the Catholic chapels and schools, and the King's printer. Horse and foot guards had to be sent in to restore order. Meanwhile William began his march towards Exeter, being joined as he went by the West Country gentry and the first of the defecting regiments from James's army.

On 17 November James set out to join his troops at Salisbury, having sent the Prince of Wales to Portsmouth for safety. Queen Mary refused to go with the child and was determined to wait for her husband in London. The following day Anne wrote to her brother-in-law, William, sending him her best wishes and the news that Prince George, who had gone with the King, would soon join him. The two vanguards met at Warminster, among them on the King's side some of Edward Purcell's regiment of foot, the Queen Consort's. The 'Chapel Royal Wagon' went with the King, but the accounts don't show which Chapel Royal or who was in it. At this juncture it would have been foolish for James to be having mass said in front of his troops, but he didn't yet know the seriousness of his position and may have needed the support of his religion.

James reached Salisbury on the 19th. The Earl of Middleton reported that he was in perfect health, but the next day he began a series of debilitating nosebleeds which, together with the prescribed treatment of being let blood, left him too weak to join his forces at Warminster, where he might indeed have been captured. This probably saved his life, since there seems to have been a plot by John Churchill to kidnap and, it was said, even assassinate him.[9] There's some dispute about this and it's unlikely that William and James's daughters were a party to any such plot. While James lingered at Salisbury unable to lead his forces in person, the number of defections was swelling daily. Anne meanwhile had shut herself up in her rooms in the Cockpit at Whitehall.

Lord Lovelace was the first to go, then Lord Cornbury, followed by John Churchill. On the 24th Prince George left Salisbury secretly in the night, after having supper with James, and went to join William, along with the Duke of Ormonde and several others. Whether Matthew Purcell was one of them, I haven't been able to discover. Two days later Edward Purcell's commander, Charles Trelawney, defected with several of his officers. Edward was not among them. Then came news that the Earl of Danby had come out in favour of William in the north and the Duke of Devonshire was raising troops in Nottingham. Civil war was imminent and James was in danger of being cut off from London as his father had been. He decided on immediate withdrawal.

James got back safely to Whitehall on the afternoon of 26 November, only to find that Anne had fled her lodgings at night with Sarah Churchill and the Bishop of London to join the Duke of Devonshire in Nottingham. 'God help me,' James cried out, 'my own children have forsaken me.' The next day he called a Grand Council and it was decided to send three commissioners, including the Earl of Halifax (known as the Trimmer, because of his ability to adjust to every political wind), to treat with William.

While the commissioners were trying to catch up with the Prince, who had set out at a leisurely advance towards London via Salisbury and Hungerford, James was reconstituting his army, filling the places of those who had defected with loyal officers. Charles Trelawney was replaced by Colonel Charles Orby, and Edward Purcell was made captain in the place of Hayman Rooke, grandson of the old parliamentarian Sir Peter Heyman and a relative of Sir George Rooke.[10] William never forgave Edward: while Hayman Rooke advanced rapidly to colonel after the Revolution, Edward stayed a captain until William died thirteen years later, then was at once commissioned major and rose rapidly to be colonel under Queen Anne.[11]

In the midst of this civil upheaval the death of a young composer, Thomas Farmer, was a further reminder that mortality was always looking over their shoulders. A member of the Catholic chapel, Farmer too had composed songs and sonatas. His second consort of four-part pieces was sold with the elegy Tate and Purcell found time to compose for him. It followed the same pattern as the one for Locke, but was less passionate and grave, and there were fewer modulations; the final chorus carried Farmer upwards on his own harmony, away from the lamenting 'sons of art' below, the mourning communion of his fellow musicians. His post was given to John Abraham in December and was among the last recorded musical acts of James's reign.

James's chief concern now was for his son, who was still in the care of George Legge at Plymouth. Legge wrote to say that he dared not send the Prince of Wales out of England, which would be treason, and that William's troops would soon be between London and Plymouth. The child was returned to London in the care of Lord and Lady Powis, and James began to plan his escape from Whitehall. This time he managed to persuade Mary to go with the baby on a promise that he would join them in twenty-four hours. On Sunday, 9 December, the royal family went to bed as usual, but then got up again. Mary dressed herself as a laundress and disguised her baby as a bundle of washing, and under the protection of a Frenchman, the Comte de Lauzun, she went out through the privy garden to where the Tuscan ambassador's coach was waiting.

The next day was spent recalling the writs for parliament and sending a message to his commander-in-chief, the Earl of Feversham, to disband the army: 'though I know there are many brave and loyal men amongst you, yet you know you yourself and several of the General Officers tould me it was in no ways advisable to ventur myself at their head: there remains nothing more for me to do but to thank you, and all those officers and soldiers who have stuck to me and been truly loyal'. One of his last acts as effective king was to issue a pass for John Abell and his family to escape overseas.[12]

Late that night James, as the Queen had done, retired to bed and then left through the privy garden, and by morning was near Faversham in Kent. Strong winds and the need to take on ballast prevented the little boat that was to carry them out to the ship for France from getting off. While they were grounded by the tide, three other boats came alongside, their occupants swarmed aboard and the King, taken for a Jesuit priest because of his black clothes and periwig, and his companions were arrested and eventually taken back by coach to Faversham.

A Council of Regency had been constituted when James's absence was discovered, for the country was now without a king. That night rioters burned the Spanish Embassy and the next day a rumour ran through the city that Irish soldiers were coming to cut Protestant throats. There was panic and confusion in London. News of James's capture finally reached the Council and he was sent his servants and an escort to bring him back to London. After washing and shaving and changing his clothes and wig, the King was able to regain some of his dignity.

He returned in unexpected triumph, riding through London to cheers, the ringing of bells and bonfires all the way to Whitehall, but William and his supporters had no intention of negotiating. They wanted James gone and were only sorry that his first attempted flight had been prevented. As it was Sunday, James heard mass and then dined in public. The following day he held a Privy Council and touched for the king's evil. That night, when he was already asleep, three lords came to give him a message from William. He was told that at nine next morning he must remove himself to Ham House so that William could enter the city, and Dutch guards were stationed in Whitehall. James refused to go to Ham House and asked to be allowed to withdraw to Rochester. William and his advisers must have known what this would mean and their agreement could only have been a conniving at his second escape. He was taken by river to Gravesend and then by coach to Rochester. On Sunday he and many of his Dutch guards heard mass.

James waited for his natural son, the Duke of Berwick, to join him and as soon as he did, staged his second escape by night and by boat. There was such a gale that after they reached the ship to take them to France, they had to lie off the Essex coast for a day. This time no one tried to stop them. When they dropped anchor off the coast of France, Christmas was already over and it was snowing hard.

·9·

When Monarchs Unite

WILLIAM HAD HOPED to be made king in his own right, but the removal of James and the way it had been effected provoked a backlash already evident in the city's welcome when James had been brought back from Faversham. William's own temperament didn't help his cause. Evelyn was soon describing him as 'morose' and ungracious to those who came to make their addresses. A convention of Lords and Commons was summoned and it was agreed that by deserting the country and carrying off the Great Seal, which he had dropped in the Thames during his first attempted flight, James had effectively abdicated. The Commons were for crowning William alone, but the Lords resisted and by 6 February a compromise was reached: William and Mary were to be crowned and to rule jointly, but William was to have the executive authority.

Life began to return to normal. Concerts started and the theatre reopened. When Anne and George came back, she aroused public hostility by wearing orange ribbons and seeming to show no remorse for her father's treatment. They were soon seen at the playhouse. The third volume of *The Banquet of Music*, which had been licensed in December 1688, contained only two songs by Purcell, one of them a drinking catch:

If all be true that I do think
There are five reasons we should drink.

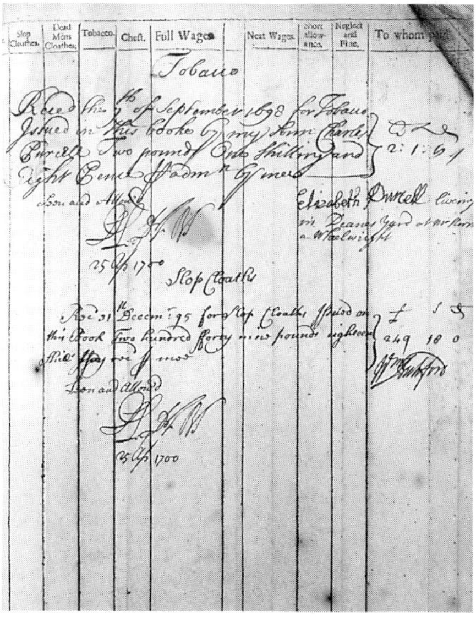

Slop Clothes.	Dead Mens Clothes.	Tobacco.	Chest.	Full Wages		Neat Wages.	Short allowance.	Neglect and Fine.	To whom paid

Tobacco

Recd the 7th of September 1698 for Tobacco Issued in this booke by my sonn Charles Purcell Two pounds One shilling and Eight Pence ... 2: 1: 8

Elizabeth Purcell living in Deanes Yard ... a Wheelwright

25 Ap 1700

Slop Cloaths

249 18 0

25 Ap 1700

Top left Henry Purcell. Charcoal sketch on lilac paper, British Museum.

Top right Daniel Purcell. Henry's younger brother composer and organist. He never married and was a non-juror under George I.

Below left Colonel Edward Purcell. Henry's eldest brother and head of the family. Gentleman usher to Charles II and a supporter of James II and later Anne.

Below right Signature of Henry's mother Elizabeth Purcell when collecting the last money due to his dead brother Charles as purser of the Tyger.

Top left James Butler, Duke of Ormonde. Colonel Edward Purcell's patron, a brave soldier and supporter of Princess Anne.

Top right John Dryden. Henry Purcell's most distinguished librettist. His conversion to catholicism deprived him of his protestant royal fervour.

Below left Mrs Arabella Hunt. A favourite performer of Henry Purcell's music to Queen Mary.

Below right Anne Bracegirdle as Semernia, the Indian queen in Aphra Behn's *The Widow Ranter*, she excelled both as actor and singer.

Tom D'Urfey, court wit, musician and poet. A favourite of Charles II he was one of Henry Purcell's chief librettists.

Corelli. Henry Purcell's Italian contemporary with whom he was often compared.

John Playford. Henry Purcell's friend and one of the most prolific and innovatory of British music publishers.

B. Smith, organ maker. Known as Father Smith but a German protestant with whom Henry Purcell worked closely on the building of several new organs.

Mathew Locke, composer in ordinary to Charles II. A prolific composer and Henry Purcell's mentor, he was also a friend of both Henry and his father.

John Blow. Henry Purcell's teacher especially for the organ, and a lifelong friend and colleague.

Dorset Garden Theatre. Site of the first production of the Purcell-Dryden King Arthur in 1691.

Patrons could arrive by land or river.

Top Banqueting House. The royal families dined here publicly to music from the private band with drums and trumpets for the many toasts.

Whitehall. The chapel royal is the lanterned building on the right. Princess Anne had lodgings in the Cockpit.

Opposite top John Dryden's dedication for Henry Purcell of Dioclesian to the Duke of Somerset showing the omissions from the printed text.

Opposite below Purcell's autograph. One of the many settings, in his own hand, that Purcell made of poems by Abraham Cowley, Charles II's favourite poet.

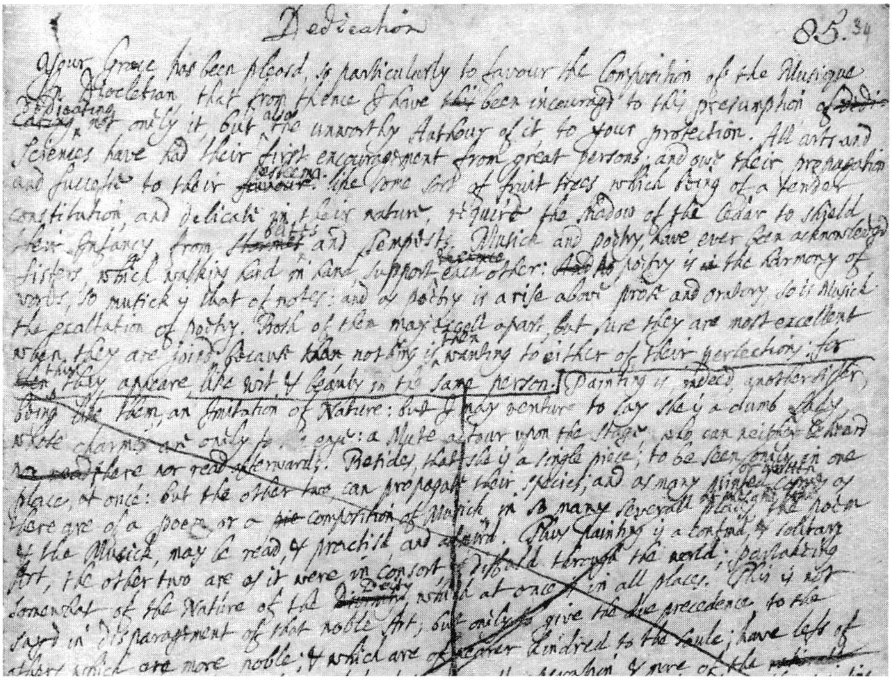

Dedication 85.34

Your Grace has been pleas'd so particularly to favour the Composition of the Musique of Dioclesian that from thence I have been encourag'd to this presumption of Dedicating not only it, but also the unworthy Authour of it to your protection. All arts and Sciences have had their first encouragement from great persons, and owe their propagation and successe to their patrons. like some sort of fruit trees which being of a tender constitution, and delicate in their nature, require the shadow of the Cedar to shield their Infancy, from blasts and tempests. Musick and poetry, have ever been acknowledged sisters, which walking hand in hand support each other: As poetry is the harmony of words, so musick is that of notes: and as poetry is a rise above prose and oratory, so is Musick the exaltation of poetry. Both of them may excell apart, but sure they are most excellent when they are joind, because then nothing is wanting to either of their perfections: for thus they appeare, like wit & beauty in the same person. Painting is indeed another sister, being like them, an Imitation of Nature: but I may venture to say she is a dumb Lady whose charms are only to the eye: a Mute actour upon the Stage, who can neither be heard there nor read afterwards. Besides, that she is a single piece; to be seen only in one place, at once: but the other two can propagate their species; and as many printed copys of them as there are of a poem or a composition of Musick in so many severall places may the poem & the Musick, may be read, & practis'd and heard. Thus painting is a confin'd & solitary Art, the other two are as it were in Consort, diffus'd through the world; partaking somewhat of the Nature of the Deity, which at once is in all places. This is not said in disparagement of that noble Art; but only to give the due precedence to the others which are more noble; & which are of a nearer kindred to the soule; [illegible]

(16)
(Mr. Cowley's complaint)
In a deep Visions intelectual Scene beneath a Bow'r for Sorrow made th'uncomfortable sha
black Yew's unlucky Green mixt the with mourning Willows carefull Gray where revrend Cha
out his famous way the melancholly Cowley Lay, and loe a Muse appeard to his closed Sight

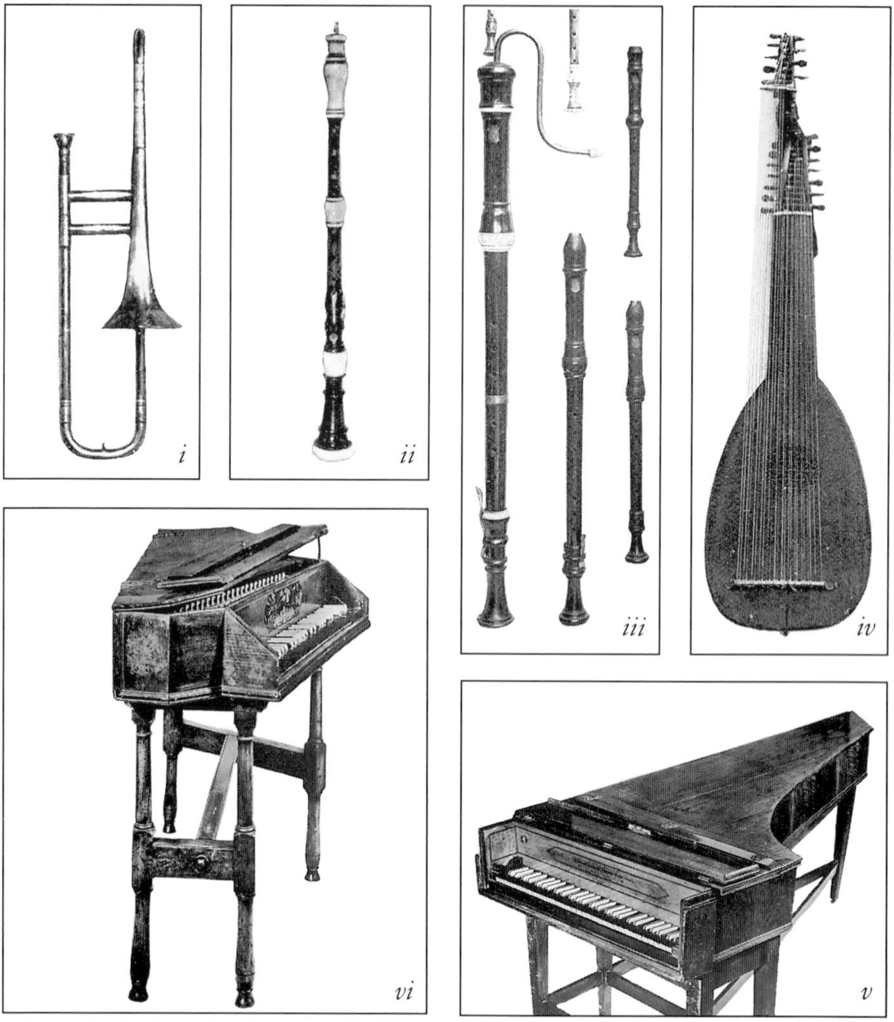

i Sackbut, being replaced during the period by the trumpet. *ii* Hautboy. Originally thought of as a military instrument but increasingly used for dancing and instrumental music generally. *iii* Recorders. The 'flutes' of the period for which Purcell wrote some of his most lyrical passages. *iv* Theorbo lute. The original solo accompanying instrument. Purcell's father was musician for the lute and voice to Charles II. *v* Harpsichord. Gradually took over from the lute for accompaniment. Purcell had several young women pupils who were accomplished performers. *vi* Spinet. In one set of accounts for lessons given, Purcell is described as 'spinet master'.

The whole country was now waiting for Mary. At last, on 8 February, after taking formal leave of the States General of Holland, she set sail. On her arrival at Whitehall on the afternoon of the 12th she 'was received with very great joy, demonstrated by ringing of bells, bonfires etc. and was waited on by most persons of quality in town, to congratulate her safe arrival'. It was Mary who could reconcile even James's strongest supporters to the change:

The murmuring world till now divided lay,
Vainly debating whom they should obey,
Till you, Great Caesar's offspring, blest our Isle
The differing multitudes to reconcile.[1]

The King and Queen were proclaimed the next day and plans were laid for their coronation in Westminster Abbey. The heralds were given their orders on 13 March, but the country was far from settled. There were doubts about the army's loyalty to the new regime and many of the soldiers deserted, some in whole regiments, at the prospect of being sent to Holland or Ireland, where Tyrconnel had raised the standard for James. Now Protestants were the ones fleeing to England as fast as they could find boats. New oaths of allegiance and association were to be administered. Charles Trelawney was among the first to subscribe and so was Matthew Purcell, but I've found no entry for Edward.[2]

There are two lists of musicians who were to attend at the coronation: one of the Private Music and another of the Chapel Royal gentlemen.[3] The lists only partly overlap. In the Chapel list there are three 'organists', Child, Blow and Purcell; in the Private one Child doesn't appear and Blow and Purcell are listed as 'composers', along with Alexander Damascene. All those on the Chapel list, among them the Dean, sub-Dean, twelve children and several servants, were to be given tickets to be admitted to 'the hall', which presumably means the dinner in Westminster Hall. The authorised account of the ceremony has no mention of anthems apart from the *Veni Creator* and the *Te Deum*. The litany was sung by the bishops of St Asaph and Bangor. It isn't clear whether the Nicene Creed was sung or spoken. Everything, including the dinner, was over by eight o'clock and the King and Queen returned to Whitehall for the fireworks and drinking of healths. Two factors may have influenced the lack of music: James's coronation had been overlong and exhausting, as Anne would have remembered; anthems, and church music in general, were open to the charge of popery. The ceremony was obviously kept simple.

Purcell had to provide 'an organ and other necessaries for the use of the Chapel Choir'. If the same plan was followed as for James's coronation, this small organ was placed on the right of the altar below the gallery for the royal vocal music, while the royal instrumentalists, under the direction of Staggins, were on the left in a large gallery and slightly lower down the transept. The gallery for the Westminster choir was on the left immediately after the transept. The organ and its loft, which contained spectators, were lower down still in the choir. The drums and trumpets were in a long gallery spanning the whole end of the choir. These six musical elements could answer each other antiphonally or circle the proceedings with a girdle of sound.[4] The Abbey was fitted with 'scaffolds' (raised and railed platforms with benches) to accommodate the nobility, civil and military officials, servants and musicians. By custom, employees of the Abbey had the perk of putting up a scaffold or seating in any area they had access to, and charging a fee to watch the proceedings. They had to recoup the cost of erecting the scaffold before they made a profit. On previous occasions all the fees collected had been paid to the Dean and Chapter for 'distribution as they should think fit'. At James's coronation, however, the only one which Purcell had known as an adult, the arrangement seems to have been that those who had the scaffold put up divided the money with the carpenter and kept their share. Shortly before the coronation of William and Mary the Dean and Chapter put in a petition to return to the old system, without informing their organist or their chaunter and petty canon, Stephen Crespion. Purcell's domain was the organ loft, which he let out for over eighty pounds. Crespion took more than four hundred.

Purcell at first disputed the demand that his money should go into the common pot, but a sharp order from the Chapter, threatening him with dismissal and the withholding of his stipend, brought both him and Crespion to heel. In the end he got back half, and received a further thirty-two pounds from the secret service moneys for the extra organ he'd provided, though he had to wait a year before he was paid.[5] The tune of 'Lilliburlero', which was said to have sung James out of three kingdoms, is almost certainly not a Purcell composition but one he set. However, a tune suggested for the song on the coronation called 'The Protestant's joy' is one of his most popular, 'Hail to the myrtle shade' from *Theodosius* of nine years before.

In spite of the air of normality created by the crowning of William and Mary, the country remained deeply divided. About four hundred clergymen and eight bishops, including two of those who had been in the Tower, Sancroft and Ken, had felt unable to take the oaths to the new rulers and had lost their places. The coronation had been conducted by the Bishop of London. Among those deprived was John Gostling's brother Isaac, into whose living at Sturry stepped a young graduate, William Sale, who the year before had been soliciting James for a place in Midley, also in Kent.

James had now landed in Ireland and taken personal charge of affairs. Although he was greatly diminished by what had happened, the English forces sent against him and those who had risen in his support were in disarray. Edward's regiment was typical. Its numbers were still being made up in April the following year when they were under orders to embark for Ireland, but had to wait for over three months for a boat to take them. The first campaign under William's commander Count Schomberg was a disaster and resulted in the loss of over half the army, mostly from disease and exposure during the winter encampment. Provisions were one of the main difficulties. At one point the army was unable to fight because the soldiers had no shoes; four thousand pairs were specially made at Northampton and shipped over. William soon realised that if he wanted results, he would have to take charge himself.

Although William had conducted military campaigns and he and Mary had experienced the political infighting of Dutch politics, they had been used to a quiet life, and neither of them liked Whitehall. William suffered from asthma and found it hard to breathe in low-lying, marshy Westminster, where the smoke from hundreds of coal fires in the winter became a smog. They preferred Hampton Court, which Wren was directed to refurbish, or the new house in Kensington they had bought from Lord Nottingham. Even one of William's chief supporters and apologists, Bishop Burnet, who had been in exile in Holland and had accompanied the invasion, appreciated that withdrawing from London and coming into town only on council days meant that 'the gaiety and diversions of a Court disappeared . . . though the Queen set herself to make up what was wanting in the King by a great vivacity and cheerfulness'.[6] The effects on English musical life were to be long-lasting.

Dryden, of course, had lost the laureateship. To keep it he would have had to revert to being a Protestant and, to his credit, he refused. His old rival Thomas Shadwell took his place and provided the words for Purcell's first birthday ode for Queen Mary, *Now does the glorious day appear*, which 'was performed before their majesties at Whitehall' on 30 April. It uses quite small forces and in a way brings to an end the series of odes begun six years before at the return of Charles II. Mary is described in one of the loveliest, most melting alto solos that Purcell ever wrote:

By beauteous softness mixed with majesty
An empire over every heart she gains.

The artists quickly realised that Mary must be their patron if cultural life was to continue. As a girl of twelve she had commissioned John Crowne's *Calisto*, which had music by Nicholas Staggins and dances by Josias Priest. In an attempt to repeat this success and to draw upon the Queen's earlier interest, Priest and Purcell decided to stage *Dido and Aeneas* at the Priests' school in Chelsea. D'Urfey wrote an epilogue and someone, perhaps D'Urfey or Tate, a prologue. Everyone had an axe to grind. Shadwell was an old man who might not have long to live, and D'Urfey and Tate could both be in line for the laureateship. Priest needed to rebuild the reputation of his school and there were young Priests who might later seek places in the Chapel Royal; one at least of his pupils was looking for financial support. Purcell had two brothers of doubtful loyalty and his place in the Private Music hadn't yet been confirmed.

The prologue and epilogue are of the same date. The epilogue was spoken by Lady Dorothy Burke (a Protestant, though her Catholic father, the Earl of Clanrickarde, was fighting for James in Ireland). She also took part in the prologue as the shepherdess Dolly. There's no point in the use of this name, the only non-mythological character's name in the prologue, unless it refers to her and her 'melancholy' situation as the daughter of an outlaw; any other name would have done as well if she weren't playing the part. The prologue was put together hastily to make the whole performance fit the occasion; it only just makes sense, though it provides splendid opportunities for Priest's pupils to show off their musical abilities. D'Urfey's epilogue displays his usual knack at knocking out a piece of competent verse to order.

Purcell had no time to write a whole opera, even a chamber one, from scratch, particularly if it was performed, as I believe, around 14 May when William had gone to Portsmouth to visit the fleet and Mary was alone. The Chelsea churchwarden's accounts for 1689 show a payment to the bell ringers, sometime between the day of the coronation in April and William's birthday in November, for ringing 'when the Queen landed at Chelsea'. Such entries are very rare: there are two or three in Charles II's reign when he stopped at Nell Gwyn's Chelsea house on his way to Hampton Court. I think it highly likely that Mary attended the performance.

Both Shadwell and Staggins lived in Chelsea, and next door to the Priests' school in Gorge's House lived the Berties, in Lindsey House. In 1705 the local historian Bowack described the school, which was still in business, as 'a large spacious house in which for many years past has been kept a famous boarding school for young ladies'. There were two other boarding-schools for girls in Chelsea. When the surgeon James Young delivered his daughter to Mrs Woodcock's in 1702, he saw 'forty young ladies dance'. The Priests', however, was the one for the nobility.

William was away again in the autumn at Newmarket,[7] but the prologue strongly suggests a spring performance. It begins with Phoebus, an icon of William, welcoming Venus. The descriptions of Phoebus are very close to those of D'Urfey's ode for the Queen's birthday the following year. Phoebus, god of the sun, was a natural image for William because the orange was his symbol, but Phoebus was also god of law and order, of cities and constitutions. That Venus, goddess of the spring, is Mary is clear from Phoebus' acknowledgement that her lustre 'half eclipses mine'. Spring arrives to welcome Venus 'to the shore', a reference not only to Mary's landing at Chelsea (Evelyn had noted what a seasonable spring it had been, with no sharp east winds), but also to her landing from Holland, which brought spring to the nation's wintry situation. Phoebus and Venus then go off to allow the Priests' pupils, dressed as shepherds, shepherdesses and nymphs, to show off their musical paces. Then follows a dialogue between Dolly and a shepherd, who asks why all the nymphs and swains are so jolly today. The reason she gives is that the sun, Phoebus, has been to court the Queen and 'tired the Spring with wooing'. It's sometimes hard to see William and Mary in this passionate disguise, but notions of their equality and devotion were part of an iconography that had to be very quickly evolved. The dialogue goes on to celebrate the fruitfulness this union brings, a theme echoed in the first birthday ode:

This does our fertile isle with glory crown,
And all the fruits it yields we now can call our own.

The final chorus brings in another bit of mythology in the person of the jolly nymph Thetis, chief of the sea nereids, who has long sought Phoebus' love. This may relate to the fact that William, who was making great efforts to take over James's naval role at this stage, was with the navy, aboard ship dining with Admiral Herbert, on 15 May, when he gave the seamen ten shillings apiece for drink: 'The seamen were very cheerful and gave his majesty great satisfaction.'[8] It was important for William to build up a relationship with the navy, as it had always been James's particular sphere. James was extremely popular with the seamen and they appreciated his competence in naval matters. When he was captured at Faversham, the sailors swore that not a hair of his head should be touched and formed a guard outside his bedroom.

D'Urfey's epilogue was published in his *Poems* (1690). The contents page identifies its provenance as the 'Opera of Dido and Aeneas performed at Mrs Priest's boarding school at Chelsey'. Much is made of the girls' virtue and Protestantism:

Rome may allow strange tricks to please her sons
But we are Protestants and English nuns
Like nimble fawns and birds that bless the Spring
Unscarred by changing times we dance and sing.

In December 1687[9] Mary of Modena had funded and opened a school for girls in St Martin's Lane, with four mistresses to teach both Protestants and Catholics. Unlike this short-lived venture, the Priests' was a long-established institution that had survived the 'changing times' of three reigns. The new Mary would have wanted to show she too was a patron of education, especially that of girls.

If I am right and what we generally now regard as the opera *Dido and Aeneas* was written about the time of Charles II's death while the prologue and epilogue belong to 1689, it's interesting to speculate on what music was used for the prologue. The music seems to have been extant in 1700 when Betterton produced the opera in four entertainments interleaved with a cut version of Shakespeare's *Measure for Measure* by Charles Gildon. What in the earlier production had been the prologue was turned into a masque within a masque, and put at the end rather than the beginning as 'the fourth entertainment', with additional dialogue. Extra dialogue was also written into the second entertainment when Aeneas and his friends debate whether to go or stay, a point where the original plot is rather thin. Purcell could easily have adapted existing music for the prologue, especially since a great deal of it is dance, like many of the pieces published in *Musick's Handmaid* in April 1689. He must have spent some time at Chelsea, revising, adapting and rehearsing during early spring.

Did he add anything to the main body of the opera? The duet 'When Monarchs unite' seems made for William and Mary, but this may have been luck. It's likely that professionals were brought in for the roles of Dido and Aeneas, which would have presented no problem to the producers. Staggins, a neighbour, may have been useful in augmenting the players, though the forces Purcell uses are well within the range of a school like the Priests' and smaller than those for *Venus and Adonis*. The version published with *Measure for Measure* ends with a 'grand dance', and that would have been appropriate for the school production. Betterton would have been able to call on Josias Priest for the choreography, and perhaps the music too, in 1700.

The operation was a success: Dorothy Burke was given a pension by Mary; Josias Priest's sons Josias and Nathaniel became Chapel boys sometime in the 1690s; the school flourished in spite of being the source for an unfortunate play by D'Urfey; Purcell was given a place in the Private Music in July and he and D'Urfey began a series of royal song collaborations; Tate got the laureateship; Purcell's brothers kept their jobs.

Mary, being of a serious cast of mind, had to make a deliberate effort to seem cheerful as a counterpoint to William's moroseness and in order to please him.[10] She had prayers twice a day and one of her first concerns in remodelling Hampton Court was for the proper refurbishing of the chapel. She ordered not only prayer books and bibles, but a new organ from Bernard Smith, who now had the post of organ-maker. The high seriousness of the opera would have appealed strongly to her. Aeneas' conflict between love and duty echoes what was perceived as William's struggle, as it became increasingly clear that he would have to leave

Mary to take personal charge of the army. She would have appreciated the emphasis on the bereft Queen and her predicament, at this early stage when his frequent absences had not yet become the source of great pain and doubt.

Luttrell records the mass oath-takings that were held in the months following the coronation. An idea of the importance of these can be gleaned from the Lord Chamberlain's instruction that Nicholas Staggins wasn't to be paid the money owing to him from the reign of Charles II unless he had a certificate proving he had taken the oaths. The members of the Private Music were sworn in between 4 and 27 July, Purcell only squeezing by towards the end with a batch of six on the 22nd. There was a great change in the career of John Gostling. While keeping his other posts, he was made a prebendary of Lincoln, minor canon of St Paul's and chaplain to King William, and began to concentrate on the clerical rather than the musical side; his address was now in the parish of St Gregory by St Paul's, where his duties increasingly lay. At St Paul's he came under the newly appointed John Tillotson, a favourite of William and Mary for a personal kindness shown to them after their marriage which Hawkins reveals as part of a story from William Gostling. According to this, there was no official appointment of Chapel Royal composer. The immediate effect was to reduce the number of Purcell anthems in the first four years after the revolution. The Gostling manuscript has none by Purcell specifically dated to this period, nor indeed any by Blow.

In June the Purcells' daughter, Frances, passed her first dangerous year and her mother was pregnant again. Sometime in July Purcell's friendship with Tate led to another work for a school: the setting of an ode by one of the pupils of Tate's friend Lewis Maidwell, a schoolmaster. (Two poems Tate had written in praise of Maidwell's teaching methods were published in Tate's 1684 collection.) The ode, *Celestial music did the gods inspire*, was performed on 5 August at Maidwell's school house in King Street, Westminster, and is almost the last entry in Purcell's autograph scorebook spanning the years 1683 to 1690. The competent verses in praise of music bring out some of Purcell's finest writing. For the opening symphony he reuses that from the coronation anthem *My heart is inditing* (which perhaps reinforces the impression that this hadn't been part of the music for William's and Mary's coronation of only four months before). Critics have been right, I think, to wonder whether this shows an element of haste in the composition. There's no evidence of it, though, in the rest of the ode, which contains some beautiful writing, in particular for recorders, and a soprano and alto solo that anticipates the later 'In vain the amorous flute', from *Hail, bright Cecilia* of 1692.

The Purcells' son Edward was born and baptised in September. Perhaps his uncle Edward got leave from his regiment to be a godfather, for although they were already under orders for Ireland, there was no sign of their embarkation. In Frances Purcell's will Edward junior was specifically left his uncle's picture. Edward had been at the army camp on Hounslow Heath in August, a custom of James's that William was keeping up. William also followed precedent by visiting Newmarket in late September, taking with him Staggins and twelve musicians for a mere eleven days. There was no welcome ode from Purcell to mark his return to London; indeed, he came only as far as Hampton Court. The new royal winter home was to be Holland House in Kensington, but official celebrations still took place in Whitehall, where at the end of October the King and Queen dined in public for the first time 'with musick, heralds, gentlemen pensioners etc. as their predecessors did'. From an entry in the royal cofferer's accounts it looks as though the musicians for these public Sunday dinners consisted of drummers, trumpeters and kettledrummers, who between them consumed six loaves of bread, six gallons of beer and two quarts of claret.[11] Not until the beginning of October were the certificates of admission to the Chapel Royal regularised; the main group, including Blow and Purcell, was sworn in on the 5th. Ralph Battell was made sub-dean and Stephen Crespion, Purcell's colleague from the Abbey, was again made confessor to the royal household and a gentleman of the Chapel, as he'd been in Charles II's time.

The winter season of royal balls began with 'a great ball at court' for William's birthday and the festivities continued next day with the usual bells and bonfires for Guy Fawkes and the anniversary of William's landing. Ten days later the birthday of the Queen Dowager Catherine of Braganza was celebrated with guns and a ball. She had wisely been among the first to present her respects to the new King and Queen, who allowed her to stay on in England in spite of pressure for her to be sent back to Portugal. Giovanni Battista Draghi had found refuge in her household at Somerset House and returned to being her organist. Most of the other foreign Catholic musicians had fled.

A week later Anne entertained Queen Mary and her ladies with a ball at Whitehall. Anne, after so many miscarriages, had produced a son on 24 July. He was christened William three days afterwards and made duke of Gloucester by his godfather. He survived several crises in his first three months of life. As the only living child of Mary or Anne, he was next in line to the throne after his mother and represented the Protestant answer to what some saw as the lawful Prince of Wales over the water whose successful birth had been followed by that of a daughter to James and Mary.

Just before Anne's ball William had issued a statement in defence of the Church of England. He expressed his determination to die in the communion of the church and to venture his life for her, a theme which would occur in several texts and in the next Purcell–D'Urfey ode, which personified the church as Eusebia. When the court took up residence in Holland House for Christmas, William licensed Robert King, one of the Private Music and a prolific composer, to set up 'a concert of musick'[12] and to have the sole control of it and the help of both the civil and military officers in preventing people from forcing their way into the meetings without paying.

An order had been issued on Catherine of Braganza's birthday for regulating the theatres, where there had been much unruly behaviour. The Duke's theatre in Dorset Garden had previously been renamed the Queen's. Now orders were given for dealing with those who tried to force free entry there too and at the Theatre Royal in Bridge Street. The second part of the order shows that opera was in the air again:

> And forasmuch as it is impossible to command those vast engines used in operas (which move the scenes and machines), and to order such number of persons as must be employed in works of that nature . . . it is commanded that no person of what quality soever presume to sit or stand on the stage or to come within any part of the scenes at either theatre before the opera or play begins, while it is acting or after it is ended.

There are also provisions to ensure quiet during the performance and to allow the officers and guards on duty outside to prevent servants from coming in with messages and such like during the performance. Any who disobeyed any part of the order were to be proceeded against as 'contemners' of the regal authority and disturbers of the peace.[13]

Betterton must have asked for such an order, though the new rise of factions in the playhouses had already alarmed the authorities, Williamite and Jacobite replacing Whig and Tory. The specific reference to keeping the stage and backstage clear for opera, its vast machines and large casts can have come only from Betterton himself. There had been no opera for four years, since the ill-fated *Albion and Albanius*, and this order shows that his mind was already running on a new production, *The Prophetess*, or *Dioclesian*, as it came to be called.

The new year began with the usual celebrations. Blow set an ode by Shadwell and 'there was a great consort of music, vocal and instrumental', before the Lord Mayor, aldermen and sheriffs and the nobility and gentry. All had come to wish the new monarchs a happy new year, the second of their reign over a deeply divided and troubled country that, after nearly twenty years of peace, found itself at war on two fronts: in Ireland and on the Continent against France.

· 10 ·

Ah, the Sweet Delights of Love!

BETWEEN PURCELL'S LAST ode of August 1689 and his next, originally scheduled for the following February but put off until 27 March because of the elections to parliament, a profound change had come over his instrumental writing, completing the process begun by the influence of Italian music in James's reign. With the *Ode for the Yorkshire Feast*, the last in the great scorebook, which was composed to words by D'Urfey for the annual gathering in London of loyal Yorkshiremen, he introduces trumpets for the first time in a choral work, backed up by oboes, or hautboys, as they were then called.

Previously both these instruments had been confined to a largely military context, although the oboe had made an appearance in both *Psyche* and *Calisto* in 1675, when a group of French wind players was in England, and had been used by Blow in two anthems.[1] The reasons for Purcell's introduction of the oboes and particularly the trumpets at this time are complex. Undoubtedly they appealed to the new King. William was to take seven trumpeters and an extra group of five oboes on his journey to Holland. There was an appropriateness about these instruments which underpinned his own liking for them. He was the first king of England to take the field since Charles I had fought against Cromwell, and a great deal of his life had been spent soldiering. Where Charles and James had been presented as bringers and supporters of peace, the public mood, and the royal iconography that embodied it, was now for war.

The other element was the increased availability and development of these instruments, especially their new capacity for more lyrical playing. In the case of trumpets this must be due to the Shore family and Purcell's connection with them. There were four of them: William and Matthias, who seem to have been brothers, William junior, the son of Matthias or William, and John, Matthias's son. All were royal trumpeters, initially under the sergeant Gervase Price.

William Shore the elder was admitted to the royal service in 1679, but his salary was backdated to 1677, which suggests that he had already been employed without fee. In 1683 an attempt was made to promote him to sergeant trumpeter, presumably over the head of Price; Either it failed or he died, for no more is heard of it or him after 1684. Matthias had been officially taken on the year before, while William junior was admitted in 1685 and John in 1688. Matthias was made sergeant trumpeter by James in 1687 on the death of Gervase Price, and he continued in the post under William and Mary.

Matthias also had a daughter Catherine, a pupil of Purcell who, according to Hawkins, taught her to sing and play the harpsichord. In the opinion of her youngest daughter, Charlotte, she 'was possessed of every personal charm that could render her attractive and amiable' in a 'perfection with which art and nature had equally endowed her'.[2] The star trumpet player of the family was John, who 'by his great ingenuity and application had extended the power of that noble instrument . . . beyond the reach of imagination, for he produced from it a tone as sweet as an hautboy'.[3] Catherine and John lived together and, so Charlotte claims, it was while he was visiting her brother that the young actor Colley Cibber heard Catherine singing and accompanying herself on the harpsichord in her chamber and promptly fell in love with her.[4] All three of them were to appear in later works by Purcell, until John was unlucky enough to split his lip while playing and had to resort to his other instrument, the lute. Catherine was eventually driven off the stage by an excess of marital passion that resulted in a plethora of pregnancies and children; according to her husband there was a new one every time he produced a new play.[5]

Purcell's connection with the Shore family and its effect on his work is first heard in the *Ode for the Yorkshire Feast*. It's a magnificent paean to William, who must surely have been present at its performance. It opens with the trumpets and oboes and then the bass begins the history of Yorkshire under the Romano-Gallic title of 'Brigantium'. The subject of the next stanza, a tenor solo with recorders, is poor Augusta (London), then a 'puny town' beside 'the bashful Thames' though now, the poet adds hastily, 'she rears her tow'ring front so high'. The performance was, after all, taking place in London at Merchant Taylors' Hall. The following ritornello for oboes and strings is a beautiful introduction to the alto solo on the Wars of the Roses, which has an unusual offbeat string accompaniment. The text goes on to celebrate Yorkshire's early contribution to the Glorious Revolution against 'Rome's slavery'. A fanfare introduces the symphony – the two trumpets raise their voices sometimes in unison, sometimes antiphonally – with such brilliance and panache Purcell might have been composing for trumpets for many years past. The ensuing duet includes the trumpets again, with a harpsichord accompaniment which Purcell presumably played himself, conducting the whole performance from the keyboard.

The tenor solo 'So when the glittering Queen of the night' is an extraordinary piece of mood music, like those passages he was to write for the seasons in the masque for *The Fairy Queen*, over an eerie ground. The chorus that follows lifts the mood again with joyous running counterpoint until it dissolves into the trumpets sounding 'the knell of falling Rome' to a simple tune the whole company could have sung. The final bass solo and chorus are punctuated by more trumpet in praise of William and those heroes who'd 'invited him in', with a final flourish for 'the city and county of York'.

Not surprisingly, D'Urfey said it was one of the finest compositions Purcell ever made 'and cost £100 the performing'. The stewards of the feast would have been happy at this point to pay for such a tribute, for the wool trade, and therefore Yorkshire and the Merchant Taylors' Company, were in the ascendance. The war with France had caused a ban on the import of French silk and the weavers, among them many French Protestants, had taken to the streets in their thousands to protest. Wool suddenly seemed English, Protestant and manly compared with the flummeries of foreign, especially French, manufacturers.

Two weeks later Purcell's brother Joseph received his certificate as a fully qualified 'chirurgeon' and his seagoing medicine chest (to which he contributed five pounds) from the Barber Surgeons' Company. His ship, the *Wolf*, was waiting for him. From now on, except when he managed to get a berth in one of the royal yachts, he would spend many months at sea like his brother Charles, with their family at home not knowing whether they were alive or dead.[6]

William's preparations for his visit to Ireland now occupied the whole country. Mary was particularly distressed that her husband and her father were to fight each other face to face. The ode for her birthday a month later from Purcell and D'Urfey, *Now does the glorious day appear*, skilfully presents her with an acceptable persona for this confrontation. Mary is Gloriana, a second Queen Elizabeth, defender of the Protestant cause against Catholic Spain, which allows D'Urfey to pun on 'Glory' in the final stanza. William is again Phoebus, the orange sun, as in the prologue to *Dido and Aeneas*, and it's his intended voyage to Ireland and its presentation as a defence of the Church of England, 'Eusebia', that saves Mary's face. (D'Urfey used the name again in an ode for William, *Cloudy Saturnia drives her steeds apace*, which is printed in his 1690 *Poems* and identifies Eusebia in a footnote.) Eusebia has to be given the role of weeping at the thought of William's danger and beg Fate to find 'some meaner force' so that Mary, in fulfilment of William's known wishes, can end the ode crying, 'Go on illustrious man, leave not thy work undone.' Whatever her private distress, confided to Bishop Burnet and perhaps others, she always had to support her husband in public.

Like the *Ode for the Yorkshire Feast*, the one for Mary's birthday begins with a trumpet flourish. After the alto solo has exhorted D'Urfey's muse to compose a mighty ode, a rich chorus brings in the Sons of Music. A new alto solo imagines the sun, 'the glitt'ring ruler of the day', calling the planets to 'wanton revels' in Mary's honour (once again echoing the prologue to *Dido and Aeneas*, which suggests that the prologue was perhaps by a somewhat rushed D'Urfey rather than Tate). This is a beautiful piece of writing by Purcell followed by two altos and a chorus wishing Mary a sprightly many happy returns.

The introduction of the theme of war brings in the bass to sober the mood with typical Purcellian word-painting: the notes fall on 'decline', then rise as Phoebus does in the text to shine 'with more lustre'. After an energetic trio, the alto weeps for Eusebia against plaintive recorders. The bass picks up the theme in duet with the alto, moving it gradually to the point where the wished-for spiritual resolution can be reached in the full chorus with delightful modulations and great richness in the texture.

The continuous invention of these two odes is all the more remarkable when they are put into context. Purcell, Betterton and Priest were hard at work on *Dioclesian*, which opened less than a month later, according to a letter from Annabel Gray to her cousin Lord Ruthyn in which she says that it has already come out by the date of her writing (30 May). Two weeks later she has seen it herself and describes it as 'all Mr Betterton's own fancy'. The pathetic dialogue between alto and bass in the ode for Queen Mary's birthday shows a strong theatrical influence that seems like a spill-over from the semi-opera.

Dioclesian is both long and elaborate and must, on analogy with the length of time that *Albion and Albanius* was in production, have been in commission when Betterton took the precaution of clearing the stage for an 'opera'. The theatre, even after the King's and the Duke's companies had joined to form the United Company in 1682, had been in decline for several years before the Revolution, forcing writers like Dryden and Aphra Behn to turn to books, and even translation, for a living. In view of the new Protestant dispensation Betterton may have anticipated the kind of attacks on the immorality of the theatre which were indeed to come and which had closed the theatres for twenty years under the Commonwealth. At that time the door had been opened again by opera – Davenant's *The Siege of Rhodes* – a form which had always interested Betterton. The theatre of the 1680s had become a warring political arena, something he was also anxious to avoid. The answer was to stage a piece that would engage everyone and offend none, even though it might contain oblique references to everyday life and contemporary politics. To some extent foreign products too were out of favour. The time seemed ripe for another attempt at an English opera. He must either have seen or known about the recent production of *Dido and Aeneas*. Here in Priest and Purcell lay just the combination he needed: the greatest English dancer and choreographer of the time, known to the Queen from her own masquing days; and the most famous English composer of his day (with the possible exception of Blow), who might equal the approved foreign composers for the form.

From Purcell's point of view it was also the right moment in the development of his art. Much has been made of how the financial constraints of the new regime pushed him towards the theatre, but although there was some royal cost-cutting, Purcell was still receiving four salaries: as gentleman of the Chapel Royal, harpsichordist in the Private Music, tuner and keeper of the organs and organist of Westminster Abbey. For some time he'd been supplementing this with teaching and composing. The reasons for his seizing this chance to compose a major work seem to me psychological and aesthetic rather than financial.

It was a move that, ambitious as he was to be the best, he must have been looking for. The last opera by an English composer had been *Psyche*, by his old friend and master, Locke, which had employed all the scenic and instrumental forces then available, including trumpets and hautboys, kettledrums and an organ. One factor in Purcell's introduction of several of these instruments into his own work at this time may have been that he'd been looking at Locke's score of fifteen years ago. If he was to equal, let alone surpass, the earlier generation (his father's generation) and those French and Italian composers whom he knew had opportunities to be both prolific and competent composers of opera, he had to take every opportunity for large-scale work.

Priest too must have been eager for greater exposure than his own pupils could give him. There's no record of his participation in public or court theatrical productions after the 1670s, but it seems highly unlikely that there wasn't any such involvement. His reputation as 'one of the greatest character dancers of the period', as expressed by the eighteenth-century choreographer and dancer John Weaver,[7] must rest on more than a career in two parts separated by a decade and a half of schoolteaching to non-professionals. What Weaver calls 'grotesque dancing' is, he says, 'wholly calculated for the stage and takes in the greatest part of opera dancing . . . requiring the utmost skill in the performer'. Describing the qualifications for such a 'master or performer', he instances someone 'bred up to the profession' and also 'skilled in music and well-read in history, ancient and modern, with a taste to painting and poetry . . . Mr Josias Priest of Chelsea I take to have been the greatest master of this kind of dancing that has appeared on our stage'. *Dido and Aeneas* had provided a showcase not only for the school, but for Priest himself.

I have no evidence to support this theory, but it seems probable that Priest kept his professional hand in during this time by choreographing either dances in plays or some of the many balls at court, which often had a professional element to them, despite the presence of the French dancing master to the court, Jerome Gohorri, throughout the 1680s. Although he had been naturalised early in the 1670s and had presumably conformed to the Church of England, Gohorri had probably reverted to Catholicism under James II and he disappears at the Revolution. Priest may have been hoping for an official post in his place, but no appointment was made until Anne's reign, when George

Hill, one of the twenty-four musicians under the master of the music John Eccles, seems to have doubled as *ad hoc* dancing master.

Betterton's decision not to employ a dramatist but to make his own adaptation of an old Fletcher–Massinger play neatly sidestepped a difficult political issue: using either Catholic Dryden or one of the Protestant group of Shadwell, Tate and D'Urfey could have cost him half his potential audience. As it was, he involved Dryden by having him provide a prologue. There's also some debate about whether Dryden was responsible for any of the songs, but given the success of the 'opera', which he acknowledged in the preface to his play *Amphitryon*, it's unlikely that he wouldn't have claimed paternity if he had been the sole author of any of them. However, his participation in the production may have meant his giving a retouching hand here and there and this has suggested his authorship of some of the lyrics to several scholars.[8] Certainly the words of the song 'What shall I do to show how much I love her?', one of Purcell's most delightful and popular, are not unworthy of Dryden.

Such an ambitious production with very elaborate machinery and scene changes was going to be expensive and Betterton needed to reach the widest audience at the highest box-office return. His subject had to be politically acceptable, but not so bland as to leave the viewers feeling cheated. The theme he chose, at the moment when William was about to embark for Ireland, was slightly dangerous since it was essentially anti-war. This was something dear to Betterton's own heart, as he was to show particularly in his rewrites to the end of *Dido and Aeneas* in the revised prologue as it appears in his 1700 version of *Measure for Measure*. Love, in Betterton's book, could and should supplant war.

With many of the male 'persons of quality' either already in Ireland or preparing to embark with William, the expected audience would be predominantly female; a 'love is mightier than war' theme would appeal to them, especially the Queen. Dryden refers to both the expense of the production and the imminent departure of the men in his prologue, which was banned after the first performance. Several lines could have caused offence. Those that speak of the departing troops as

Never content with what you had before;
But true to change and English Men all o'er

could have been interpreted as Dryden's strike against the change from James to William. Further on he describes them going to Ireland to grow rich on vanquished rebels and bring back both men and women as slaves to supplant 'the fashion of our blacks'. Finally, he uses the absence of the men to speak in what could be seen as praise of the 'Female Regency' such as Mary was to exercise in William's absence. She began 'to act' according to Narcissus Luttrell, on 13 June, having heard that William had, at last, sailed on the 11th.

The epilogue, which is anonymous but is usually taken to be by Betterton, also refers approvingly to female government. The sense is quite hard to follow. One or two lines seem to suggest that Tate or some other Irish writer is being spoken of:

No wonder Irish fogs obscure our light
When such as scarce can read presume to write.

Perhaps its very obscurity preserved it from the censor, or else its authorship did. Betterton was acknowledged to be the finest actor of his generation and a scholar who didn't meddle in practical politics.[9]

The story of *Dioclesian*, the emperor who resigns in favour of his nephew to enjoy a retired life with his first love, Drusilla, had a subliminal message for the audience. If James would only resign in favour of his son-in-law, William, then war could cease. Best of all would be his return to his faithful Drusilla, that religion he had been brought up in and that had always supported him, even when he cast her off for the haughty Aurelia. Betterton's version follows the original closely, but the masque inserted just before the end, which gave Purcell his second chance to write an extended score, is all new material. So too are the songs, scattered throughout, including the beautiful love lyric

'What shall I do to show how much I love her?' The message of the play is encapsulated in the words sung by a faun in the masque, representing the natural order:

Let monarchs fight for pow'r and fame,
With noise and arms mankind alarm;
Let daily fears their quiet fright,
And cares disturb their rest at night.
Greatness shall ne'er my soul inthral
Give me content and I have all.

Opinions have differed ever since about how financially successful the production was, but there's no question about its *succès d'estime*. Both prologue and epilogue speak of the great cost in scenery and costumes. Dryden, who'd been through it all before, describes the risk graphically:

Money the sweet allurer of our hopes
Ebbs out in oceans and comes in by drops.

With the men all away at the wars, the enterprise had a potential for disaster as great as that of the opening of *Albion and Albanius* on the day of Monmouth's landing. Betterton must have calculated the risks very shrewdly, since the King's departure for Ireland had been planned for months. According to Colley Cibber's memoirs, the semi-operas didn't make as much profit as expected, but Downes, the old prompter, whom Cibber was assisting at the time, says 'it gratified the Court and City'. One thing Cibber praised unreservedly was the singing of Charlotte Butler.

By 10 May Edward Purcell's regiment had reached Belfast, where Lady Donegal's house was being prepared for the King. William took with him 'an itinerant house', designed by Sir Christopher Wren, which could be carried in pieces on a wagon and quickly reassembled. D'Urfey's ode 'excellently set by Mr Henry Purcell', *High on a throne of glittering ore*, once again sees Mary as Gloriana but now alone, ruling as regent in William's absence. It's a baroque, Protestant apotheosis in which Mary has displaced both Mary of Modena and the Virgin Mary, and is 'exalted by almighty fate':

The dazzling beams of majesty
Too fierce for mortal eyes to see
She veil'd and with a smiling brow
Thus taught the admiring world below.

Virtue is still the chiefest good.

The final stanza completes the picture, like one of Verrio's paintings for the remodelled Hampton Court:

She spake whilst gods unseen that stood
Admiring one so great so good,
Flew straight to Heaven and all along
Bright Gloriana was their song.

The last line is repeated as a joyful chorus of praise.

D'Urfey's *Poems* (1690) contain, as well as the one above and the epilogue to *Dido and Aeneas*, two bawdy catches by Purcell: 'The old fumbler' and 'Young Colin cleaving of a beam', both of which became immensely popular, judging by the number of times they turn up in songbooks. There's also a missing ode 'excellently set' by him: *To pretty Mrs HD upon the sight of her picture standing amongst others at Mr Kneller's*. The volume offers several interesting pieces for which D'Urfey must have written the music himself, including the touching song 'sung to the Queen at Kensington' 'Valiant Jockey's marched away', presumably meant to comfort her for William's absence, together with a catch to drink William's health, the previous year's ode on his birthday and a version of 'Cold and raw the North did blow'.

Mary had moved to Whitehall on William's departure, but returned to Kensington when she could. Luttrell presents a lonely picture of her being rowed up river to Chelsea in the evenings, which was designed to show she wasn't spending her time in dancing and gaming while the country was at war. Almost at once her guardianship of the country was put to the test, for the French fleet set sail in an attempt to surprise and burn the English ships in Plymouth harbour. It was becalmed for eight days, giving the English time to put to sea. A declaration from James called the people to rise in his favour and restore the 'rightful sovereign'.

In the ensuing panic several people were arrested and imprisoned in the Tower, among them Samuel Pepys and the two Catholic bishops, Leyburn and Bonaventure Gifford. The English and Dutch fleets under Admiral Torrington engaged the French, but the brunt of the action was taken by the Dutch. Torrington was accused of cowardice and he too was sent to the Tower. Mary showed great presence of mind in all this, summoning the Lord Mayor to call out the London militia against an expected invasion. William meanwhile was engaged in the battle of the Boyne. On 1 July the river was crossed in force. James retreated to Dublin. In the action William lost his commander-in-chief, Count Schomberg, who had always had a low opinion of the English officers, though a high one of the English soldiery. His appointment of the Earl of Scarborough and then Count Solms in Schomberg's place, instead of Marlborough, was to lay the seeds of future discontent. Edward's commander, Colonel Trelawney, had been made governor of Dublin by William and quartered there with six regiments after taking part in the Boyne crossing.

James abandoned Ireland and returned to Paris ready, it was thought, to join the French fleet in an invasion. The London militia was drawn up for Mary's inspection in Hyde Park: nine thousand largely untrained men. At first William believed he should come back to England at once, but he changed his mind and laid siege to Limerick. Not until a new fleet and reinforcements under Marlborough were ready to sail to Ireland, and he was forced to abandon the siege because of the flooding of the trenches, did William return to England, on 6 September.

It seems strange, in the middle of all this, that the book of *Dioclesian* was announced in the *London Gazette* in the second week of June. The advertisement is misleading, since it implies that the book includes

Purcell's music, which wasn't published until the following year by Purcell himself. The publisher of the book was Jacob Tonson, Dryden's publisher. Even more strange, given the political climate, was Purcell's decision to undertake his first piece of work with Dryden, *Amphitryon*, which was advertised in October. It suggests that Purcell thought himself above politics as a musician or that he was hedging his bets, or both.

Affairs of state were so shaky that it looked as though James could be restored at any time if he made certain concessions and came without a French army and a horde of wild Irish. Although Mary was liked and admired, William had failed to move hearts. Leading politicians were known to keep a constant line open to James at St Germain. Charles had been restored, so why not James? Those whose livelihood depended on royal favour or court patronage were wise to tread a middle road as Betterton did.

Dryden's dedication of *Amphitryon* to Sir William Levison-Gore makes his position clear. He has chosen a patron 'of a different persuasion' because he knows Levison-Gore's even-handedness and because Levison-Gore had been kind to him in the past and entertained him at his home in Trentham. Dryden speaks openly of the loss of the laureateship as 'the ruin of my small fortune', but says, 'I suffer no more than I can easily undergo.' As long as he is a patient sufferer 'and no disturber of the government' and has his liberty, 'which is the birthright of an Englishman, the rest shall never go near my heart'. He goes on to praise Purcell's music for the play and to give him the accolade of recognising him as the person in whom 'we have at length found an English man equal with the best abroad'. The greatest poet, the acknowledged arbiter of taste and culture, is publicly crowning the greatest composer.

Dryden implies that he and Purcell had worked closely together on the songs and states that it was Purcell's music 'and particularly . . . the composition of the pastoral dialogue' that the 'quire of fair ladies gave so just an applause on the third day'. The crucial third performance was the one the author received the first box-office payments for. The music is grand and lush, with rich string writing as befits the classical story of Jove's seduction of Alcmena under the guise of her husband, Amphitryon. Dryden's only sadness, as he says in the dedication, was the absence of Berenice, Jane Levison-Gore, a great favourite of his, who had married the brother of the Earl of Rochester, Mary and Anne's uncle, and a useful contact in difficult times.

Queen Mary, joined in her box by her maids of honour, was present on 21 October and three weeks later saw *Dioclesian* without the prologue. The country was quieter and William was beginning to make preparations for another visit, this time to Holland and the campaign still being fought on the Continent against France. The great success of *Amphitryon* ensured that every playwright would now be eager for a contribution from Purcell to any new play, and Betterton would also call on him to rekindle interest in the many revivals that took place in between.

There had been great rejoicings to mark William's triumphant return from Ireland, but I've been unable to identify any piece of music that might have been played at them. The anthem *My song shall be alway of the loving kindness of the Lord* is dated 9 September 1690, on the copy in the Bodleian Library, and would seem to fit the occasion; it is the only one belonging to this period. Nor did Purcell contribute to the St Cecilia celebrations, but this is hardly surprising since his theatre work increased all the time and the team of Betterton, Priest and Purcell, with the addition of Dryden, was already making plans for a new opera.

For William's birthday there was a concert of music at court and a play after the King and Queen had dined publicly before 'a great resort of nobility and gentry'. Surely something by Purcell must have been performed, even though he was no longer officially harpsichordist in the Private Music, following a retrenchment earlier in the year to finance the war.[10] Edward must have been home from Ireland for Christmas, since his was one of the regiments that was to accompany William to Holland. The brothers would have had a chance to discuss the ever changing political situation and speculate on the future.

· 11 ·

Fairest Isle

WILLIAM'S BAGGAGE WAS shipped off in December and on 7 January 1691 he himself set out, but he was forced to return to Kensington by frost and an east wind, and it wasn't until the 16th that a second, successful attempt was made. As well as reinforcements for the confederate army which included Edward Purcell and their cousin Matthew in the ordnance train, he took with him a group of musicians from the Private Music. Staggins went with seventeen others, a keeper of the instruments and a chamber keeper, seven trumpeters, among them all three Shores, a kettledrummer and five extra hautboys. A couple of confusing, undated lists in the papers of Charles, Earl of Dorset, the lord chamberlain, have given rise to speculation that Purcell might have gone to Holland, but references in Andrew Ashbee's *Records of English Court Music* make it almost certain that he did not. William took instrumentalists, some of whom could double as singers if necessary. Blow would have remained behind to oversee the Chapel children, and there was no need of a harpsichordist on what was essentially a military expedition. If a composer were required, Samuel Ackroyd among the group would do. Performing vocal music would have meant singing in a tongue foreign to the Dutch hosts and, as William's allies were Lutherans or Catholics, English church music would also have been inappropriate.

At the last moment Robert King, the royal favourite who had been given a patent for his concerts, was substituted by Henry Eagles,

Francis Cruys went in place of John Banister junior and Samuel Ackroyd stood in for William Hall. One musician, Richard Tomlinson, died during or shortly after the trip.

There's no payment in the records for Blow's or Purcell's 'riding charges' for Holland as there is for those I've mentioned and the rest of the group. In addition, Purcell had to write and rehearse the ode for the Queen's birthday in April, a fortnight after the expedition returned, and to write and rehearse *King Arthur* by the end of May. Attractive as the idea of his visit to Holland may be, all the evidence seems against it. It's true that Dryden already had the Urtext of *King Arthur*, since it had been almost finished when Charles II died, but, as he makes clear in his letter of dedication to the Marquess of Halifax, it required extensive rewriting to fit it to the changed times and for Purcell's music.

Amphitryon had been followed by Elkanah Settle's *Distressed Innocence, or The Princess of Persia*. Purcell wrote an overture and act tunes for this and for Thomas Southerne's *Sir Anthony Love, or The Rambling Lady*. He also set three songs, of which 'In vain, Clemene' with hautboy is the most engaging, apart from the delightful instrumental *Ground* with its 'Scotch Tune' allusions perhaps intended for a dance. Comparing this music with his first theatre music of ten years earlier for *Theodosius*, which has many echoes of *Venus and Adonis*, it's easy to hear how far Purcell had travelled since.

William's campaign in Flanders hadn't been a success, but it had to be presented as one to justify its great expenditure of taxpayers' money. The delay in setting out and in getting the confederate troops together from Holland, Spain, Savoy and the German states while William was visiting his old home, Het Loo, for the hunting had allowed the French to make the first move and invest Mons, which fell three days later before William could attempt to relieve it. At best the expedition could only be presented as a stalemate.

When William came back to London in April, he found Whitehall severely damaged by a fire; it had begun in the little Duke of Gloucester's apartments, which had once glittered for the Duchess of

Portsmouth. Just before his return Elizabeth Villiers, known to be his mistress, though it has never been sure how physical their relationship was, had been married off to Lord O'Brien with a wedding supper and ball given by Mary at Kensington, and a dowry of five thousand pounds from Their Majesties.

No records give any hint of what music might have been played during William's first Dutch visit, though they are eloquent on the fireworks and the triumphal arches. New commanders were appointed from among his Dutch friends and Prince George, who hadn't been allowed to go to Holland, was preparing instead to join the fleet. On his return William embarked on a series of public relations dinners with his supporters among the English nobility. He waited only for Mary's birthday on the 30th, and then set out for Flanders again the following day. This time he was content to use the trumpeters, drummers and hautboys that had recently been appointed to the various regiments.

The ode *Welcome glorious morn*, which Purcell produced for the Queen on her birthday this year, has an anonymous, better than competent text. Its opening splendid trumpet flourish leads into an overture which delightfully mingles all the instruments and voices. After a duet for tenor and bass a lovely ritornello intervenes, ending in a joyful chorus. The following melting duet for alto and bass moves straight into a tenor solo over a syncopated bass ground. A trio leads on to a chorus and ritornello with the return of the trumpet. The tenor solo 'And lo, a sacred fury swelled her breast' becomes almost a *da capo* aria, taken up by the chorus. The high spot of the ode, which begins as a soprano recitative 'My prayers are heard', is reminiscent of the opening of Dido's lament. This then becomes a fluent aria over a throbbing ground bass, which dissolves into a chorus using an echo effect on 'no more' and culminating in a kind of florid joy with a drawn-out 'happy hour'. The whole section is masterly. A staccato military duet, 'He to the field', leads to yet another modified *da capo* and into the final jubilant 'Sound all ye spheres' in which trumpets lead the entire ensemble.

Welcome glorious morn is fluid, fluent and immensely rich. The only element missing, for those addicted to them, is an alto solo lyrically wandering above a ground bass. At the end of February the music for *Dioclesian* had been advertised in the *London Gazette* as being ready for its subscribers, another indication that Purcell was in London not Holland, at that time. There had been problems with the printing which caused it to be later than intended and now, Purcell apologised, it had swollen 'to a bulk beyond my intention'. As usual, he had applied his meticulous standards 'to the examination of every sheet' in an effort to make it, only the third 'opera' score to be printed, 'as correct as any extant', as he'd promised his subscribers. Now he was afraid that it was underpriced and there would be very little financial return from the initial subscriptions.

The way to make money from publication, as well as through sales, was to find a patron for the work who would pay for the privilege of a dedication. Dryden's exchange in his letters to the Earl of Chesterfield shows how the system worked. If the dedication was accepted, a present followed. Dryden suggests in a letter to his publisher Tonson that subscription copies were individually named and lists of subscribers printed.[1] For the patron of *Dioclesian* Purcell chose Charles Seymour, Duke of Somerset, and Dryden wrote him a dedication. The first sheet of Dryden's working draft of the letter is preserved in the British Library – which is remarkable, given how little autograph material exists by either of the people involved.[2]

It differs considerably from the final printed version. Dryden took the opportunity to write a piece of his typical cut-and-thrust cultural polemic, which I believe Purcell made him modify in certain places. In the middle of the sheet there is a long excision, cutting out a favourite hobby-horse of Dryden's, a comparison of the arts of painting, poetry and music, which Dryden himself probably thought too discursive for this purpose. Purcell's modifications, as I see them – indeed, I can imagine him standing over Dryden and saying, 'That must go' – are in the following section on the development of English music. The printed text reads:

> Poetry and painting have arriv'd to their perfection in our own country: Musick is yet but in its Nonage, a forward child, which gives hope of what it may be hereafter in England, when the masters of it shall find more encouragement. 'Tis now learning Italian, which is its best master, and studying a little of the French air, to give it somewhat more of gayety and fashion. Thus being further from the sun we are of later growth than our neighbour Countries, and must be content to shake off barbarity by degrees. The present age seems already dispos'd to be refin'd, and to distinguish betwixt wild Fancy and a just numerous Composition.

The manuscript's 'a prattling foreign forward child' has been replaced by 'a forward child' and 'than what it has hitherto produced' by 'when the masters of it shall find more encouragement'; the clause 'and leave the hedge notes of our early ancestors', which followed 'content to shake off our barbarity by degrees', has been deleted. The effect of Dryden's original remarks is not only to denigrate Purcell's contemporaries, particularly Blow, and the previous generation, including Locke and Lawes, but also to reduce the Tudor musicians he so much admired, Orlando Gibbons, Tallis and Byrd, to sparrows chirping untutored in a hedge. The Dryden who wrote the defence of Grabu in the preface to *Albion and Albanius* would have had no qualms about this; Purcell would. The expression 'a prattling foreign forward child' suggests that music hadn't existed in England before it was brought in by Grabu, Draghi, Matteis and other foreigners, which again was a belief not held by Purcell, whose respect for the English tradition forms a vital element in his work. It was, however, a view reinforced in Dryden by his conversion to Catholicism, even though it went against the grain of his own 'Englishness'.

Dryden had already praised Purcell at the expense of his contemporaries, and it was a theme he was to maintain:

> *So ceased the rival crew when Purcell came*
> *They sung no more or only sung his fame.*

Blow was generous enough to set these words in Dryden's ode on Purcell's death. Dryden, while speaking in the person of Purcell, though, couldn't voice such views; in any case, I don't believe Purcell shared them, although he did share Dryden's admiration for the Italians, which appears in both printed version and draft. Nothing has been added to the printed text, which again makes me believe that the changes, apart from the long excision from the comparison of painting and the other arts, were made at Purcell's instigation.

The second interesting element in this dedication is the choice of patron: Charles Seymour, 'the proud duke', as he was called. An anecdote or two can explain this title. On one occasion his second wife tapped him with her fan to attract his attention, upon which he turned and said, 'Madam, my first wife was a Percy and she would never have dared to behave so.' When he went out in his carriage, he was preceded by outriders to clear the way so that no one would look on him. The story goes that once in a country lane, a farmer driving his pigs was ordered out of the way so that the Duke wasn't seen, but the farmer refused to stand aside, saying, 'I will look on him and so shall my pig', and he held the animal up by the ears until the coach had passed.

This seemingly unattractive person was a great patron of poetry and music, as the dedication says, but, more importantly, he was very powerful. He had been a gentleman of the bedchamber to Charles II and was therefore known to Edward and Thomas Purcell. He had lost his various appointments under James for refusing to introduce the papal nuncio at court, and had gone over to William at the Revolution. Now, however, he had become one of the 'Cockpit group' -- those who took the part of Princess Anne in the worsening relations between her and the King and Queen. They had begun to sour when parliament voted Anne a pension of twenty thousand pounds while pinching William, and this had been exacerbated by William's refusal to allow Prince George to dine with him when they were in Ireland. Relations were to deteriorate throughout this and the next year. When Mary ordered Anne out of her lodgings in the Cockpit, Charles Seymour gave her and George Syon House and refused to eject them even when asked to do so by the Queen.

The choice of dedicatee was always a public statement and noted as such. It's no accident that William Seymour, later to be Edward's commander under Queen Anne, was a member of the same family, and that Frances Purcell dedicated one publication after Purcell's death to Seymour, acknowledging or reminding him of past favours, and another to Anne. Edward's tombstone speaks of 'the much lamented death of his late mistress Queen Anne', and Anne gave both him and Frances a pension on her accession.[3] Frances, in her dedication, speaks of Anne's support for Purcell's 'performances' and says that his 'greatest ambition' had been to have her as his patron, implying that circumstances had prevented this: that is, Purcell's employment as a royal musician in an immediate relationship with Mary and the bitter quarrel between the two royal sisters, which meant that, after their complete estrangement, they didn't meet for several years before Mary's death.

In March Tom D'Urfey had brought out a new play, but there was no music by Purcell in it. D'Urfey had spent the previous summer staying at the Priests' school in Chelsea and he now produced *Love for Money, or The Boarding School*, which offended the Priests and gave the scandalmongers a handle to try to drive a deep rift between him and the Priests. Opinion is generally agreed that D'Urfey wasn't malicious. On this occasion he seems to have been merely silly, and not to have realised the implication of what he was doing. The play depicts the school, run by a female Squeers, as a kind of 'Do the Girls Hall', where the girls are half starved and bullied, and resort to sexual liaisons in retaliation. One comment must have been seen as particularly damaging:

'This comes of putting girls in a boarding school.'

'Aye, they hop and dance till they set their blood afire and then they quench it with the next puddle they come at seriously.'

D'Urfey claimed in his preface that he had squared things with the Priests before publication and that the Queen had enjoyed it. The play was a great success, partly because of the comic acting of Thomas Doggett, but also partly because of the subject-matter and the circumstances of the dispute between the Priests and D'Urfey which gave it added publicity. Purcell was to be dragged into this storm in a teacup through his music for *The Fairy Queen*, in which the Priests got their own back on D'Urfey in the character of 'the scurvy poet' Stutter. For a few months afterwards D'Urfey and Purcell produced no new work together.

Meanwhile Dryden, Purcell and Josias Priest were hard at work on *King Arthur*. Unfortunately, there are no letters from Dryden of this date that refer to what must have been a longish period of close collaboration. It seems hard to believe that such an elaborate production could have been less than four to six months in the making. In the dedication of the *Dioclesian* score Dryden–Purcell speaks of the town being 'so indulgent to my first endeavours in this kind' that it has encouraged him 'to proceed in the same attempt, and your favour to this trifle will be a good omen not only to the success of the next' – a clear reference to the imminent *King Arthur* – 'but also to all the future performances'.

Dioclesian is essentially, I believe, a play with music and a masque. *King Arthur* is a true semi-opera, a *Singspiel*, close to *The Magic Flute* in its integration of music into the text. It's long, elaborate and brilliant, and, according to the prompter Downes, it was the most successful (he means in terms of box office) of the three semi-operas (*Dioclesian*, *King Arthur* and *The Fairy Queen*). The men were still away in Flanders, and the plot contains exactly the right mixture of love and war for an audience deeply interested at that moment in both topics. It's an infinitely better text than *Albion and Albanius*, a true play rather than just a piece of propaganda. Though Dryden may have seen Charles II mirrored in Arthur, that doesn't prevent the relationship between Arthur and the blind Emmeline from being deeply affecting, as is Dryden's witty and delicate exploration of her blindness.

Purcell's score has moved on again from *Dioclesian* – by which I do not mean to imply a progression like climbing a ladder, which I don't believe is the way art works or should be described, simply that *King Arthur* is different from its predecessors. Purcell is continually exploring, innovating, making his own blend of baroque, which now combines the greater density of Italian scoring with the invention, the constant surprise and lyricism of the English tradition, in which Dowland is his great forerunner. He now increasingly has both strands to call on, giving him enormous flexibility and expressiveness compared with, say, his contemporary Corelli, who's more bound by what Dryden would have called, approvingly, 'a just and numerous composition'. Purcell hadn't abandoned the 'wild fancy' of Locke, but he was refining it to make his art the most subtle and delicate of instruments, yet with an added robustness.

Ensemble writing, both vocal and instrumental, is what he concentrated on for *King Arthur*, producing music that's complex and supremely confident, as if the knowledge that he's working with the greatest acclaimed poet of his age has removed any remaining anxieties. The growing importation of professional singers into the theatre may have presented him with a practical challenge: how was he to use these additional forces to create a texture that's like a piece of brilliantly woven tapestry? The oboe parts also make a particularly rich contribution.

From its conception *King Arthur* had been intended as an opera in the 'English' mode, which was endlessly dilated on, from the staging of *The Siege of Rhodes* (which had first employed recitative) and thereafter for the next fifty years by, among others, Locke, Dryden and North: the problem was, quite simply, how much should be sung. It was believed that the English so liked their drama that they wouldn't accept something that was completely set to music. Subsequent developments proved this wrong: they would accept all-sung opera, preferably foreign, once the stage was in decline and under attack after 1700. What was developing before that was something that would now be called a multi-media event, and closely allied to the modern musical. It had the potential, in the hands of Dryden, Purcell and Priest, to become a popular art form of the highest quality, to broaden the range of its appeal – unlike foreign opera, which would hasten the split between 'popular culture' (pantomime and music hall) and 'high art' (opera and ballet).

King Arthur isn't an adaptation like *Dioclesian* and the later *Fairy Queen*, but an original for which Dryden did considerable research into British and Saxon customs, as he says in the dedicatory letter. The text in some respects belongs to that side of the seventeenth-century mind that could spawn the Royal Society and publish a treatise on Stonehenge. When the foundations of Charles's palace at Winchester were being dug (and the opera was in its first drafting), great interest was aroused by the artefacts, especially Saxon, that were turned up. The opera was intended as a serious celebration of British history finding its apogee in Charles II. By the time it was produced in 1691 that particular identification had to be transferred to William, who had become 'English' in something the same way as by the fusion of Briton and Saxon.

The reuse of the overture from the ode for the Queen's birthday of the year before suggests that Purcell ran out of time after composing the main body of the work with Dryden, who complained a little tetchily in his prefatory letter that he'd had to roughen up some of his lines in order to suit Purcell's musical requirements. The opening musical scene, the Saxon sacrifice, anticipates Bellini's *Norma*. Pagan rites fascinated the people of the period, embroiled in their own religious disputes, and also gave Dryden, the anti-clerical Catholic, a chance for a swipe at priests of all kinds.

The story of *King Arthur* is simple, but allows enough twists and turns for variety. Arthur and the Saxon Prince, Oswald, are both in love with the blind Emmeline, and she's in love with Arthur. The two princes both have their magicians: Merlin and Osmond, each of whom has a ministering spirit. Philodel is an airy Puck to Merlin's Oberon, and Grimbald the earthy demon who carries out Osmond's orders. The action takes place, symbolically, on St George's Day. The text derives ultimately from *A Midsummer Night's Dream* and *The Tempest*, but is still Dryden's own invention, and his handling of the romantic fairy idiom is masterly. Of all Purcell's works after *Dido and Aeneas*, *King Arthur* cries out for a full production with both text and music. 'Come if you dare the trumpet sounds' introduces real trumpets, and the effect of drumming in the vocal and instrumental parts is a powerful piece of military evocation that would have found an immediate response in its audience. Next, in Act II, there is a soprano solo, supported by oboe and chorus, which becomes a duet, as Philodel and Grimbald try to entice Arthur to follow them, with the fairy music, 'Hither this way'. An almost anthem-like section precedes one of Purcell's, and Dryden's, loveliest songs, in praise of the pastoral life, 'How blest are the shepherds', while the shepherds sing and dance to entertain Emmeline in Arthur's absence. The spirit of Charles II, with his hankering after the Arcadian life of pleasure, hovers over the song as over the later song 'Fairest isle'. This is Britain mythologised as Venusground. Oboe and bassoon take up the theme of 'Hither this way' and lead into the soprano duet that prefaces the brilliant, throbbing, erotic ensemble 'Shepherds lead on'. Oswald seizes Emmeline, who cries 'A rape, a rape', and he carries her off.

In Act III Merlin frees Emmeline and gives Philodel, who has been immobilised by Grimbald, but manages to free himself and freeze Grimbald instead, a philtre to pour on Emmeline's eyes to cure her blindness. In Act IV Arthur, still in pursuit of Oswald, is deceived by a scene of water nymphs, who invite him to take his clothes off and skinny-dip with them, and then by the apparition of a tree which appears to hold the metamorphosed Emmeline. He frees her and is about to take her in his arms when Philodel appears, strikes her with his wand and reveals the true shape of Grimbald.

The fight between Arthur and Oswald finally takes place in Act V; Arthur wins and everyone is reconciled by the Masque of Britannia, showing how Saxon and Briton will some day fuse into one nation.

The recitative that calls the Genius of the Isle to awake from sleep indicates how easily Purcell could have set the whole text. The bass aria in which the Genius casts off his frozen sleep over a staccato ground of cold strings is a showy piece of imitative writing and must have brought the house down for its daring – an aspect of Purcell's style that Roger North particularly appreciated, and which he was to elaborate on in the Masque of the Seasons in *The Fairy Queen*. There are whole sections in the string writing of *King Arthur* which anticipate Vivaldi's 'Four Seasons' so closely that the listener is driven to wonder if the younger composer could have heard them. Dryden's sons were in Rome at this period under the protection of Cardinal Howard, in correspondence with their parents – they were, of course, Howards on their mother's side. It's not impossible that they could have provided a channel for the music to reach Italy.

At times the strings give an almost visual effect of showering notes, like a bursting rocket shooting stars, to be followed by a limpid, melting duet for two sopranos in complete contrast, or the lyrical tenor solo with chorus 'How happy the lover', whose endlessly inventive accompaniment slides into the duet 'For love every creature'. The composition of the odes, for which he had to provide contrasting sections and find fresh, innovative ways of embodying the same sentiments year after year, had trained Purcell for this full-scale work; in effect the odes are mini-operas, and their ritornellos foreshadow the act tunes and instrumental sections of, in particular, *King Arthur*. For the final masque a ground march with trumpets brings on the bass to sing 'Ye blustering brethren of the sky' and to calm the winds to an accompaniment of recorders, which is unusual for the low voice. The horns of elfland duet towards an ensemble of quiet ecstasy, interrupted by the rollicking haymakers; Purcell adapts or invents a morris dance for them, 'Your hay, it is mow'd'. Dryden takes the opportunity to underline the unpopularity among countrymen of tithes to pay for 'blockhead' Anglican clergy. Both of them obviously enjoyed the chance for a bit of buffoonery.

As if he hadn't done enough, there are two soprano solos: 'Fairest isle' and the recitative 'You say 'tis love', which becomes a love duet in the seduction tradition of the dialogue song, with the voices mingling in: 'I'll be constant, you'll be kind . . . ' A variation on 'Come if you dare' allows St George to enter, and a robust chorus leads to the 'grand dance', usually a chaconne or pavane, which closed the musical part of such entertainments. It only remained for Mrs Bracegirdle, who had returned to the stage after an absence from *Amphitryon* and perhaps *Dioclesian*, and was now playing Emmeline, to speak the epilogue, which refers to her own recent absence:

My wisest way will be to keep the stage
And trust to the good nature of the age;
And he that likes the musick and the play
Shall be my favourite gallant today.

The work was a huge success and put Purcell beyond the reach of his contemporaries. Dryden said he had composed the music 'with so great a genius' that he need only fear the ignorant. Why, then, didn't he publish it as Dryden did the text? The main reason, I believe, was its sheer size. In her vocal score edition Margaret Laurie lists forty-three separate pieces. Purcell had been out of pocket over the publication of *Dioclesian*. With his insistence on the highest standards, the sheer labour of preparing *King Arthur* for the press would have been daunting in itself. He had many things to occupy him in the remainder of 1691; and Betterton, in his desire to keep up the theatrical momentum, was planning another opera in the following year.

Politically, *King Arthur* had been given the royal approval before production. After the banning of his prologue to *Dioclesian*, Dryden, not completely reassured by the easy passage of *Amphitryon*, had taken the precaution of getting his patroness, the Duchess of Monmouth, to recommend it to the Queen, who had been 'graciously pleased to peruse the manuscript of this opera and give it her blessing'. Its ability to be read as conducive to national integration and harmony would have pleased her, particularly coming from a Catholic and avowed Jacobite who in the dedication nevertheless rejected the idea of a new invasion of 'Gauls'.

About a fortnight after the opening of *King Arthur* Purcell's sister Katherine – lying blatantly about her age, since she was twenty-nine and appears in the licence as 'about twenty-two' – married William Sale, the young clergyman who'd taken Isaac Gostling's parish of Sturry when he was put out for refusing to take the oath of allegiance to the new monarchs. There's something strange about this whole episode. Isaac was John Gostling's brother, and it's almost certain that John performed the wedding ceremony, on 18 June, since the couple were married in his parish church, St Mary Magdalen, Old Fish Street, which had been combined after the Great Fire with St Gregory by St Paul's, where Gostling was now living and serving as sub-dean in the rising cathedral. It almost looks as if William Sale had been a plant in Isaac's old parish. Sale was a great collector of benefices and curacies, having not only Sturry, but also Bapchild, Westbear, Sevington and Sheldwich between 1689 and 1696. After the ceremony there would have been feasting and dancing until the couple were put to bed, perhaps in Purcell's own house in Bowling Alley East. Sometime this year they had taken on the lease of a second house next to their own and their rates had almost doubled, so there was plenty of room.[4]

Edward was still in Flanders. Perhaps Daniel came back for the occasion from Oxford, where he had settled down as organist, composer and punster in residence at Magdalen College. He showed no sign of marrying. Unless they were between ships, Charles and Joseph were at sea. Charles was probably married by this time: a 'Mr Charles Purcell' had married Frances Dawson in Barbados in 1684.[5] Since there's no record of children being born to them there, it looks as if this was a marriage of non-residents, for neither of them appears in any other registry entries in the area, and Charles was a widower with two young children when he died.[6]

Edward almost certainly returned from campaign during the winter when the two armies retired into their respective camps. There's a story in Luttrell, which bears this out, of the abduction of the thirteen-year-old heiress Mary Wharton by two young officers back from Ireland the previous November. Unless they were due for relief, the ordinary soldiers stayed put, but Luttrell also records that the Duke of Ormonde, Edward's patron, returned on 20 October with other lords and volunteers; entries in the state papers indicate that this was the annual pattern as long as the war against France continued.

William's campaign hadn't gone any better after he had returned to Flanders in May, but his arrival in England in autumn 1691 was greeted as a triumph, largely because Limerick had been taken by Ginkel, obscuring the less than satisfactory state of the King's military affairs on the Continent. William landed at Margate and travelled by coach to London through cheering crowds, together with his Dutch favourite, young Count Bentinck, and John Churchill, the Earl of Marlborough. Going over Shooters Hill, the coach was overturned and they were all thrown out. Marlborough thought he'd broken his neck, but William assured him that since he could still speak, it must be intact. Dazed by the accident, they drove on into London through more cheering crowds, salutes from the Tower cannon, ringing bells and bonfires. At eleven o'clock they reached Whitehall and Mary, who immediately whisked William off to their newly decorated apartments in Kensington.

The combination of Guy Fawkes' Day, the King's birthday, his and the Queen's wedding anniversary and William's landing in 1688 was celebrated first with a sermon. Then, Luttrell says, the royal pair dined in public and the night concluded with a great ball and dancing at court. 'The court was all in their splendour, the queen very rich in jewels; and all the great officers attended.' The separation of the two elements of the 'great ball' and 'dancing' suggests again that there was a professionally performed balletic part followed by general dancing.

Purcell's music must have had a place in all this and probably Priest's choreography too. A few days later a fire at Kensington, caused 'thro the carelessness of a candle', destroyed the lodgings of the Duke of Ormonde and others in the stone gallery.

King Arthur was still playing in December, and Purcell was also involved in a production by Dryden's protégé, Thomas Southerne, *The Wives' Excuse*, for which he wrote four songs. These and another song from Southerne's earlier *Sir Anthony Love* were published in the next *Banquet of Music* (licensed in February 1692), which also contained 'On the brow of Richmond Hill' by D'Urfey, 'Underneath this myrtle shade' (a setting of *The Epicure* by Cowley) and a song for a revival of *The Indian Emperor* (Dryden's sequel to *The Indian Queen* which he had written with his brother-in-law Sir Robert Howard), 'I look't, and saw within the book of fate'. Altogether there were nine songs by Purcell. To complete the Dryden spin-offs, Purcell also provided instrumental music around this time for a play by Dryden's correspondent and friend, William Walsh, *The Gordian Knot Untied*. This included first and second tunes, during which the audience was expected to come in and settle down, the overture, which usually began on a strong, attention-demanding chord, and five act tunes, among them a fine chaconne and minuet.

At the beginning of December someone whom Frances describes as one of Purcell's patrons and thanks for his 'many favours' to him[7] was married at St Martin's in the Fields, and it seems very likely that Purcell took part in this event. It was Nathaniel Crewe, third Baron and bishop of Durham, Purcell's old supporter as dean of the Chapel Royal in James's time, now in disgrace with William, and preserved from expulsion from his see only by the intercession of the new archbishop of Canterbury, Tillotson. Crewe's entry in the *Dictionary of National Biography* is vituperative in the extreme. He'd been made dean of the Chapel Royal and, worse, a member of the suspect ecclesiastical commission by James and remained at heart an unrepentant Jacobite although he took the oaths. He was probably also involved in Daniel Purcell's appointment to Magdalen College, along with Bonaventure

Gifford. As Baron Crewe of Stene he had a family seat in Northamptonshire, Dryden's native county, and as a member of the Inner Temple he was a friend of Gilbert Dolben. Gilbert's son John was to be not only appointed sub-dean of the Chapel Royal, but also made a prebendary of Durham by Crewe. The story goes, according to W. H. Cummings, that it was a John Dolben (presumably his uncle of the same name, son of the former dean of Westminster) who, with Sir Christopher Wren, took a death mask of Purcell. In spite of the general disapproval in which he was held and his having gone down in history as a high Tory, Crewe was a generous contributor to charity, and especially, on his death, to the poor of Durham. Frances's acknowledgement of his kindnesses to the Purcells isn't surprising, but it does place the Purcells as inclining away from the Whig position.

Crewe had been a favourite with Charles II and, according to his modern biographer, it was Crewe who had brought Gostling and Turner into the Chapel Royal. He was an enthusiastic performer on several instruments, although Anthony à Wood, who detested him, said he wasn't very good. He had been one of the original Oxford Music Club and was a friend of William Fuller, bishop of Lincoln, several of whose devotional poems Purcell had set in *Harmonia Sacra*.[8]

The year closed with a sour note for the future of the theatre. On 15 December a riot broke out which ended in four lords being punched and knocked down. They complained to William, who referred the matter to the House of Lords. The House asked the King to suspend performances. A week later the Lords considered the matter, sending for the captain of the soldiers who was supposed to keep order at the playhouse, but he 'excused himself therefrom'. A bishop called for the complete suppression of the theatre as a 'nursery of lewdness'. The secular Lords rejected this on the grounds that it was too harsh and likely to interfere with their own pleasures, but they got the Lord Chamberlain to suspend the players from acting for the time being.[9] Realising the risk they were running, the actors begged their lordships' pardon and the ban was lifted. It was, however, an indication that all wasn't well with the theatre and a foretaste of the attacks that were to come.

According to Colley Cibber, it was the theatre owners, the patentees, who emphasised opera in the hope of making large profits, rather than Betterton, yet Betterton's own interest in opera and even, later, in foreign singers and dancers is well attested. Whoever was the driving force, the publication of the next operatic production, *The Fairy Queen*, had already been entered in the term catalogues of the Stationers' Company by November 1691. It was to be the most lavish yet.

· 12 ·

'Tis Nature's Voice

AT CHRISTMAS PURCELL left Bowling Alley East and his mother-in-law, Amy Pieters, took over the house.[1] My belief is that the family went first to stay with the Priests in Chelsea, as D'Urfey had done, in order to work on the new opera. Frances's widowed sister, Amy Howlett, almost certainly moved in with her mother, who paid the rates for both houses, but let one to a family called Davis and a Madam Carhile. The Purcells didn't return to a house of their own in Westminster for two years. It's possible that Frances and the children stayed with her mother, at least from time to time, but she and Purcell were certainly together early in 1693, when their last child was conceived.

Already plans were being made for the next year's military campaign. Resentment at the promotion of so many Dutch officers and the neglect of the English was mounting, and early in January 1692 Edward Purcell's regimental commander, Charles Trelawney, resigned his commission in protest, to be followed by several others; his brother Henry was appointed in his place. The Christmas festivities continued with the usual heavy gaming by the King and the groom porters on Twelfth Night, a scene Pepys had once witnessed with some amazement and disgust, followed by a great ball, which William passed doing his accounts in the Treasury. On the following day the Queen took Catherine, the Queen Dowager, to see *King Arthur*.

The Earl of Marlborough had been openly critical of William's Dutch promotions and on 26 January, shortly after helping the King into his shirt in his capacity as gentleman of the bed chamber, he was sacked from all his posts. He was also suspected of being a supporter of James. Anne had certainly written to ask her father's forgiveness just before Christmas, and it has often been said that this was meant to pave the way for Marlborough, had James been restored. There was, however, another element to the problem. Sarah Churchill's sister was the wife of James's Irish commander the Duke of Tyrconnel, and there were those ready to allege that military information passed between the sisters. Mary demanded that Anne should also sack Sarah, and relations rapidly worsened. Although there was a ball at Kensington for Anne's birthday on 11 February, a week later Anne left her Whitehall lodgings in the Cockpit for Charles Seymour's Syon House, where she was soon visited by Seymour and his relative by marriage the Duke of Ormonde. She was, in effect, setting up an alternative court.

A series of petty retaliations followed. When Prince George attended a debate in the House of Lords, he wasn't given the usual guard of honour and the drums didn't beat for him as he passed through St James's Park. George, indeed, was one of the causes of the rupture, for even his attempts to ship on board as a volunteer with the fleet had been thwarted and he was forced to kick his heels at home, when, however limited his intelligence, he was known to have great personal courage in battle. This coldness between the royal sisters was to create problems for all those who had somehow to stay in favour with them both. Purcell seems to have had a strong loyalty to and liking for Mary, but the family generally inclined towards Anne.

At the beginning of March William took his leave of everyone, except, presumably, Anne but including Catherine of Braganza, who was now at last to go back to Portugal. Mary accompanied him as far as Brentwood and then went to Kensington; after hearing that he had sailed, she returned formally to Whitehall to take up the government. This year he didn't come back for her birthday. The other officers followed him to Holland at the end of March; a big new kettledrum on a gun carriage headed the artillery train and there was a new royal standard. Reinforcements for Edward's regiments left the Downs for Holland at the same time.

A week later Dryden's new play *Cleomenes*, to which Purcell had contributed the delightful soprano song 'No, no, poor suffering heart' and which was due to open in the second week of April, was banned 'by order of the Queen' as 'reflecting much on the government'. Dryden had been ill for several weeks in the previous autumn and had asked Tom Southerne to finish the last act for him. Now his friends rallied round to try to get the ban lifted, in particular the Queen's uncle, Lawrence Hyde and his wife, and the Lord Chamberlain, the Earl of Dorset. Someone had obviously advised Mary that the play was dangerous – perhaps the rancorous Shadwell, whom D'Urfey claimed had persecuted him for many years and who had been thought by some to be behind the banning of Dryden's prologue to *Dioclesian*. Betterton must have been relieved that Dryden hadn't provided the text for the expensive opera then in rehearsal. Attempts were made to bring the opera forward to fill the gap left by *Cleomenes*, but such an elaborate production wasn't to be hurried.[2]

The efforts of Dryden's supporters were successful by 18 April, and *Cleomenes*, with the offending passages left out, was acted 'to great applause'. The ill feeling between Mary and Anne deepened. Anne had moved into Syon House in the last weeks of pregnancy, worrying about her son, William, left behind at Kensington. Not surprisingly, her baby lived for only a few hours. An adamant Mary came to see her to insist that she dismiss Sarah Churchill. In tears, Anne refused. They were never to meet again and Anne and George went down to Bath to pass the summer.

The Fairy Queen was advertised to open on 28 April, just before Mary's birthday, as a graceful compliment to her, but in the event the ode for that occasion, *Love's goddess sure was blind*, which Purcell had composed and simultaneously rehearsed with *The Fairy Queen*, got in first. The words were by Sir Charles Sedley, father of James II's witty Protestant mistress Catherine and a supporter of William, who quipped at the Revolution: where James had made Sedley's daughter a countess, Sedley had made James's daughter a queen. Sedley was a better than average lyric poet and dramatist, and the text is one of the most lyrical and original of all the odes Purcell set. The birthday was a grand occasion, Luttrell reported; the full court of nobility and gentry, the Lord Mayor and aldermen were all present. For the first time Luttrell mentions the ode.

The beginning is very regal and grave; the second movement of the overture is a running melody that ends on a slow introduction for the countertenor solo 'Love's goddess sure'. A short bass solo leads to a countertenor duet with treble recorders, 'Sweetness of nature'. A soprano sings in further praise of the Queen and this is taken up by the chorus. Then the harpsichord introduces a ground bass, the folksong 'Cold and raw', over which the soprano briefly explores several themes: the Queen's attempts to improve public manners and morals, the absent William and the political factions at home. The countertenor returns for a duet with string bass; Purcell is at his most subtle, complex and inventive when setting 'Many, many such days'. The ode seems to be closing with a choral plea for Mary's long life, but dissolves into a meditative quartet anticipating her death.

> *we below shall mourn*
> *Our short but their eternal choice.*

Surprisingly for this period, there are no trumpets, even in the section that brings in William, and the whole piece requires very few, though highly accomplished, players and voices. It looks as if the large forces needed for the opera had gobbled up the available rehearsal time and left Purcell to produce a jewelled miniature. I wonder whether something so exquisite would have been suitable for the occasion Luttrell describes, which must, in the custom of the times, have had the usual flourishes of trumpets and drums. Perhaps the ode was performed privately for Mary before the grand ceremonial, reminding her of things she valued: her gentleness (except with Anne) and her genuine piety.

According to a Hawkins tale which comes from the Gostling camp, the piece contains a private joke between Purcell and the Queen. The story has it that Mary, wanting some musical entertainment one day, sent for Gostling, the soprano Arabella Hunt, a great favourite of hers, and Purcell. After hearing several songs by Purcell, the Queen asked Arabella Hunt to sing 'Cold and raw', which she did to her lute, leaving Purcell twiddling his thumbs at the harpsichord. Clearly this is the version as told by Gostling to his son William, but it needs some looking at.

If, as Gostling says, 'Cold and raw' was used as the ground bass in the ode as a direct reference to this incident, which is said to have taken place before Gostling became sub-dean of St Paul's, then it happened immediately after the previous year's ode, a long time for such a slight or preference to be remembered. On the other hand, D'Urfey had a version of 'Cold and raw', the *Scotch Tune*, to naughty but not vicious words, and his songs were often sung to the Queen. The impression which the story gives of Purcell getting in a pet because Mary wanted one song, and that a folksong, as a change from his, doesn't accord with other reports of his character. It's more likely that he put it in because he knew she liked it, and the music accreted a slanted version of the story. What seems to be true is that such musical happenings, involving Gostling, Hunt and Purcell, did take place. Indeed, all three of them could have been part of the small forces used for the ode: Hunt as soprano, Gostling for the one bass solo and Purcell as harpsichordist and countertenor.

The text of the ode was printed in full without the music in a new publication which had been started in January, the *Gentleman's Journal*, the first arts magazine in Britain and forerunner of the more famous eighteenth-century publication, the *Spectator*. Its editor was a young French Protestant, Pierre Antoine Motteux, who had come to England in 1685 and was a poet and dramatist. Motteux says that the ode was sung to the Queen on 29 April, the day before her birthday, which also ties in with its intimate nature. In his first issue he'd included a song of his own set by Purcell, 'Stript of their green the groves appear'; it praises winter, which brings back William, and Motteux hoped it would be sung before the Queen. There were no more songs by Purcell in the next four months while he was working on *The Fairy Queen* and the birthday ode, but as soon as these were over he was back again (in June) with one of his most beautiful and popular songs, 'If music be the food of love', a setting of words by Colonel Heveningham.

The Fairy Queen appeared at last on 2 May: 'the clothes, scenes and musick cost 3000 L'. Taking Staggins's or Blow's salaries of a hundred pounds a year to be equivalent to twenty thousand nowadays, the relative cost was well over half a million pounds. The opening music is full of menacing magic. These aren't the pretty fairies of nineteenth- and twentieth-century children's stories, but creatures of often sinister power and beauty. The book is an adaptation of Shakespeare's *A Midsummer Night's Dream*. There seems no reason to suppose that Betterton himself wasn't responsible for it, especially since it was published anonymously as many of his adaptations were. After its huge success any other adapter would surely have claimed it, unless the representation of D'Urfey as the drunken scurvy poet Stutter made anonymity advisable. He had been portrayed as such in the anonymous pamphlet *Wit for Money* of 1691, which reflected on his boarding-school play and was probably by the satirist Tom Brown. An added hit in *The Fairy Queen* came in the lines on D'Urfey's ambition to be the next laureate:

And as I hope to wear the bays
I'll write a sonnet in thy praise.

This strongly suggests that this scene, which is sometimes thought to be an insertion for the run the following year, was put in at least before Shadwell's death in November and Tate's appointment, which ended any hopes that Poet Stutter might have to become laureate. The house must have rolled about at this satire, but D'Urfey bore no malice and soon worked again with Purcell and Priest. The immediate effect of the scene is to introduce an element of hobgoblin caricature into the comedy as the fairies pinch the poet 'black and blue'.

Act II offers the beautiful countertenor solo, imitative of bird song and flight, 'Come, all ye songsters of the sky', precursor of so much similar writing in Handel, particularly *Acis and Galatea*, and in Mozart's *Magic Flute*. In the following duet the voices and trumpets echo each other. The next song, 'Sing while we trip it', was sung by Mrs Ayliffe, one of the professionals recently brought into the theatre. Dryden mentions in a letter that she was not as good on that occasion (D'Urfey's *The Richmond Heiress*) as Mrs Bracegirdle, his own favourite. Next comes what is effectively another masque within the whole work: the lulling asleep of Titania, begun by Night and carried forward by another of the newcomers, Mrs Dyer, as Mystery, who sings the second night music; it leads to the entry of Secrecy, sung by the countertenor John Freeman, for the erotic 'One charming night'. The bass solo for Sleep completes this section with the help of a chorale-like chorus and a slow hypnotic dance for the fairies.

After the act tune for Act III and the rehearsal of *Pyramus and Thisbe* by Bottom and company, Titania brings in her new lover in his ass's head to be entertained by a fairy masque against elaborate scenery of a wood, a river, arching dragons and, in the distance, two swans on the river. Mrs Dyer sang again – 'If love's a sweet passion' – and then a symphony played while the swans came closer and a ballet of fairies affrighted by savages was danced. 'Ye gentle spirits of the air' seems to have been inserted after the first production before the comic duet of Corydon and Mopsa, sung by John Pate and Freeman in drag. Venetian opera, no doubt influenced by carnival, also used drag for comic roles; it was to transfer into British pantomime and, indeed, become a staple element of the form. 'Now the maids and the men' is a burlesque of rustic seduction. A new feature of *The Fairy Queen* is the introduction of knock-about comedy – evident in the mock morris in *King Arthur*, but now developed much further, and picking up the mood of Purcell's many catches of robust slapstick.

Charlotte Butler, who'd been such a success as Philodel in *King Arthur* that Roger North remembered her performance in detail several years after, sings 'When I have heard young maidens complain', then comes a haymakers' dance and Mopsa and Corydon sing of the delights of the bed:

> *A thousand, thousand ways we'll find*
> *To entertain the hours;*
> *No two shall e'er be known so kind,*
> *No life so blest as ours.*

Act IV begins with drums and trumpets for Oberon and Puck. The play carries the story to the point of Titania's awakening and disgust at having been 'enamoured of an ass'. Bottom is restored and while he sleeps again the fairies celebrate with the Masque of the Seasons for Oberon's birthday, introducing a celebration of William in his icon of the rising sun, which all salute. Once again the scenery is lavish: a garden of cypresses, statues, columns and a magnificent fountain ejaculating a twelve-foot jet into the air.

Phoebus appears after a song in which the countertenors imitate 'the fifes and the clarions', followed by real trumpets and drums, ushering in Phoebus' own aria; it celebrates the benefits of the sun, 'great parent of us all' in his life-giving warmth – the familiar image of William bringing freedom and vigour to the nation. The winter had been particularly hard and the Thames had frozen again, and the praise of Phoebus' potency works on both a realistic and an iconographic level. The seasons make their contributions in turn, Charlotte Butler taking on spring and John Pate the sprightly summer. The melancholy of autumn in 'See my many coloured fields' is particularly evocative; in the spectacular 'Now winter comes slowly' the cold notes drag themselves out of the strings before the bass takes up the frozen theme.

After the resolution of the rest of Shakespeare's plot in Act V, Oberon introduces the Masque of Juno, who descends in a chariot drawn by peacocks, like an animated painting by Verrio. William has had his tribute as Phoebus, now Mary has hers as the goddess of conjugal love:

Be to one another true
Kind to her as she to you.

In later performances there was a further insertion here while the ravishing lament 'O let me ever, ever weep' is sung. Then Oberon transforms the scene to a Chinese garden and Chinese men and women enter, dancing to celebrate the golden age of the natural world before the introduction of labour and trade, 'which fools on each other impose'. The first song, for countertenor with trumpet obbligato, 'Thus the gloomy world', anticipates a similar section in Purcell's next St Cecilia ode.

A Chinese couple sing in praise of free love until the monkeys come in for one of the grotesque dances Priest was famous for, representing the animal nature of love. The soprano takes up this theme in celebration of sexual passion; 'kind cupids' clap their wings in triumph in the bass while she climaxes ecstatically. Hymen is supposed to regularise this excess with marriage, but he complains that his torch is out, extinguished by 'loose dissembled vows',/Where hardly love outlives the wedding night'.

Two women persuade him to change his mind and he joins them in 'They shall be as happy as they're fair' while the Chinese men and women dance in support. The whole company twines and intertwines in the 'grand dance', a splendid chaconne that's both stately and constantly in motion, and all join together for the final chorus. As with the two earlier semi-operas, it's the continuous flow of invention, in both the melody and its rich accompaniment, that takes the breath away.

The audience loved it, but what were they seeing? It's possible to dismiss *The Fairy Queen* as an enjoyable pantomime, not worthy of the musical effort expended on it. The cost of a modern production is as prohibitive as that of its first, and in consequence we have to be content with concert performances that merely reinforce this impression. I believe that, if properly produced, it would show itself for what it is: a great work of erotic art that explores the full range of sexual passion – which is, after all, the theme of Shakespeare's original.

There is, though, something questionable about the production of *The Fairy Queen* at that time. It's as if the whole nation had refused to consider the everyday realities of war and civil unrest and was hankering for a golden age of pleasure which had never existed, but which some now began to see as the reign of Charles II; as if the women left behind were indulging in a collective fantasy and had been spirited away in imagination to fairyland, where they could give their erotic conscious and unconscious free but harmless play. The sexual conventions of the time demanded that men pursue and that women resist or succumb: 'be kind'. Rules governed exactly how far everyone could go. Abduction, although it took place, was frowned upon as the violation of another man's property. Seduction wasn't. This kept society in a state of almost perpetual sexual excitement, which made the drama seem so lewd to later generations. As with modern pop songs, sex in all its mutations was the explicit material of most of the lyrics.

A few days after the opening of *The Fairy Queen* there was a new rumour of a French invasion. The trained bands were called out and Admiral Russell put to sea with the part of the fleet that wasn't already engaging the French in the Caribbean. John Churchill, the Earl of Marlborough, and many others were arrested, allegedly for 'conspiring the death of the queen and endangering the officers and soldiers of their majesties guards'. The naval victory at La Hogue towards the end of May crushed any idea of a French invasion, and William set out to relieve the besieged town of Namur, but in spite of all his efforts it finally fell to the French in June. The strain of unremitting conflict at home and abroad began to tell on Mary. She left Whitehall and retired to Kensington, it was said, 'to drink the spa waters'. Marlborough had been in the Tower since his arrest, but was finally bailed by Halifax and

Shrewsbury, who were at once struck off the Privy Council. Then in July came the defeat of William's confederate forces with appalling losses on both sides at Steenkerke, in which the British troops were cut to pieces and MacKay, their commander, died of his wounds. It's a mark of the overall number killed in this campaign that Edward Purcell had already been given two new ensigns in the field at Villé in June.

In the preface to the published text of *The Fairy Queen* Betterton, the probable author, reflected sharply on the situation of the opera in Britain and the difficulty of staging large productions without a state subsidy such as the ones given by the Republic of Venice and the French King. The arguments he deploys are remarkably familiar:

> What encouragement Seignior Baptist Lully had from the present King of France is well known . . . In Italy especially in Venice . . . the noble Venetians set 'em out at their own cost and what a confluence of people the fame of 'em draw from all parts of Italy to the great profit of the city . . . Many of the English gentry are sensible what advantage Paris receives by the great number of strangers which frequent the Opera's three days a week throughout the year. If therefore an Opera were established here . . . it would be some advantage to London considering what a sum we must yearly lay out among tradesmen for the fitting out so great a work.

If not by Betterton, this plea to 'the nobility and gentry' (rather than the royal purse, which was fast being depleted by the war) might be by one of the patentees, either in themselves or through a suitable mouthpiece. I'm inclined to Betterton, however, because of his long involvement with spectacular drama and opera. Whoever wrote it is very niggardly with any praise for British talent: 'I dare affirm if we had half the encouragement . . . you might in a short time have as good dancers in England as they have in France, though I despair of ever having as good voices among us as they have in Italy.' The writer ends with a comment on the cost that bears out both Downes's and Cibber's doubts about the financial viability of *The Fairy Queen* in spite of its popularity, 'considering the mighty charge in setting it out and the extraordinary expenses that attends it every day 'tis represented'. The additional two songs in the 1693 edition, along with the 'new music' for the drunken poet's scene, may have been intended to persuade people to see it again.

A certain Thomas Cross hurried into print with *Philomela*, a collection of songs from *Dioclesian* and *King Arthur*, forcing Purcell to issue a selection of his own from *The Fairy Queen*. His could be bought either from Henry Playford or at the theatre in Dorset Garden, and a second edition was needed later that year. Once again he published no full score; the copy manuscript disappeared for over two hundred years, only to turn up in the Royal Academy of Music. North commented, though he believed it was just *King Arthur* and not *The Fairy Queen* that was missing too, that it was 'no wonder it's lost; for the English have no care of what's good, and therefore deserve it not'.

There was nothing from Purcell in the *Gentleman's Journal* for July, but the August issue included a song which had been sung by Mrs Ayliffe in John Crowne's *Regulus* in June: 'Ah! me to many deaths decreed'. Motteux described it as being 'set in the Italian way', by which he means it was a recitative lament with much imitative ornamentation. Its theme of the lover going to the wars struck at many hearts, including Mary's. Motteux praised Mrs Ayliffe's performance: 'had you heard it . . . you would have owned that there is no pleasure like that which good notes, when so divinely sung, can create'. In fact, the Italian it most resembles is the Monteverdi of three quarters of a century before and, as Franklin Zimmerman and others have pointed out, however it was perceived at the time, it is ineluctably Purcellian.

Again he contributed nothing in September, and October only contained a reprint from *Dioclesian*, 'Let us dance, let us sing'. *Dioclesian* had earlier provided music to celebrate the victory over the French at sea, for its 'Let the soldiers rejoice' was converted in a broadsheet broadside to 'Valiant Protestant boys'. The lack of any new music for this period and the fact that his mother-in-law had taken over the

Purcells' home in Bowling Alley East make me think that if Purcell wasn't still staying with the Priests in Chelsea, he was even further out of London. Those who could tended to leave the city in the summer and look for cleaner air. Dryden usually retired to his native Northamptonshire, particularly when he was ill. It strongly suggests some concern for the health of one or more members of the family.

Anne and George had gone to drink the waters in Bath, where they were subjected to the same petty discrimination they had suffered at home: the Mayor and local officials had been instructed by Mary not to wait on them or to recognise their presence even by attending them to church. While they were away, they rented Berkeley House, which had been damaged by a fire earlier that year, had it 'fitted up' against their return and took two houses nearby for their servants. By the middle of September the exhausted armies on the Continent, who had spent six months in bloody but inconclusive warfare, were stabilising their positions for the winter, and Mary went back to Whitehall in expectation of William's arrival. William, however, unwilling to leave until he saw that the French had indeed decamped to winter quarters, changed his plans and Mary returned to Windsor. From there she drove out to dine with a reinstated Halifax and with Sir Robert Howard at his magnificent house, Ashtead Manor near Epsom; one of its most noteworthy features was Verrio's staircase, which showed Astrea presiding over the Golden Age.[3] William meanwhile had gone to their old home at Het Loo again to hunt. The troops were starting to embark at the beginning of October and the volunteers had already returned when the French commander, Boufflers, suddenly laid siege to Charleroi and William was forced to go back to the army and stop the embarkation. James's much publicised decision to go to Fontainebleau at this time, after the birth of a daughter in July, seems a deliberate piece of propaganda; there 'several operas were being prepared for their entertainment'. The childless Mary could only give her sister Anne's little son a jewelled sword and herself gird it about his waist.

On 13 October the second of the several tragedies this year that were to affect the future of the theatre took place during a revival by Dryden and Lee of *Oedipus*: Samuel Sandford, believing that he had a retractable stage dagger in his hand, ran George Powell, with whom he was acting, three inches deep into the body. Earlier in the year the actor Williams had died after killing his opponent in a duel. Duelling had become much more common; it was hard to enforce laws or moral sanctions against it when men were killing each other in thousands legally every summer. Crime of all sorts was rising, especially clipping the coinage; since it was categorised as treason, it was punished by death, and women clippers were burned. The numbers of highwaymen had increased too. Whereas James had liked to exercise the royal prerogative to pardon offenders, the sterner Protestant monarchs were less forgiving. Mary announced her intention not to pardon while she was governing and William issued a proclamation that he wouldn't pardon highwaymen.

This tragic production of *Oedipus* had new music by Purcell, including one of his best-known songs (made so famous by Alfred Deller), 'Music for a while', which has a plangent, hypnotic accompaniment. Once again, although as far as I'm aware there are no songs by Dowland among the copies of earlier music which he made, it's the Dowland of 'I saw my lady weep' who seems its closest predecessor. Another likely revival for this year is Shadwell's *The Libertine*, which, surprisingly, since it's a version of the Don Juan story, has the song most beloved of girls' choirs earlier this century, 'Nymphs and shepherds, come away'. It also contains an innovative solemn march for trumpets preceding the devils' scene, so it is all the more regrettable that Purcell hadn't the opportunity for a full setting of this 'Don Giovanni'.

William finally returned on 20 October and Mary went out as usual to meet him and bring him home to the customary joyful accompaniment, the crowds running alongside the coach shouting huzzahs and smashing any windows that weren't showing a welcoming light. The next day the whole court assembled at Kensington and the City rulers came to invite him to dine at Guildhall. Prince George came too and paid his respects. The next event was the Lord Mayor's Show; the King and Queen and 'most of the nobility', but not the Denmarks, dined. It was a particularly splendid occasion. Theophilus Fitz was paid twenty-one pounds, one shilling and sixpence for the violins and his fee. Since Fitz was a member of the Private Music, it looks like the royal musicians were hired for the occasion.[4]

For William's birthday this year the shops were shut, the guns fired and 'their majesties dined openly' in the Banqueting Hall with the knights of the garter in attendance. At night there was a great ball, for which an extra six hautboys were engaged. There were two rehearsals, and Purcell must have been heavily involved in the event, both as composer and as accompanist. William liked the hautboy and it was to assume an increasingly important place in music. Purcell wrote superbly for it, turning it from being simply a martial accessory into a sensitive and flexible instrument in its own right.

A fortnight later Dryden's old enemy Shadwell died at his son's house in Chelsea. In its November issue the *Gentleman's Journal* recorded *The Volunteers*, a new comedy by him acted after his death. If D'Urfey had hoped 'to wear the bays', he was disappointed. Tate had been assiduously producing poems in the royal praise and in October the *Gentleman's Journal* had puffed his educational aid *The Complete Tutor*, which would have given him the right kind of weight with Mary. D'Urfey, who was an equally loyal Protestant propagandist, was still perceived as rather a gadfly. The same issue which announced Shadwell's death contained the notice of one of Purcell's most flamboyantly confident odes, *Hail, bright Cecilia*; the words are by Tate's friend, collaborator and fellow Irishman, Nicholas Brady.

Motteux's account is ecstatic, not just about the setting and the 'universal applause' that had followed its two performances, but about Purcell's own singing of the second stanza for countertenor solo, ''Tis nature's voice', with 'incredible graces'. Brady was an adequate occasional poet and his versions of the Psalms were no worse than Tate's.

He was also deeply immersed in musical and, particularly, sacred life, as well as the St Cecilia's Day celebrations. Motteux had been enjoined not to name him, but contrived to let the name slip out in a later number of the journal.

From the opening symphony with trumpets and its unequivocal jubilant statement, Purcell laid claim to dominance both for himself and for his beloved art. As once the odes fed the dramatic work, so now the theatre fed back into this most dramatic of odes, which uses the fullest forces available to him: chorus, orchestra with trumpets, oboes, organ, harpsichord and lute, and a full complement of soloists.

Strictly speaking, ''Tis nature's voice' is the third stanza, a bravura piece requiring not only complete control of the voice, but great expressiveness. The words in praise of music, I believe, are Purcell's credo:

> *We hear and straight we grieve or hate, rejoice or love*
> *In unseen chains it does the Fancy bind;*
> *At once it charms the sense and captivates the mind.*

To hear it sung by its composer must certainly have made it seem so. The stanza is effectively a love song to music, and it has to be assumed that Purcell endorsed its views of the fundamental and natural position of music in the universe and in human life, since otherwise he could have altered them. He had no qualms about altering Dryden, as Dryden himself says. Here there was no dramatic framework or persona into which the text had to fit. He didn't have to set and perform what he didn't believe, and it's therefore fair to say that this was how he perceived his art.

Brady's image of music binding up the 'scattered atoms . . . the jarring seeds of matter' gives Purcell an opportunity for some forceful word-painting for chorus and orchestra before a soprano celebrates the music of the spheres to oboes and bassoon. Seventeenth-century cosmology and science having been given their place, religion enters in a celebration of St Cecilia's own instrument, the organ, embodied in the instrument Purcell would have set up for the occasion in Stationers' Hall. This leads to the bass aria 'Wondrous machine', which is slightly dotty in its oompah sprightliness. The lute yields to the organ, and then the 'airy violin', used to sing of love and war. The amorous flute and guitar try their luck in a sensual duet of 'wanton love'; the inevitable triumph of 'seraphic flames and heav'nly love' closes the delightful meandering air, whose recorders are finally overtaken by the drums and trumpets of war, with the tenor echoing and answering the trumpet. The vocal sections lead into each other without the ritornellos of the earlier odes, which were derived from the anthems written under the influence of Charles II.

A complex canon blends all the previous instruments in a 'conflict' that resolves itself into the great chords of the final chorus of celebration, bringing the ode back to its opening, 'Hail, bright Cecilia', in a perfect musical sphere, before the ecstatic meditation on 'With rapture of delight' allows the movement to float free. Then at last the chorus and trumpets bring it to a triumphant end. The whole ode is three quarters of an hour of variety, richness and continual invention that foreshadows Handel's oratorios. No wonder that, according to Samuel Johnson's friend Richard Savage, when someone suggested that a movement in *Jephtha* reminded him of 'some of old Purcell's music', Handel is said to have replied, 'O Gott the teffel, if Purcell had lived he would have composed better music than this.' The St Cecilia's Day celebration now began with a service and sermon at St Bride's in Fleet Street, and adjourned to Stationers' Hall for the concert followed by the feast. Unlike some feasts, all was conducted with great decorum.

Three weeks later many of those who'd been present to hear this banquet of music were shocked by the murder of a leading actor and fine countertenor, Purcell's friend Will Mountfort. Among the officers returned from Flanders (as well as Edward Purcell) were the fifteen-year-old Charles, Lord Mohun, and his friend Captain Richard Hill. Hill had become besotted with Anne Bracegirdle as, Colley Cibber claimed, many did, 'it being a fashion among the gay or young to have a taste or *tendre* for her'. When she repulsed him, however, Hill went so far as to abduct her and tried, with a party of soldiers, to force her into his coach. This was foiled by her mother and Gwyn Page, whose house she had been visiting, at which point the two young men wandered the streets with drawn swords and followed her to her home. When Will Mountfort, whom Hill believed was responsible for Anne Bracegirdle's refusal of him, appeared, Hill, probably drunk, took offence, struck Mountfort, ran him through and fled. Mohun was arrested and eventually tried for murder; though convicted by the judges, he was acquitted by his peers in the House of Lords, Evelyn thought, 'in commiseration of his youth . . . though [he was] exceedingly dissolute'.

Mountfort, a great favourite with Queen Mary, was buried on 13 December, at night, as the custom was, at St Clement Danes. Purcell played the organ and the Chapel Royal choristers sang an anthem. Luttrell says that a thousand people were present and many of the nobility sent their escutcheoned coaches. Captain Hill's mother went to the King to intercede for her son, who had fled, but was told that it was 'a barbarous act and that he would leave it to the law'. Mohun's acquittal in February must have angered the cultural and theatrical world in spite of the funeral tribute to Mountfort, who had been very popular and a talented performer of many Purcell songs written with him in mind. Cibber took over some of his roles, but admitted that he was unable to perform the musical part as well.

A week after the funeral the comedian Anthony Leigh, who had played Mercury in Dryden's *Amphitryon*, also died. Nokes, another comedian, had died earlier in the year. As far as music was concerned, an even greater loss was Charlotte Butler, though the circumstances were financial rather than tragic. Cibber's version of events was that in spite of her fine performances, Charlotte Butler (whose first name, according to him, had been given her by Charles II) was only paid forty shillings a week. At this time Joseph Ashbury, a Dublin impresario and the master of the revels, was trying to rebuild his company after the civil war, and make Dublin a theatrical centre second only to London. A letter to the

Lord Lieutenant in Dublin from Betterton and Alexander Davenant of 22 March 1693 complains that Ashbury has enticed away two or three of their best performers, contrary to law, among them Charlotte Butler. Butler's surname suggests that she may have been Irish, the illegitimate daughter of one of James Butler, of the Duke of Ormonde's family, which would account for the royal favour she was shown.[5] The departure of someone who combined both singing and acting, as Mountfort had, intensified the move towards a separation of the roles.

Motteux predicted gloomily that the theatre 'was like to be without new plays' because of the deaths of Mountfort and Leigh, though one by Southerne was promised. The December issue of the *Gentleman's Journal* closed the year with a new song by Purcell, 'Corinna is divinely fair', to words by that typical late seventeenth-century figure, 'a person of quality', and songs by Blow and a German composer from Hamburg, Johann Franck; who, along with the Moravian musician Godfrey Finger, was beginning to make his mark. At the end of 1692 no new opera was in preparation, but Purcell's reputation was at its height. In so far as any artist can ever be satisfied, he must have felt that with this year's work he had attained even his own high standards.

· 13 ·

Tell Me, Some Pitying Angel

SOMETIME TOWARDS THE end of 1692 and the beginning of 1693 Aphra Behn's *Abdelazer* was revived with new act tunes by Purcell. It's only a pity that he didn't set her best song, 'Love in fantastic triumph sat'.[1] He also contributed several songs to other revivals, some of which are printed in the anthologies, such as *Comes Amoris*, *Joyful Cuckoldom*, *Thesaurus Musicus* and *Deliciae Musicae*, which had sprung up to fill the gap left by Henry Playford's and his father's anthologies, and which are often the only record, apart from Frances's posthumous collection *Orpheus Britannicus* and the *Gentleman's Journal*, of Purcell's theatrical contributions.

In January John Dyve, the father of one of Purcell's pupils and clerk to the Council, died. His place was given to William Bridgeman, Purcell's old friend and former St Cecilia steward. In February his eighteen-year-old daughter, Annabella (who, according to Luttrell, was maid of honour to Princess Anne), married, as if on the rebound from her father's death, a much older man, Sir Robert Howard; she was his fourth wife. Sir Robert was Dryden's brother-in-law and sixth son of the Earl of Berkshire. He had grown rich as the auditor of the Exchequer, and this had enabled him to buy and rebuild Ashtead Manor. Satirised by Shadwell as Sir Positive At-All, he was often despised for what were seen as his literary pretensions; when his plays were reprinted in 1692, he made it clear that he had allowed this new edition only at the insistence of the printer-publisher, Henry

Herringman. In his preface he repeated the arguments against the use of rhyme in plays which had caused him to fall out with Dryden in the seventies, after having collaborated with him in the hugely successful *Indian Queen*. Annabella Howard is 'the Honourable Lady Howard' of Frances Purcell's 1698 dedication of *Orpheus Britannicus*. As well as putting up Purcell's memorial, she had become the family's supporter.[2]

Annabella was Purcell's pupil, as the dedication makes clear: 'that dear person whom you have sometimes been pleased to honour with the title of your master' and some of his songs had 'been designed for your ladyship's entertainment'. Purcell had set some songs by Sir Robert Howard. One of them, 'Love, thou canst hear though thou art blind', is attributed to Sir Robert in *Orpheus Britannicus* and by the time of Frances Purcell's dedication there was also the music to *The Indian Queen*. Whether these two Purcell patrons were brought together by him no one has recorded. Sir Robert, said by Luttrell to be seventy, seems to have been very happy with his new young wife and he speaks of her with affection in the will he made in 1697 just before his death (and Frances's dedication, in which he left her all his personal wealth.

The household at Ashtead included Sir Robert's son by a previous marriage, Thomas, who was in his forties, his wife, Diana, and their two children, Diana and Thomas. Since a John Dyve witnessed Sir Robert's will, it looks as if Annabella's brother was living there too. The younger Diana, who was about seven in late 1693, became Purcell's pupil: the household accounts record payments for tuning 'Misses spinet' and fees of two pounds, three shillings and sixpence a month to 'Mr Purcell' for February and March 1694, and again in February and April the following year.

Another of Purcell's pupils appears in one of Frances Purcell's dedications: Rhoda Cavendish, née Cartwright, who must have come to him through Nathaniel Crewe, bishop of Durham. Crewe's niece Armine had married Rhoda's brother Thomas Cartwright of the manor of Aynho, a few miles from the Crewe family seat at Stene in the south-western part of Northamptonshire. The household accounts of the

Cartwright family indicate that Rhoda was taught by Purcell from at least November 1691, when the accounts begin, until August 1693. At the same time Purcell had as a pupil the Eton scholar John Weldon. Eton allowed five pounds for two quarters' teaching. Comparison with the twenty pounds paid by another pupil, young Hodge, for a similar period shows that Weldon didn't board with Purcell, but simply went to him for lessons.

Rhoda Cartwright, who paid two pounds a month to 'Mr Henry Purcell the spinet master',[3] must have been living in London or nearby for her to have five months of weekly or fortnightly lessons during the spring and summer of 1693, when Purcell was also teaching Weldon and had no house of his own. I believe that the family was probably still lodging with the Priests while Purcell worked on the alterations to *The Fairy Queen* at the end of 1692 and the beginning of 1693. Queen Mary saw the new version in February with the maids of honour.

The Cartwright family had a house at Barn Elms, where Rhoda might have been staying; or she may have been a pupil at the Priests' school, but I've found nothing in the accounts to substantiate this. The journey from Chelsea to Barn Elms is very short and could be made by river, although probably not in March in any comfort. Weldon too could easily have got to Chelsea from Eton, making the Purcells' continued residence there even more likely. Chelsea, of course, was very convenient for Kensington, and the Queen. By the time of Frances's dedication of Purcell's *Ten Sonatas* in 1697, which praises Rhoda's musical skills, Rhoda had married, rather against her mother's wishes, Henry, Lord Cavendish, son of the Duke of Newcastle.

Purcell's known pupils fall roughly into two categories: boys who would become professional musicians, such as Weldon, Jeremiah Clarke, Peter Hingestone (John Hingestone's organist nephew) and 'Mr Hodg' (who, as mentioned earlier, had caused Purcell so much trouble and may be Robert Hodge, organist of Wells and St Patrick's, Dublin, and later Christ Church), and girls from good or rich families, for example Annabella Dyve, Diana Howard and Rhoda Cartwright. The exception is Catherine Shore, who was a family friend and daughter of a fellow musician and who, for a time at least, also became a professional performer as Catherine Cibber.

Purcell's boy pupils were proud of their master, but the girls clearly adored him. It was for them that the various harpsichord and spinet pieces were composed or adapted. They were music's handmaids. His writing for them shows great patience, borne out by his teaching of Sir Robert Howard's seven-year-old granddaughter, Diana. His own daughter Frances was the same age. To teach such young children requires gentleness. The writer Robert Gould in his elegy testifies to Purcell's great warmth of personality and gift for friendship, the 'conquering sweetness' of his expression, 'in life so much ador'd'.

It would be too easy to see the Annabellas, Dianas and Rhodas as simply spoilt little girls dabbling in music. Yet there's a very real sense in which they, just as much as the boys who were to become professional musicians, were equipping themselves for their jobs and, indeed, gaining employment by their self-marketing skills. Without marriage, they remained at home as powerless dependants. As marriageable commodities they enriched and strengthened the family network; as wives they entered into their own business as managers of families, houses and spheres of social influence, without which their husbands couldn't function in politics or build their own empires. Both Pepys and Evelyn make clear the importance of music in this context and the very high level of skill expected and often attained by young girls. Evelyn's daughter performed before the King and was taught and praised by such masters of music as Matteis.

Once they were married, the girls had to provide a cultural ambience not only for their children but also for entertaining, the serious background against which other business was conducted. They were, in effect, the public relations departments of the family concern; they could even gain for themselves a place at court or, if widowed, patronage and support. Arabella Hunt is an interesting example. Her marriage was unhappy, but by leading a life in which even the scandalmonger could find nothing to fasten on and exercising her talents, she managed to support herself. According to Hawkins, she spent the summers virtuously in the house of a Mr Routh at Epsom, where she was on hand to entertain Mary at Hampton Court, Kensington or at one of the grand houses nearby, such as Sir Robert Howard's Ashtead.[4]

Purcell's long absence from a settled home in Westminster must raise questions about the family's health. Ashtead was reputed to be very healthy, and especially beneficial in the treatment of consumption. It was also close to the waters of Epsom Spa, and the racecourse, which attracted royalty and everyone else. Although there's no record of Purcell's staying at Ashtead and although by the time of his lessons with Diana Howard the following year (which could equally well have taken place in the Howards' Westminster residence) the Purcells had taken a new house in Marsham Street, Frances continued to be involved with the family in the early 1700s, as a payment to her maid in the accounts shows, and it's possible that they were there at the time of Sir Robert's marriage to Annabella. Unfortunately, the accounts which survive aren't those of Sir Robert or Annabella but of his son Thomas and his wife, Diana.

Edward Purcell had returned with his commander, Henry Trelawney, and his commander-in-chief, the Duke of Ormonde. Ormonde and Charles, Duke of Somerset, were among those who dined privately with William in January 1693 while the Denmarks were being ostracised and forced to go to St James's, Piccadilly, for their religious observance. At least they could hear a good organ there, built by Renatus Harris for James's Catholic chapel and donated to the church by Mary. On Twelfth Night there was the usual heavy gaming and a great ball at Kensington. The New Year's greeting, with an ode by Blow and Tate, had also taken place this year at Kensington.

The January *Gentleman's Journal* included two songs by Purcell from Southerne's *The Maid's Last Prayer*, which Motteux praised for its wit and purity of diction. One of the songs was by Congreve: 'Tell me no more I am deceived'. The other, 'Though you make no return to my passion', was by Southerne, while 'No, no, resistance is but vain' is attributed to Anthony Henley. Motteux said the play had been acted four times already. The duet 'No, no, resistance is but vain' is a little cantata in itself. There are problems with dating the issues of the *Gentleman's Journal* of this time since it was running several weeks late, and when Motteux says 'this' week, it's hard to know whether he means the originally intended week or a week in the month of actual publication. In the February edition he prints a drinking catch by Blow and a song by Purcell that doesn't seem to belong to any play, 'No watch, dear Celia, just is found'.

William was now anxious to leave for Flanders in order not to be caught unprepared by the French as he had been the year before. The regiments, among them Edward Purcell's, were recruiting in March, but when he set out, William was forced back by contrary winds. He finally sailed on 4 April and Mary took up residence in Whitehall. She was now the effective ruler of the country for half of every year. Edward Purcell and Henry Trelawney were given passes, along with their servants, to follow William from Harwich ten days later. This annual departure of his brother, the head of the family, for the uncertainties of battle must have been disturbing to Purcell, to whom Edward was close. It was a lonely business for Mary too. Whatever William's faults in other people's eyes, she loved and missed him and longed for his return, as she wrote in her letters to him. She took up her annual burden with a service in the chapel 'with full regalia' and a fortnight later was distributing the Maundy money in the Banqueting Hall, where the crowd was so great that two people were crushed to death.

The ode for her birthday this year, *Celebrate this festival*, was much larger and more elaborate. Evidence for how precise in their meaning contemporary poets could be comes in Evelyn's description of the 'extraordinary wet' spring in his entry of just three days before the royal birthday. Nahum Tate brings this into the ode:

April, who till now has mourned,
Claps for joy his sable wing
To see within his orb return'd
The choicest blessings he could bring:
Maria's birthday, and the Spring.

Motteux printed the text in full and at the end of the April issue included a version of the last stanza as a solo song. Purcell reused the overture from the St Cecilia ode of the previous year, which allowed him to begin with trumpets. As usual, he introduces new ideas, especially in the vocal solos and his writing for the soprano. This makes me wonder whether it was on this occasion that he came to the defence of the boy soprano Jemmy Bowen (often just known as 'the boy' in his earliest appearances). Antony Aston in his supplement to Cibber's *Apology* has a story that when the other musicians were trying to tell Bowen how to ornament his part one day, Purcell cut in with, 'Oh, let him alone. He will grace it more naturally than you or I can teach him.' This little episode seems to me to fit in well with the performance of a royal ode rather than a piece for the theatre. It's generally held that Bowen was the chief soprano for *Celebrate this festival*. He was perhaps as young as six at his first known appearance a year before in *The Libertine*, when he sang 'To arms, heroic Prince'.[5] Bowen had no Chapel training and the royal musicians probably felt they could give him some good advice. (He must have been a boy prodigy, such as Aled Jones or Ernest Lough in this century.) Purcell usually wrote out his ornamentation in full, so he may simply have been trying to prevent others from interfering with what he had already prescribed as enough.

The opening of the birthday ode of 1693 sounds like music for a procession. There follows a soprano and trumpet duet, ''Tis sacred, bid the trumpet cease', and an extensively graced soprano solo. The alto then sings above a mysterious cello bass in 'Crown the altar'. Bearing in mind Purcell's performance in the last St Cecilia ode, it's tempting to think that he might have sung this alto solo too. In a rather joky bouncing tune, the bass introduces the first stanza about the late spring:

Expected Spring at last is come
. . . .
and pleads for her delay:
She's waited for Maria's day.

The ode is characterised by an inventive use of repetition on 'Maria's birthday' in the next stanza and the penultimate one, but also by increased use of melisma. The trumpet writing is exceptionally fluid as it duets with both bass and soprano. The high tenor solo, 'Return fond muse', is set against organ and recorders until it is ended by all the soloists' lovely echoing repetitions of 'Maria's name'. The final soprano solo, 'Kindly treat Maria's day', leads into a tender closing chorus. The last notes create an impression of a final bow.

The *Gentleman's Journal* gives the 30th, the Queen's actual birthday, as the date of performance, but Luttrell says that since this was a Sunday, the formal business of congratulation took place the next day, followed by a great ball at court. The whole tone of the ode is gentle and intimate, suggesting again a private performance for Mary. Even the trumpets are lyrical rather than martial as the words reject 'the thoughts of war'.

The same issue of the journal mentions the production of Tom D'Urfey's new play *The Richmond Heiress*, which Dryden saw and reported on in a letter to his friend William Walsh. He found it 'woeful stuff', except for the mad duet 'where the scene was in bedlam', which was 'wonderfully diverting'. Purcell's music for this was performed by Anne Bracegirdle and Thomas Doggett. Dryden said that 'the singing was wonderfully good, and the two whom I nam'd sung better than Redding and Mrs Ayliffe whose trade it was'.

The play ran for only four nights and Dryden thought it had been 'kicked off forever', but D'Urfey revised it and brought it back later, when it was more successful. A claque against it had been organised by the dukes of Richmond and St Albans, presumably because of its anti-war stance, as epitomised in the chorus to 'Behold the man':

> *Then mad, very mad let us be,*
> *For Europe does now with our frenzy agree,*
> *And all things in nature are mad, mad, mad,*
> *And all things in nature are mad too as we.*

Purcell's contribution to D'Urfey's new play so soon after the drunken poet addition to *The Fairy Queen* shows that the two of them hadn't seriously fallen out over the satire.

Dryden too mentions the very bad spring in his letter to Walsh. He was writing what was to be his last play, *Love Triumphant*, to which Purcell contributed a song. Dryden also discusses the political situation and the failure of William's confederate army to achieve any spectacular success. Dryden, still hoping for the restoration of James, was, of course, a very partial reporter.

Mary's birthday ball was followed by a concert on board Matthias Shore's pleasure boat, moored at Whitehall, recalling John Abell's earlier floating concert for her father. No account of what was played has survived, but both Luttrell and Motteux record it as a spectacular event which 'pleased the most judicious lovers of that art'. Motteux published no new song by Purcell in May, and printed Johann Franck's contribution to what seems to have been a rather dreary version of Molière's *Les Femmes savantes* by Thomas Wright, the machinist at the theatre, instead of Purcell's 'Love, thou art best', perhaps because this was a duet for sopranos.

The June issue publicised the second volume of *Harmonia Sacra* by printing the satirist Tom Brown's commendatory verses on 'His unknown friend Mr Henry Purcell'. Motteux himself wrote: 'I need not say anything more to recommend it to you than that you will find in it many of Mr Henry Purcell's admirable composures . . . which charm all men and are universally extolled and even those who know him no otherwise than by his notes are fond of expressing the sense of his merit.'

Brown's superscription is rather strange. Unless he means that Purcell is his friend by virtue of his work, it suggests that the true modern equivalent should be 'unknown relative.' Brown came from Stifnel in Shropshire, where he was surrounded by Purcells, with whom his family could have been connected. It sounds as though he believed he and Purcell were related. Brown was known for excessive tippling among cronies at The Hole in the Wall in Baldwin Gardens, Holborn. Purcell almost certainly became known to Brown after this and the verses were prefixed to the book, which came out in July. There were therefore two years in which they could have become friends before Purcell's death. Robert Gould, a satirist himself, speaks of Purcell's 'flashing wit', which suggests that he would have been able to keep up with Brown on his own terms.

Hawkins implies that Purcell became one of Brown's drinking companions and connects him too with Owen Swan's tavern in Bartholomew Lane, known as Cobweb Hall, and a drinking house in Wych Street that came to have Purcell's head, in a brown full-bottomed wig and green nightshirt, as its sign. Hawkins takes the opportunity to condemn the words of many of Purcell's catches as 'wretched ribaldry'. Three paragraphs on he is condemning Frances Purcell for locking her husband out after just such an evening's drinking.

Brown's praise is quite specifically for Purcell as a composer of settings for sacred texts. This is interesting because it comes at a period when it's usually thought that Purcell had almost ceased such composition in favour of the theatre. Charles Burney's father, who was a young man in the last years of Purcell's life and remembered him perfectly, but unfortunately wrote nothing down, told his son how packed the church was whenever a new anthem by Purcell was to be performed, yet the Gostling manuscript has only two pieces by Purcell for this period. However, it also has only two by Blow, who was very much known as a sacred composer. It may be that Gostling's removal to St Paul's has distorted the record in that these are the only works he was called on to perform for this period, and copies of others may have been lost in the great fire that burned down Whitehall in 1698.

The poem's praise extends to a comparison with the Italians Corelli and Bassani and ends with a swipe at D'Urfey:

> *Sweetness combin'd with majesty, prepares*
> *To raise devotion with inspiring airs*
> . . . .
> *And surely none but you with equal ease*
> *Could add to David, and make D'Urfey please.*

This second volume of *Harmonia Sacra* has five pieces by Purcell, only one by Blow, one each by Daniel Purcell, Wanley's friend Berenclow and Robert King, and three by the young Jeremiah Clarke, who had only just left the Chapel. The texts of Purcell's contributions are one by William Fuller, 'Lord, what is man?', Cowley's *Resurrection*, two by Tate and *Saul and the Witch of Endor* ('In guilty night'), which had previously been set by Nicholas Lanier. This last and Tate's *The Blessed Virgin's Expostulation* ('Tell me, some pitying angel') are the most spectacular and dramatic, though they are all bravura pieces. Between them, Tate and Purcell have produced in *The Blessed Virgin's Expostulation* an equivalent in sound to Bernini's *St Theresa*, a flight of high camp baroque, lush and ornate. The picture of Mary being visited in her 'cell' is strongly reminiscent of the statue.

Both this and 'Lord, what is man?' have the same structure: an elaborate recitative ending with an *arioso* section. In the setting of Fuller's text, just when everything seems to have been said there's a burst of alleluias that brings the fate of man to a triumphant, orgasmic climax, while *The Blessed Virgin's Expostulation* declines into unanswered sorrow. Purcell's word-painting in his contributions to this second volume, published at a time of national doubt and disgust, is unsurpassed. The volume ends fittingly with Tate's and Purcell's meditation, by two terrifying basses, on the last things as the dead are summoned to judgement: 'Awake and with attention hear'.

The June *Gentleman's Journal* also contained a song by Purcell, 'We now, my Thyrsis', with words by Motteux, which seems to have been intended for concert or private performance, and an interesting song by 'Signior Baptist', with English words, 'Never complain that my flame I discover'. This looks like something by Giovanni Battista Draghi, but it's hard to tell whether it is an old tune of his or a new one. He was still in the country and hadn't returned to Portugal with the Queen Dowager, Catherine, the year before or when most of her servants were paid off in August.

William had at last made disastrous contact with the French. Britain had already lost most of the Turkish fleet of merchant ships through a misunderstanding of the position and strength of the French fleet under Admiral Tourville, which had left Sir George Rooke to fight a superior force alone. Now William was in the same situation on land. On 22 July news came that the town of Huy had fallen to the French and that 'coll. Trelawney's regiment of English' were 'all made prisoners of war and stript of their clothes'.[6]

The battle of Landen followed, described by Sir Winston Churchill in his life of Marlborough as the bloodiest before Malplaquet; the confederates lost an estimated twenty thousand men and the French half that number. William fought at the head of his troops with great personal courage and was wounded. His commander, Count Solms, who had presided over the butchery of the British at Steenkerke the year before, was killed and Ormonde was wounded and taken prisoner. He had tried to resign earlier in the year, but William had insisted that he couldn't do without him. Ormonde couldn't be left behind at home to intrigue with Anne and Churchill. On the French side, James's natural son, the Duke of Berwick, was captured. From the British point of view, it could have been worse. William managed to gather his forces and fresh recruits, and the French under the Duke of Luxembourg failed to follow up their advantage. There were many families at home waiting anxiously for news. When the Queen heard that William was safe and recovering and that something had been retrieved from the defeat, she ordered a national thanksgiving, to which both Blow and Purcell contributed, Blow with the anthem *Thy righteousness, O God* (dated August in the Gostling manuscript) and Purcell with *O give thanks*. Luttrell recorded on 10 August that next week would be a general thanksgiving for the 'preservation of his majesty in the late fight'.

Perhaps it was this occasion and the need for special commissions that caused Mary to lament the lack of church music and to agree with Dr Tillotson that 'ours fell short of what it had been in the preceding reign'. Tillotson mentioned this conversation to Gostling on a journey to Hampton Court, where Gostling was to do his chapel duty. According to his son, William, in Hawkins's version, Gostling replied 'that Blow and Purcell were as capable of composing at least as good anthems as most of those which had been so much admired, and a little encouragement would make that appear'. Hearing this later from Tillotson, Mary approved posts for two composers and proposed a salary of forty pounds a year each, but the war continued to swallow up all available money and both she and Purcell died before the idea was implemented. Blow, however, was made composer in 1699 and the second place, which went to Purcell's pupil John Weldon, was added in 1715.

Anxieties about Edward – whether he was alive, wounded or could be exchanged without payment of a ransom – were compounded by their brother Charles's shipping as second purser on board the *Tyger* for service in the Caribbean on 3 August. She was a large ship with a complement of two hundred. It was a dangerous voyage not only because of the French fleet and the increased number of privateers of all nations who were operating under licence of war, but also because of the high incidence of sickness and death in those waters. Their cousin Charles had already died off the coast of Guinea, a similarly sickly area.

Neither Luttrell nor the state papers follow up the story of what had happened to Edward's regiment. Great soldiers such as Berwick and Ormonde, who were swapped for each other, tended to be exchanged quickly, but others could be imprisoned for many months. Whether the family knew it or not, Edward Purcell was safe; on 1 August he was given a new lieutenant, so if he had been among those captured, he had been freed.[7]

Thinking that the campaign was over for the year, William decided to return to England, but the French, having recovered from their costly victory at Landen, now renewed their activities. Parliament was prorogued until October, a sign that William wouldn't be coming back yet, and Mary quelled a near mutiny among the seamen's wives, who, as a result of a rumour that their husbands' arrears of pay were postponed, 'came in clamorous manner to Whitehall'.

While the court waited for William's next move, Motteux and Purcell contributed a new song, 'I envy not a monarch's fate', to the September issue of the *Gentleman's Journal*. Motteux made a revolutionary decision to have the next number devoted to and largely written by women; this shows their great importance in cultural and social life, which had been enhanced, as is so often the case, by the long years of war. Towards the end of September Mary moved back to Kensington to prepare it for William's return, but contrary winds kept him in Holland until 29 October. As usual, Mary set out to meet him in Essex and on Tuesday morning the formal levee 'to congratulate his majesties return' took place at Kensington. Presumably Edward Purcell came home too. He would have been relieved to hear that his younger brother Joseph had secured a surgeon's place in a safe berth on the royal yacht *Mary*, William's customary transport to Holland, at the beginning of October.[8] From her, he moved in January to the *Fubbs* and then in March to the *Katherine*, all easy short commissions. He must already have been under the patronage of Sir George Rooke, who recommended him strongly for a post when he left the *Kent* in 1697.

Mary was at Guildhall on 29 October while William was crossing from Holland. Whatever the complaints of the Jacobite gentry, the City had continued to support William and provide him with money to carry on the war, and Mary was careful to involve and support the 'rulers of London'. The London merchants realised that it was essential to their trade that France should be contained, particularly in the struggle over who should control the world's new and desirable consumer goods on which civilisation was to be increasingly dependent and which would give it its cultural veneer: the spices, silks, china, teas, coffee, wood and metalwork of these exploding markets. Many of the richest merchants were Protestant refugees from France or Flanders, as their names show: Coutts, Houblon, Lethulier, Weyman, Vanbrugh and Pieters itself.

During late October Purcell was involved, unusually for him, in a theatrical flop: Congreve's new play, *The Double Dealer*. Dryden, who sent a copy to William Walsh, said it had 'been much censured by the greater part of the town and is defended only by the best judges who, you know, are commonly the fewest . . . the women think he has exposed their bitchery too much and the gentlemen are offended with him; for the discovery of their follies and the way of their intrigues, under the notion of friendship for their ladyes husbands'. It had, even so, been acted eight times and the music must have helped: Purcell provided a full set of overture and act tunes and the delightful seduction song 'Cynthia frowns'. That Mary commanded a performance of it should have helped it too. The instrumental music, which included minuets and hornpipes, was suitable for both serious and grotesque dancing.

For the annual ball at Kensington to celebrate William's birthday six extra hautboys were engaged. The musicians rehearsed twice, which again suggests there was a balletic formal element before the general dancing. (An entry in the *Post Boy* of May 1696, describing a ball at Kensington at which William was present with the French ambassador, tells how a French dancer, currently performing at the Playhouse, was sent for 'and perform'd his part very dextrously'). The King's birthday ode, *Sound a call, the tritons sing*, was by Tate and Staggins. The round of autumn events continued with the St Cecilia's Day Feast. This year the ode was by Theo Parsons and Godfrey Finger. Ralph Battell, sub-dean of the Chapel, preached the preceding sermon at St Bride's on 'The Lawfulness and Expediency of Church Music Asserted', and the stewards were quickly ordered to print it.

These sermons had now become a permanent feature of 'the anniversary meeting of Gentlemen, Lovers of Musick'. Several of them have survived, and all exhibit the same defensiveness in the face of Puritan criticism; they appeal to both the Old Testament and the New as well as to later authorities, including, in Ralph Battell's case, Ambrose of Milan's *Te Deum* (with instruments) and bishops Baxter and Hooker from the more recent radical Anglican wing. It was the instrumental music so beloved of Charles II which was looked on with suspicion by the new puritanism, a view which seems to have been favoured by Mary. In more and more anthems the emphasis was on virtuoso vocal music harking back to Tallis and Byrd, accompanied simply by the organ. If King David had only his harp, why should anyone else need more than a ground bass of some sort?

Whether they were in their new home in Marsham Street before Frances gave birth to their daughter at the beginning of December isn't clear. I suspect that she may have had the baby under the eye of her mother, Amy Pieters, who was still occupying the house in Bowling Alley East, since the baby was christened Mary-Peters Purcell in Westminster Abbey on 10 December. A Mary Peters, aged about twenty-two, had been buried 'by her mother' in the Abbey in 1688,[9] and the memorial to her shows the Peters arms as used by Frances's brother, John Baptist, and for herself. It looks very much as if their new child was named in remembrance of Frances's other sister, who is mentioned in the original Dowgate poll. Unlike little Frances, she wasn't baptised in St Margaret's as well. If Frances was staying with her mother, and Purcell was away, they must nevertheless have moved very soon after, for they paid highway rates on Marsham Street from Christmas that year. Frances's sister Amy Howlett took over the remainder of the lease of Bowling Alley East, which suggests that their mother moved to the new house with the Purcells to help look after Frances and the new baby.

Meanwhile D'Urfey had rejigged *The Richmond Heiress*, which was having a new run, and he was promising a play based on Cervantes' novel *Don Quixote*. A new play by Dryden, which he'd decided was to be his farewell to the theatre, was also expected. The *Gentleman's Journal* for December included two new songs for a revival of *Dioclesian*: the sensual 'When first I saw the bright Aurelia's eyes' and 'Since from my dear'. The theatre had recovered from the tragedies of the previous year and before Christmas Purcell was also at work on two new odes.

· 14 ·

Come, Ye Sons of Art, Away

AT THE END of December Prince Lewis of Baden arrived at Gravesend for a state visit. He was one of the confederates' most able commanders and a strong supporter of William, and the English court's intention was to make much of him. He should have been at Whitehall in time for the New Year's Day celebrations, but was too ill to travel until 2 January, when he came up river in the royal barge. He was given Mary of Modena's old apartments, a guard of twelve and forty dishes of food a day. That night he went to Kensington. An ode, *Light of the world*, had been prepared for what looks like New Year's Day, but it isn't clear whether it was performed then. The words were by the royal secretary and favourite Matthew Prior, written at the Hague before his return with William (over two months previously). The first published version of it, which appeared on 19 January, says 'intended to be sung'; the second, in 1709, says 'sung' before Their Majesties. Both say 'set by Dr Henry Purcell'.[1] It sounds as if the ode was in the press before it was performed, which may account for the discrepancy.

There's no evidence that Purcell was ever given a doctorate, yet Edward Chamberlain's *Angliae Notitiae* makes this claim in the eighteenth edition of 1694. A further mystery about this ode, apart from the fact that the music is lost, is why Purcell should have set it at all when it was Blow's prerogative to provide the New Year's ode as it was Purcell's to provide that for Mary's birthday. Blow had had a difficult year. His only son, a boy of great promise also called John, aged fifteen, had died in June. Perhaps he hadn't recovered from that loss, and there had been some question about his ability to provide a suitable composition this year. Nevertheless, Blow did set the ode, *Sound, sound the trumpet*, but at what seems very short notice, for Motteux complained in his *Gentleman's Journal* he had had 'so little time allowed me to write'. This *Hymn to the Sun*, as Prior calls it, clearly wasn't the official New Year's ode but an adjunct to it. Staggins was paid the large sum of forty-five pounds and five shillings for having the music copied for both the ball in November and the festivities in January, which suggests there were several pieces. Maybe the provision of two odes was simply the effect of William's obvious desire to fête Prince Lewis. If so, it shows that Purcell was now acknowledged as the leading composer of his day, and this is borne out by his intense involvement in the activities during the intended fortnight of the Prince's visit. In the end it stretched to six weeks as he was entertained by the nobility as well as the court, and then further delayed from returning home by an attack of gout.

On 11 January Prince Lewis saw a revival of *Dioclesian*, with additional songs, and five days later he was present at a concert of Purcell's instrumental and vocal music, which included his last St Cecilia ode, *Hail, bright Cecilia*, and a song by Motteux and Purcell, 'Sawney is a bonny lad'. Less intellectually demanding diversions were provided by a bull-and-bear baiting in St James's Park, a treat at the Sun Tavern by the Hamburgh company, a city tour in a hackney coach and a visit with the King to Windsor, where he was invested with the garter. When the King returned to Kensington, Prince Lewis stayed on with the Duke of Ormonde, who took him to Oxford University, 'of which he is Chancellor'.[2]

Ormonde was also chancellor of Dublin University, which on 9 January celebrated the secular centenary of its refounding by Queen Elizabeth. According to James I, Elizabeth's main intention, ironically, had been to promote learning in the Irish language. Tate was a graduate of Trinity and also, of course, poet laureate – the first Trinity had had, so it's not surprising that he should have been asked to provide a celebratory ode, *Great parent, hail*, which Purcell set to music. The occasion was of great political significance. Trinity was a Protestant foundation. James II had used it as a barracks during his occupation of the city, forcing most of the scholars and staff to flee. The library had been preserved by the joint efforts of two Roman Catholic priests, Dr Moore and Father MacCarthy. The centenary celebrations marked the full restoration of the college to its proper function as a place of learning. They were also an obvious attempt by the college authorities to raise the profile of the university and gain the necessary patronage and, incidentally, to help in the propaganda task of re-establishing the Protestant Anglo-Irish ascendance. As chancellor, Ormonde's role in all this was crucial. The operation was successful as far as Trinity was concerned, in that her sons subsequently filled the Irish Episcopal Bench, and ten of them became bishops. Furthermore, William reduced all the crown and quit rents due on the college lands to ten pounds for three years from 1693.[3]

On 30 December Trinity's bursar had been instructed to lay out such money as was necessary for the celebration. If this was the first Tate and Purcell knew of their commission, which had to be composed and transmitted by sea and land, it gave them very little time. I therefore think that preparations must have been under way before this, and again I see Ormonde as central. Not only was he Edward Purcell's patron, but he was closely involved in the entertainment of Prince Lewis, in which Purcell's work figured so prominently. His wife was D'Urfey's patron, as is clear from the dedication of *Don Quixote*, which was in production early in the year and whose rehearsals the Duchess attended. I believe Ormonde himself may have commissioned the ode, which has a penultimate section in praise of him and his father.

At this date Trinity had a modest musical establishment. Prayers were usually said and once a year the musical forces of Christ Church and St Patrick's combined to celebrate Trinity Sunday, as it were on the college's behalf. According to tradition, an organ was finally provided by Ormonde in 1702; it had been looted from the Spanish port of Vigo in an operation for which one of his chief assistants was Edward Purcell, by then a major. However, by 1694 the college already had an organ, which suggests that Ormonde merely added to it later.

Purcell's music is carefully fitted to the forces he could expect: for the instruments, strings, an organ, recorders and a harpsichord, but no trumpets or oboes; for the voices an accomplished chorus and, among the soloists, a skilled bass and soprano. The instruments could have been augmented from the Theatre Royal, Dublin (or Smock Alley, as it was commonly called). Purcell was used to rehearse and direct his music himself from the harpsichord. In this case he had to compose something which could be sent overseas and performed out of his control and yet, apart from the necessary tailoring to the musical resources available, there's no suggestion of any lowering of standards in the writing. He expected the best from the performers and gave them his best, especially in the choruses and the bass and soprano solos.

The day of celebration began with prayers and a sermon in the cathedral, followed by an anthem said to be by Blow, *I beheld, and lo a great multitude*. After dinner at two o'clock and a performance of instrumental music, there were speeches in honour of Elizabeth, the two Charleses and previous chancellors, and then came a pastoral on the revival of the college by William and Mary. Most of these were, of course, in Latin. 'A thanksgiving ode was then sung accompanied by instrumental music.' There were more Latin speeches, verses, a debate on the greater indebtedness of the arts or the sciences to the ancients or the moderns, a poem by the son of the Bishop of Meath, Anthony Dopping, a potentially dire 'humorous speech' on the increase in university studies, the formal closure by the provost and a procession from the building which was followed by 'a skilled band of musicians'.[4]

Who would have been responsible for realising, rehearsing and performing the ode? The most likely candidate is Peter Isaac, a member of an extensive musical family,[5] who had been a child of the Chapel under Captain Cooke and therefore a contemporary of Purcell. After leaving he had stayed a pupil of Cooke and in 1673 had become vicar choral of St Patrick's; when he was deprived of this post by James in 1688, he retired to Salisbury. In 1691 he was invited by the Dean and Chapter of Christ Church to return to Ireland. (The Peter Isaaks who was given a pass for Holland in May 1693 may be another person of the same name, or it may be that he went to consult Ormonde about the centenary celebrations. Before being wounded and captured the previous summer, Ormonde may have been planning to attend.) Another possible candidate is Purcell's old pupil Robert Hodge, now working in Dublin.

The ode begins with a sprightly symphony, which leads into a trio and chorus for 'Great parent, hail', with repeated triumphant 'hails'. Purcell immediately uses his characteristic word-painting: the grave music for 'last distress' breaks cheerfully into 'joyful year'. Then the alto, in a rather low part of its register, sings a meditative *arioso* to the organ. The tenor duet 'After war's alarms' has the voices imitating the absent trumpets while the harpsichord acts as percussion. A string ritornello in its turn echoes the trumpet effects of the voices. 'Awful matron take thy seat' is a bass aria in the tradition of Purcell's 'frost' music for that voice, but without the shiver. Great sustained control is required for its long measured phrases, which invoke the 'alma mater', who is also Hibernia, and introduce praise of the college founder, Elizabeth. This continues in the tenor solo and chorus with the extraordinary repetition of 'mute, mute' that also suggests 'lute, lute'.

Poet and composer take the opportunity of seeming to honour 'succeeding princes' in the next duet, while pointing out that it's only art that can give them fame:

To save 'em from oblivion's might
Is only in the Muses' pow'r.

A jaunty chorus praising William and Mary then becomes a leisurely flow for an evocation of the Boyne and Shannon rivers. Recorders introduce the soprano to lament beside the tomb of the first Duke of Ormonde and invoke his shade before switching to a brisk martial air, like a tune on the fife, for the second Duke's 'hero's glory'. The final chorus asks the 'sons of art', scholars and participants to make it a memorable day with their contributions:

> *Those blessing to bequeath that may*
> *Long, long remain your kindness to repay.*

This rather suggests Tate knew that the 'contributions' were all to be deposited in the library. The ode lasts about twenty-five minutes and encapsulates most of the themes of the surrounding discourses. Motteux praised the ode, of which he had obviously seen a copy: 'Mr Tate who was desired to make it has given Mr Purcell an opportunity by the easiness of the words to set them to musick with his usual success.'

January also saw the not particularly successful production of Dryden's farewell play *Love Triumphant*; it contained a song by Congreve and Purcell, 'How happy's the husband'. It was Dryden's intention to devote himself to his translation of Virgil, which he could do quietly wherever he was without the stress of the theatre, and without any involvement in its often complicated affairs and factions. Southerne's *Fatal Marriage* followed in February, with two songs by Purcell: 'I sighed and owned my love' and 'The danger is over'.

Purcell began teaching Sir Robert Howard's granddaughter Diana in February. The Ashtead Manor Accounts are, in a sense, misleadingly named, since they also include accounts for the Howards' London expenses in Westminster. The children had a schoolroom in Ashtead, but it seems most likely that Purcell taught Diana at their Westminster home. There are payments for tuition from February to April, one via Matthew, the Howards' steward, who frequently travelled between Ashtead and London on various commissions. It's clear from various entries that the children were taken or sent to London on several occasions, so Purcell probably did not travel to Epsom to teach 'little mis' there at this time.[6]

Mary and William were at Kensington on the morning of her thirty-second birthday in April and he left, presumably after hearing the ode

Come, ye sons of art, away, for Whitehall and Gravesend to embark for Flanders. However, once more contrary winds forced him back and he returned to Whitehall the next evening. The ode is in praise of music as much as of Mary, and the fact that William makes only a brief appearance in words that hint that he is already 'in the field' suggests an uncertainty about his movements.

The symphony offers a particularly glorious piece of writing for the trumpet before the poignant adagio on the strings. As in the Trinity ode, Purcell again uses voices to evoke instruments, particularly hautboy and trumpet: 'the instruments of joy' in the alto duet 'Sound the trumpet'. The alto solo 'Strike the viol' which follows the repeated chorus is another lyrical piece of writing which Purcell could have 'graced' himself, full of those runs that later writers found too baroque.[7] The ritornello is a duet between recorders and strings in a graceful dance. A bass solo anticipates Handel's 'O ruddier than the cherry' in giving the dark voice a brisk melody, which is taken up by the chorus. Then the mysterious soprano solo, in duet with the hautboy, here an instrument not of joy but of meditation and prayer, invokes Mary as a high priestess on her throne in personal communion with 'the eternal'.

Another bass solo over a harpsichord ground allows Tate to make the obligatory obeisance to William and 'his righteous cause', though he is secondary to Mary, who draws 'immortal pow'r' to his support with her 'sacred charms'. The ode ends with a vigorous duet and rich choral writing for 'See nature rejoicing'. Drums and trumpets round the whole piece off triumphantly.

When William set out again, hoping to sail from Harwich, he was forced down to Gravesend. He was still unable to leave, and the royal couple retired to Canterbury to wait for a fair wind. It came at last on the 6th; William embarked at Margate and was soon out of sight, while Mary returned to take up her lonely rule at Whitehall.

Purcell's work as a teacher is encapsulated in his revision of John Playford's *Introduction to the Skill of Musick*, which he largely rewrote this year for its twelfth edition. He has made it his own to such a degree that it can safely be assumed that what he didn't rewrite he endorsed. The definition of music reveals his complete dedication to his art: 'Musick is an art of expressing perfect harmony, either by voice or instrument, which Harmony ariseth from well-taken concords and discords.' The emphasis on discords is typical of his method and his theory: 'imperfect chords are more pleasant and less cloying to the ear than many perfect chords'. He reinforces this in dealing with counterpoint, when he politely rejects Christopher Simpson's *Rule in Three Parts for Counterpoint*, in favour of flexibility, as being 'too strict and destructive of good air which ought to be preferred before such nice rules'. Whereas Simpson says that all three parts should run together, Purcell wants the alto to move gradually in thirds with the treble: 'though the other be fuller this is the smoothest and carries more air and form in it'. Not surprisingly, he praises the practice of 'the Italians in all their musick either vocal or instrumental which I presume ought to be a guide to us'.

Sonatas, he says, 'are the chiefest instrumental musick now in request where you will find double and treble fugues also reworked and augmented in their canzonas with a great deal of art mixed with good air which is the perfection of a master'. For church music he insists on 'smoothness and decorum'. When he comes to canons, Purcell, after praising the Welsh composer Elway Bevin's book published as long ago as 1631, 'to which I refer the younger practitioners', goes on to quote a 'Gloria patri' canon of four parts by Blow, 'whose character is sufficiently known by his works of which this very instance is enough to recommend him as one of the Greatest Masters in the world'. This tribute, at the height of his own achievement and fame, shows his generosity of spirit and his continuing appreciation of his old master.

'Composing upon a ground', he says, is 'a very easy thing to do and requires but little judgement', though he also speaks of the 'pretty diverting grounds of whom the Italians were the first inventors . . . which to do neatly requires considerable pains, and the best way to be acquainted with 'em is to score much and chuse the best authors'. His well-attested modesty comes out in the last lines in this section on composition; he hopes that what he has said 'may be as useful as 'tis intended, and then 'twill more than recompense the trouble of the author'. Such instruction was particularly important for those who, like his pupil John Weldon, were studying composition, but there's also good advice for the student of the voice or instrument. 'Let the sound come clear from your throat and not through the teeth by sucking in your breath for that is a great obstruction to the clear utterance of the voice . . . The young practitioner must take care to sing or play with one that is perfect in it and shun those which are not better than himself.' He also speaks of the importance of time as 'so necessary to be understood that unless the practitioner arrive to a perfection in it he will never be able to play with any delight to himself or at least to a skilful ear'. He recommends beating time to the slow motions of the pendulum of 'a large chamber clock'.

The book, being a combination of practical and theoretical elements, gives the only insight, apart from the music itself, into Purcell's own ways of working and teaching. The sheer quantity of his music to a ground shows how easy indeed he found this technique, and the elaboration that required 'more pains' to make it 'pretty' and 'diverting' is evident in the dozens of more complex pieces. Though the book is short and the section on composition even shorter, he manages to say something on every category in which he worked: recitative, church music, instrumental and vocal.

Most interesting is his use of the word 'air' to mean both melody and something more, as Roger North was to explore at some length in his *What is Ayre?* of about 1710. Thomas Morley, the originator in 1597 of the text that Purcell was rewriting, says that 'every key hath a peculiar air proper to itself' and that these 'airs' are what 'antiquity termed *modi*'. Purcell had to adapt this notion to a music no longer based on modes but, increasingly, on tonality. With his own facility and ear for melody, it was natural that for him this should be its primary meaning, as is apparent when, in writing about the composition of chaconnes, he says, 'they regard only good air in the treble and often the ground is only four notes descending'. Immediately the 'Great' chaconne reverberates in the ear as having been a 'very easy thing to do'. But 'air' also carries with it a subtext of rightness, of natural sequence and, for Roger North, an indefinable quality akin to what in people was called presence.

The *Introduction to the Skill of Musick*, simply because it is a rewrite, shows again how Purcell continued to see himself as part of the English tradition which was taking on, in both senses, the best of the Italian. He saw his own art, and music itself, in process of constant evolution and because of the beliefs of his time, the late seventeenth century, he also saw it as capable of perfection.

The *Gentleman's Journal* for April has two Purcell songs and the following number gives an extract from the Queen's birthday ode. John Crowne's new play, *The Married Beau*, had been a great success and he remained a favourite with Mary. Purcell set 'See where repenting Celia lies' for this play, which may have had a command performance. In May D'Urfey's *Don Quixote* was 'still impatiently expected', and the first part must have been produced either in the final week of May or at the beginning of June. It too was a huge success, and D'Urfey quickly followed with a second part, which must already have been in production since it was performed soon after the first. There are no new Purcell songs in the June *Gentleman's Journal*, presumably because he was too busy with these productions to compose much else; as proof of his many-sidedness, however, a book of Psalms revised by him also appeared this year. He had given up teaching Weldon and Diana Howard at the end of April.

D'Urfey's text struck the right chord with his audience. It enabled them, through Quixote, to laugh at war and chivalry, to indulge a growing cynicism without betraying the ostensible causes of the war – the defence of Protestantism and resistance to French aggression – or those who were fighting for them. Purcell's contribution, in terms of both the quantity and quality of his music, to the play's success was massive. The texts he set had been carefully inserted by D'Urfey as vehicles for music, and were extrinsic to the plot. They could therefore have been altered for Purcell's musical requirements, but also, I believe, for his philosophical and political views if he'd wanted. It seems fair enough, then, to accept that he endorsed what he was setting: it was tagged with his name, which by now was indisputably the greatest. The other chief composer of vocal music for these two parts of *Don Quixote* was the rising young musician John Eccles, who contributed five songs to Purcell's seven. What isn't known is who wrote the very considerable instrumental music, and perhaps it was D'Urfey himself. The titles of the eleven dances strongly suggest Josias Priest was their choreographer. I suspect that the Purcells were again staying with the Priests during this early summer since a 'Mary Pursell' was buried in St Luke's, Chelsea, on 30 June. After her baptism seven months before, Mary-Peters Purcell disappears from all records, most importantly from Frances's own will, which makes me think that this Chelsea burial is probably hers.

According to D'Urfey, the hit of the play was a song by Eccles, 'I burn, I burn', but its success owed a great deal to Anne Bracegirdle's performance. In his dedication of the second part to the Earl of Dorset D'Urfey described it as 'so incomparably well sung and acted by Mrs Bracegirdle . . . that 'tis the best of all that kind ever done before'. By comparison with Purcell's contributions, 'I burn, I burn' is a simple piece. Apart from his second contribution, 'When the world first knew creation', and 'Lads and lasses', which is a jolly song for the soprano Mrs Hudson, Purcell's are long, complex and often cantata-like. They were sung by the professional singers, among whom must be included Purcell's pupil Catherine Cibber (née Shore), who performed, with John Freeman and her brother John on the trumpet, the song 'Genius of England'. It's almost as if Purcell is deliberately setting out to push the form as far as it will go, combining recitative, aria, solo and duet in long chains of music, the most extended of which lasts nearly ten minutes.

The play had a male drag role, played by 'Leigh', probably Anthony's son Francis; Cibber himself had a part and the singers were Mrs Ayliffe, John Bowman, Freeman and John Reading, as well as those already mentioned. Significantly, there was no Letitia Cross and no Charlotte Butler, who seems already to have left the London stage. Purcell's first song, the duet 'Sing, all ye Muses', is a description of the soldier's life, which would inevitably have brought his brother Edward to mind.

Yet see how they run at the storming a town
Through blood and through fire to take the half moon;
They scale the high wall whence they see others fall
. . . .
Though death's underfoot and the mine is just blowing.
It springs, up they fly
Yet more still supply
As bridegrooms to marry they hasten to die.

The apparent heroism of the beginning alters in the second part, with an echoing change in the music, as the town falls and the 'martial hero' becomes a looter and rapist.

The text of his second song, 'When the world first knew creation', is equally cynical, a bass solo of a Hogarthian harshness; the jauntiness of the tune mimics the satire. 'Let the dreadful engines' is another bass solo of jealous rage against Lucinda, the ingrate: 'I glow but 'tis with hate.' The fierce recitative turns to *arioso* when the singer remembers an earlier happy occasion and then again to angry staccato with a cry of anguish on 'rail', only to come back to short violent phrasing until the final harsh 'goodnight', which has the effect of a curse.

The trio 'With this sacred charming wand' is one of Purcell's finest and longest invocations of the mystery and power of magic, drawing the greatest variety out of D'Urfey's skilful text and the three voices, with a conviction that again anticipates Mozart's music of enchantment in *The Magic Flute*. There's nothing soft about this magic. The soprano sings of her 'little spirit . . . . basking his limbs ready for murder' with sprightly malice, while the bass calls on the hellish kitchen where the 'fat fiends' feast on 'a garbage of souls' and 'boil rashers of fools for a breakfast on coals' with rough vigour.

Purcell's first song in the second part is a satirical dialogue. Reading, as a country boy, tries to convince his sweetheart, Mrs Ayliffe, that 'Since times are so bad' he must go off to the city to better his fortune as others have done, while she tries to dissuade him. D'Urfey paints a bitter picture of contemporary life as the boy considers the various professions: courtier, soldier, pimp, gambler, lawyer and, in the sharpest words, priest, whom his sweetheart describes as 'black cattle'. They join lyrically in a duet to accept the country life as the best.

The masque to entertain the Duke in Act V of the second part allows some respite from this so far grim view: a patriotic interlude of St George and the Genius of England offers some of Purcell's most prolonged and melodic trumpet writing for John Shore. Praises of the soldier are sung in what is almost a recruiting song – at a time when the nation was growing increasingly weary of war, the lack of any perceivable success, the privations required to carry on the annual campaigns and, above all, the heavy taxes needed to pay, or bribe, the soldiers and seamen.

Then follow brave boys to the wars,
. . . .
Who brings home the noblest scars
Looks finest in Cęlia's eyes.

Purcell's last contribution is a piece of cheerful naughtiness describing Willy's attempts to seduce the singer. It's one of the immensely popular genre of Scots songs and the last in the play – the only one of Purcell's that would have sent the audience home humming cheerfully. Bracegirdle could certainly have performed it to great applause, which would then probably have made 'Lads and lasses' the one to be singled out by D'Urfey as the greatest hit, rather than Eccles's 'I burn, I burn'. But most of the rest are too complex and demanding for instant popular success.[8] He was going further and faster than his audience could follow.

In April and July this year, 1694, the *Gentleman's Journal* published songs with music by Purcell to which words had been fitted, and D'Urfey's *Songs Compleat* of 1719 have several of the same kind. This would suggest Purcell was so naturally prolific that he often produced music which he or someone else could adapt later rather than always composing to a specific text or occasion.

In June, in order to provide a solid financial base to carry on the war, the Bank of England was set up. The first subscribers were Mary, for ten thousand pounds, and Sir Robert Howard and his son Thomas, for eighteen thousand between them, which gives some idea of the wealth Purcell's ex-pupil had married into.

Early that month the British, under Tollemache, had tried to storm Brest, with disastrous results; the commander died of his wounds. It was obvious that the French had been waiting for them and there had been an intelligence leak. The following month part of the British fleet bombarded and burned Dieppe and Le Havre. This new method of warfare, which, the British comforted themselves, had been first used by the French, added to the growing unease. Bombing civilians wasn't chivalrous and, as Evelyn remarked to his diary, it didn't seem to end the war any more quickly.

Purcell resumed his teaching of Diana Howard in August, but for some reason Frances collected his fee of two guineas. He may have been at Chelsea while Frances was visiting Westminster. The entry in the Ashtead Manor Accounts gives no precise detail of what the money is for, as it usually does, saying simply, 'Paid Mrs Purcell 2 gins.' Purcell had been getting his songs from *Don Quixote* ready for publication, and organising extensive repairs and alterations to the Westminster Abbey organ, in conjunction with Stephen Crespion, the chaunter. Bernard Smith was to be paid two hundred pounds for 'new making' the instrument and Purcell and Crespion were to oversee and approve the work.

The confederates were at last rewarded with some success in September when they retook Huy. Matthew Prior, who had gone with

William to Flanders, wrote a celebratory poem on the event which was published by Motteux in his summer double issue. Sinisterly, the issue also included three poems on the smallpox, which, along with the very wet summer, was making life both difficult and dangerous.

Sometime about now Purcell contributed two songs to a revival of Dryden's *Tyrannick Love*: another duet for spirits, 'Hark, my Damilcar', and the soprano song 'Ah! how sweet it is to love', one of Dryden's and Purcell's most delightful love lyrics, whose words are for once equal to the music.

A song by Purcell, 'Good neighbour, why?', was used in a long delayed production of *The Canterbury Guests* by Edward Ravenscroft which finally took place early in November,[9] and the *Gentleman's Journal* published another song by him, 'Dulcibella'. The first is a cat fight set to music and resolved by the intervention of the husbands. 'Dulcibella' proved a popular song and was reprinted a few months later in *The Pleasant Musical Companion*.

William missed his birthday celebrations this year because contrary winds held him in Holland. He was at last able to make the crossing and Mary met him at Dartford on 11 November. After dinner they returned to Whitehall, taking the ferry at Lambeth, where the bells were rung for them and throughout the city; from Whitehall they retired home to Kensington. Since it was a Sunday and the anthem which Purcell wrote to celebrate the King's return, *The way of God*, is specifically dated to that day in the Gostling manuscript, it would seem that the King and Queen heard the anthem at evensong in the Chapel Royal. Gostling had been brought from St Paul's to sing the bass part, which is the voice of the warrior, while the countertenor and high tenor seem to represent Mary as the guiding spirit hovering round him. It's a beautiful flowing composition using only an organ ground, and a fine alleluia chorus closes it. The text had been carefully chosen with William in mind, and a little wishful thinking:

> *Thou hast girded me with strength unto the battle;*

Thou shalt throw down mine enemies under me.
I will smite them that they shall not be able to stand,
But fall under my feet.

In spite of suffering from what sounds like recurrent asthma attacks, William was fêted with his birthday ball on the 15th; once again there were extra oboes and music was specially copied out for the event by Nicholas Staggins. It would surely not have been complete without songs and dance music by Purcell, but his next certain engagement was the one which would spread his fame furthest: the performance of the *Te Deum* and *Jubilate* at the service in St Bride's which preceded the St Cecilia's Day Feast and concert. They were given again on 9 December in the Chapel Royal at Whitehall before the King and Queen. The response was modestly described by Frances, when she published the two anthems three years later, as a 'kind reception'. On St Cecilia's Day a public thanksgiving for William's safe return and the success of the British forces had been ordered for 2 December in London and two weeks later throughout the kingdom. Mary and William also received the news of the death of Tillotson, their favourite cleric and archbishop of Canterbury, on St Cecilia's Day. According to Bishop Burnet, Mary spoke of him 'in the tenderest manner and not without tears'.

Tudway, writing of the *Te Deum* and *Jubilate* in his introduction to his collection of church music for Lord Harley over twenty years later, says:

> He brings in the treble voices or choristers singing 'To thee cherubims and seraphims continually do cry'; and then the great organ, trumpets, the choirs and at least thirty or forty instruments besides all join in most excellent harmony and accord; the choirs singing only the word 'Holy'; then all pause and the choristers repeat again 'continually do cry'; then the whole copia sonorum of voices and instruments join again and sing 'Holy'; this is done again three times upon the word 'Holy' only changing every time the key and accords; then they proceed all together in Chorus with

'Heav'n and Earth are full of the majesty of thy glory' . . . I dare challenge all the creators, poets, painters etc. of any age whatsoever to form so lively an idea of choirs of angels singing and paying their adorations.[10]

Both works alternate rich full baroque ensembles with sections of fluent meditation. 'Vouchsafe, O Lord' for alto is as eloquent as any comparable passage in the odes. The *Jubilate* opens with the alto and trumpet being joyful together before the alto and trebles pour out a liquid melody for 'be ye sure that the Lord he is God . . . we are his people'. With death all around, from barely understood sickness or bloodily in war, Purcell reached for all his resources to bring comfort and an idea of beauty and purpose into life's chaos and dissolution.

Tudway's contemporary account shows how visual the response to music could be. He lets the reader see a great baroque ceiling with angels ascending and descending. The Muses were still united in their eternal dance, and it was appropriate to call up poetry and painting as sister arts when speaking of music. He points out that this was the first setting of its kind in English music; he preferred it to all that came after, finding Handel's version too theatrical, whereas Purcell's was 'nobler and more elevated'. According to Tudway, Purcell had meant the two works for the opening of St Paul's Cathedral. If this is so, he must have seen how behindhand the project was and fortunately decided not to wait. Tudway's collection, which includes both composers in its pages, provides a direct link between Purcell and Handel.

Disintegration was threatening the theatre as well as the country, unsuccessful in war and divided at home. In spite of the opera's popular success, the patentees (or owners) were heavily in debt, and their solution was to reduce the actors' wages and to promote new young members of the United Company into the roles usually associated with such people as Betterton and Elizabeth Barry, who were paid more. The actors complained to the Lord Chamberlain, and all the parties were summoned to meet at Sir Robert Howard's house on 17 December to try to patch things up. Howard was particularly anxious for a resolution because preparations for an operatic version of his and Dryden's play, *The Indian Queen*, were already under way.

Smallpox had by now reached epidemic proportions and on 22 December Mary, who had never had the disease, was unwell. The next day she felt better and the day after was well enough to go out, but in the evening she was again so ill that she shut herself in her closet and went through her papers, burning many of them and putting the rest in order. Two days later the characteristic symptoms of smallpox appeared. William was distraught; he ordered his bed brought into her chamber and spent hours at her bedside. From the beginning he feared that she was dying. He called Burnet into his closet and burst into tears, saying that there was no hope for her and that 'from being the happiest he was now going to be the miserablest creature on earth'. On Christmas Day Mary felt better again and it was thought it might, after all, have been only the measles, but at night she relapsed.

Thomas Tenison, the newly appointed archbishop of Canterbury, took William aside and explained that he could not do his duty unless he was able to tell her the danger she was in. William gave his consent. She received the news without any sign of fear, saying she had always been prepared in her own mind for death and she had nothing to do but to submit to God's will. She was given communion, despite being a little worried that she might not be able to swallow the bread.

The usual remedies were applied: bleeding, which must have weakened her resistance, and cordials, which might at least have made her more comfortable and briefly oblivious. Anne sent messages of sympathy and asked to be allowed to see her, but Mary was too ill and wanted to die in peace; she even avoided a final meeting with William, who was suffering so much that everyone was amazed to see the courageous soldier of Landen 'fainting often and breaking out into most violent lamentations'. Mary ordered Archbishop Tenison to continue reading and praying until at last she lost consciousness. She died on 28 December at one in the morning. She had felt herself already old, yet she was only thirty-two.

· 15 ·

Mourn, All Ye Muses

AS AT THE death of Charles II, the nation's poets reached for their pens and the elegies poured off the presses. There was even a poetic round-up of them all, in which D'Urfey was castigated for his lack of a contribution to the general mourning. Congreve's was judged the finest and William paid him a hundred pounds for it at the beginning of February 1695. One of the most interesting, however, is by Purcell's friend James Talbot, to whom he gave a copy of *Dioclesian*. Talbot was a Latinist and regius professor of Hebrew at Cambridge; he was also rector of Spofforth in Shropshire, which suggests a family connection with the Talbots, dukes of Shrewsbury, although his own father was said to be from London. He'd been an undergraduate at Trinity, Cambridge, and an exact contemporary there of Charles, Dryden's son. Talbot's tutor was Leonard Welstead (chaplain to the elder John Dolben when archbishop of York), whose son of the same name would later marry Frances Purcell, Henry's daughter.

Talbot's patron, to whom the elegy 'Instructions to a Painter' is dedicated, was Charles Seymour, Duke of Somerset, 'the muses' glory and the muses' friend . . . head of that worthy body whereof I am an unworthy member and of that noble family which by your grace's favour I have the honour to depend on'. This web of relationships makes plain the network of combined patronage and friendship that at this period was necessary to sustain life and position for those who weren't themselves rich. Talbot's poem, which seems to have been written after

Mary's funeral, since it speaks of 'the dismal pomp of grief' being 'done', also praises 'valiant Ormonde' and makes its obeisance to Anne as 'Elisa, great in sorrow as in blood'. He speaks of Purcell's funeral music, although not by name:

Whilst mournful musick in melodious sound
The ravish'd sense at once delights and wounds;
Here artist wish thy skill could paint each strain,
Which in sad notes so sweetly did complain.

In his copy of *Dioclesian* Talbot called his friend the priest of the Muses (*musorum sacerdotus*) and said that when Purcell died many had wept, but none more than his friend and admirer. Tonson, Dryden's publisher, also published Talbot's elegy for Mary.

She had left instructions for a quiet funeral and at first this was the intention, but public grief had to be assuaged. The people had been denied their desire to mourn as they had wished for Charles II; now they demanded a state funeral. Any attempt to shrug Mary off would have been deeply resented while so much was being spent on the war. William and the Privy Council acquiesced, although it meant he couldn't return to Flanders until it was over. To find a precedent, the committee in charge had to go back to the funeral of James I. Mary was embalmed, the state and private apartments of all their palaces were hung with mourning, clothes and drapery were commissioned and music was written and rehearsed. Her body lay in state in Whitehall from 21 February.

The theatres had been closed since the onset of Mary's illness, which gave time for all the rumbling discontents to surface. The meeting at Sir Robert Howard's had resolved nothing and the leading actors now petitioned the King, through the Lord Chamberlain, to allow them to set up a new company. William, still deeply and genuinely grieving, referred the matter for legal advice. It was exactly the sort of dispute that Mary had resolved with great diplomacy.

William could have seized this ideal moment and problem as an opportunity for beginning to involve Anne in public affairs. They had been officially reconciled and had wept together over Mary's death, but he showed no sign of taking her into the government in Mary's place, even though she was to be chief mourner at the funeral. He had retired to a private house in Windsor so that Kensington could be put into mourning. His closest acquaintances feared for a time that he might follow Mary, his grief was so great. The argument between the actors and the patentees must have sounded trivial to him at such a time, but he seems to have shown great patience over the dispute.

Mary's funeral took place on 5 March. The Earl Marshal's instructions differ in several respects from a French version printed in Amsterdam for circulation in Holland, where there was genuine grief, and throughout the Continent. The scale of this state occasion made several important political statements about the popularity of the Protestant monarchy, the humanity of William and the wealth of the nation and its king. To accompany the body on its journey from Whitehall to the Abbey on a carriage drawn by eight horses, each with a leading groom, Purcell used the march from *The Libertine*. It was bitterly cold, as it had been all winter; the sky was overcast and a light snow was falling. They passed through streets whose crowded balconies were hung with mourning black. Three hundred poor women provided with money and new gowns for the occasion led the way. In one account they are followed by two trumpets; in another preceded by two drums and followed by three trumpets, described as 'flatt', which were used instead of the older curtals and sackbuts of earlier processions, but there's some disagreement among scholars about what the term means. Presumably when the march was first played in the stage version ordinary trumpets had been used. In the Earl Marshal's instructions the boys of the Chapel Royal choir, which came after the Union banner and the grooms of the stable, were to be 'singing all the way', though it's hard to see how they could have sung against the nine or eleven trumpets and four muffled drums. Both houses of Parliament and the London civic dignitaries took part in the procession, along with all the Queen's household and the royal regalia, the ornaments of state.

At the Abbey door the body was transferred to a dais carried by eight gentlemen and attended by the clergy and choir of the Abbey, which was lit by thousands of wax lights and hung in black velvet. It seems likely that they sang some of Purcell's early set of Funeral Sentences as Mary was carried up the choir for the funeral rites and the sermon by Archbishop Tenison, who told the listeners the very moving story of her illness and exemplary death in simple yet graphic words. Then Purcell's anthem *Thou knowest, Lord* was sung. Purcell had deliberately chosen a traditional form which departs from classic polyphony only in its continued use of the flatt trumpets. Tudway, describing the occasion, says: 'I appeal to all that were present . . . wither they ever heard any thing so rapturously fine and solemn and so heavenly in the operation, which drew tears from all.' He applies this particularly to another anthem of Purcell's, *Blessed is the man*, which he states was also sung at Mary's funeral. In the Gostling manuscript it occurs as a separate insert on smaller paper before Blow's anthem *Thy righteousness, O God*, dated August 1693.

The body was taken, accompanied by both choirs, to Henry VII's chapel, to be placed in the vault; the appropriate part of the burial service and Purcell's canzona for trumpets were heard as it moved towards interment. The bells tolled in all the churches for three hours and the guns at the Tower were fired at one-minute intervals, and from the ships at the Nore and Blackstairs. 'Aussi n'a-t-on jamais vu la Cérémonie plus triste, plus grave ni plus pompeuse.' The crowd was 'inconceivable'.[1]

Purcell's setting of the elegy 'Incassum, Lesbia' by a 'Mr Herbert', together with Blow's version of its translation, and Purcell's 'O dive custos' were published in May as a final tribute to Mary at a time when Purcell would normally just have composed and performed her birthday ode. Both lamentations reach unashamedly down into the depths of grief. 'Incassum Lesbia' is an alto solo which Purcell might have performed himself, 'O dive custos' a duet in which the voices intertwine against an organ continuo. Where he had once set 'Maria' as a tender yet joyful call, here it becomes a cry of anguish. The contrast with the restrained emotion of the funeral anthems is so strong that it's as if Purcell had only half done his mourning with the earlier pieces and now had to complete it with these two more lushly expressive elegies. Tudway probably found them 'too theatrical'. The choice of Latin texts was meant, I believe, to ensure their widest appraisal beyond the shores of Britain, a deliberate bid for international status both for himself and the country.

On 25 March Betterton and his group of rebelling actors were given a licence by William to set up and perform plays in a new and separate theatre. Many 'people of quality' subscribed twenty or forty pounds to erect a building for them within the walls of the old tennis court in Lincoln's Inn Fields. Meanwhile the patentees had lost the bulk of the most experienced members of their company and were forced to offer salaries as high as five pounds a week to attract those who were left – mainly the young performers, including Colley and Catherine Cibber.

They decided to reopen in April with Aphra Behn's *Abdelazer*, her only tragedy, and it may be for this production rather than an earlier one that Purcell composed new music. Cibber disliked the play and called it 'poorly written'. The theatre was full on the first night and half empty on the second. Cibber admits that it might have been the actors rather than the play that failed. Betterton replied within three weeks with Congreve's *Love for Love*, such an instant success that 'they had seldom occasion to act any other play to the end of the season'. There was no music by Purcell. Congreve was offered, and accepted, a share in the new company.

Mary's death, with the consequent stop on theatrical and social life, had contributed to the collapse of Motteux's *Gentleman's Journal*, depriving historians of a valuable record. The split between the theatres meant that Downes reported only on his own, that is, Betterton's company. It's therefore more difficult to give precise dates for the plays in this last year that contained music by Purcell, since most of them were for the patentees. Cibber, who must have known, is silent on the subject – so much so that I'm led to suspect an antipathy between the two. Perhaps he found Mrs Cibber too admiring still of her teacher, or perhaps Purcell had joined with the Shore family in opposing his marriage to Catherine. Cibber, although he remained with the patentees at Drury Lane and Dorset Garden, is basically on the side of the rebels. He had resented the fact that the singers and dancers in the operas were paid more and better clothed, and thought it was 'the necessary fitting out these tall ships of burthen', the operas, that had caused all the problems.

Most of the singers, apart from Mrs Bracegirdle, had stayed with the patentees, who could afford the more lavish shows they appeared in, and naturally Purcell was drawn to them. Cibber doesn't mention the production of Howard's *The Indian Queen*. I incline to think it took place earlier rather than later in the year, since the music of the songs was published before November and publication didn't usually take place until at least a month after production.

Purcell's teaching of Diana Howard came to an end in April after he was 'paid in full'. He'd given her lessons in February, but she seems to have had an ear infection in April, for she was treated for deafness and didn't resume her lessons until the following year under an unnamed 'harpsicall master'.

The Ashtead Accounts record a payment by Thomas Howard, Sir Robert's son, of five guineas to Anne Bracegirdle in January.[2] Is this some compensation for not playing the lead in *The Indian Queen* as she could have expected, or just a New Year's gift? She had been a hit as Semernia, the last female Indian role, in Aphra Behn's *The Widow Ranter* and was a natural for Zempoalla. Instead it seems to have been played by her friend Frances Mary Knight, who had been with her when she was attacked by Hill and Mohun; she had elected to stay with the patentees for more money and bigger roles than if she had been in competition with Barry and Bracegirdle in Betterton's new company.

John Freeman and Miss Cross certainly took part in *The Indian Queen*, as well as 'the boy' Jemmy Bowen. The long prologue section before Act I, which begins 'Wake, Quivera', shows Purcell reaching after a continuous operatic setting of the text and recalls Tudway's remark that had he lived until the time of true opera 'he would never have ceased till he had equalled if not outdone' the Italians. Many of the songs in *The Indian Queen*, among them some of his most famous set pieces, such as 'Ye twice ten hundred deities' and the ravishing 'I attempt from love's sickness to fly' (sung by Letitia Cross), are built on complex structures, and the instrumental passages carry on the standard set by the richly orchestrated overture. The scene of pagan sacrifice once more gives a foretaste of *The Magic Flute*.

The last masque, of Hymen, was set by Daniel Purcell, who had given up his full-time post at Magdalen College this year and was sharing his salary half and half with Benjamin Heicht. The record is missing for the previous year, but by 1696 he had left completely. Some scholars have suggested that he'd returned to London to help his brother out, either because of Purcell's workload or because he was already ill. I suspect, however, that Daniel was bored with college life and wanted to come back to London and attempt to make a wider career for himself. A mock letter to him later in his life suggests that he liked to drink and philander: 'I perceive the tenor of your life to be chiefly in taverns where you never leave drinking a treble quantity, till your hand quavers . . . Time was we could both of us have played upon the virginals; and particularly you have been a man of note for your many compositions upon them.' He had been contributing more and more songs to the anthologies, and had probably realised that his job as college organist was a dead end and he could go no further unless he took orders. He had written a St Cecilia ode to words by Thomas Yalden for the Oxford version of the annual celebrations in 1693. From now on, until he was able or forced by lack of money to take the job of organist to St Andrew's, Holborn, and St Dunstan's, he would try to make a living and a reputation in the theatre.

Purcell's own songs for *The Indian Queen* were effectively pirated by one of his own usual publishers, May and Hudgebit. Somehow they had got hold of a score, which looks from the number of his songs included in the publication to have been John Freeman's, and issued it on the grounds that they knew Purcell's own 'innate' modesty would inhibit him from publishing them himself. Their justification was that this would prevent the music from being printed in poor editions or published as 'a common ballad'. They relied on Purcell's 'accustomed candour and generosity . . . to pardon this presumption', and seemed to believe that it was now open season for the press. I've found no order or change in law to support this view, though the older arrangements through the Stationers' Company were certainly breaking down at this time. Unless all this is simply a blind to cover a naked piece of money-making, the words suggest two things about Purcell: that he was reluctant to publish not because of the labour and cost, but because of modesty, so *Dioclesian* and, indeed, the early sonatas were exceptions to his general practice; and that he was known for his honesty and generosity of spirit. These both tie in with Robert Gould's comments on him quoted earlier, and it is, I think, also significant that Blow too published so little until after *Orpheus Britannicus*.

On 8 June the *Tyger* finally reached home from Barbados. On board was the governor, Colonel James Kendal, an admirer of Purcell's music who would one day solicit Charles Sergison of the Navy Board, another admirer, for a post for Joseph Purcell as surgeon,[3] but there was no Charles Purcell – only the entry 'DD' in the pay book, meaning 'discharged dead'. The log doesn't say when he died, but the probate record which granted custody of his children, Henry and Elizabeth, to his mother, Elizabeth Purcell, later in June says 'in partibus Barbados'. The children are described as 'freeborn', which suggests that they might have been born in Barbados, but I've found no other record of them either here or there.

William had sailed for Flanders on 11 May in his new yacht the *William and Mary* and under the convoy of Sir George Rooke. A fortnight later it was feared that the little Duke of Gloucester had caught smallpox. Five physicians attended him but he managed to recover. He had become even more the nation's hope since the death of Mary, and William was genuinely fond of him. After Mary died, Anne had been confirmed in the succession on William's death, but he was the 'little rising star' of the ode Purcell set for his sixth birthday on 24 July.

The brisk overture gives plenty of opportunity for the trumpet, played by John Shore. He had been admitted to the Private Music without fee in March, to come in with fee as soon as there was a vacancy. In addition to being the best trumpeter, he was a skilled lutenist; his affiliations were to the Denmarks rather than to William. At some time before the end of the century he became trumpeter to Prince George and he is described as one of Princess Anne's musicians in the account for playing at a ball for the King's birthday which she'd organised in 1698.

Little William was a frail but spirited child, and the music shows a mixture of tenderness, reflecting Purcell's liking for children, and a martial playfulness. It exists in Purcell's own hand, with the names of the singers, John Howell, John Freeman, Alexander Damascene and Anthony Roberts.[4] Apart from a correction to the final phrases, the manuscript is so clean that either it's a fair copy or it shows how easily Purcell composed. It also shows that sometime before this he'd gone back to the open, modern 'e'. As well as the trumpet, oboes form part of the band, but the forces were small enough to be easily transported to Richmond House in Kew, where the celebration took place. They probably took a boat and were rowed up the Thames, making music all the way.

After the overture, the alto introduces the theme:

Who can from joy refrain, this gay
This pleasing, shining wondrous day?

The chorus and instruments take up the phrase 'wondrous day'. Then the text begins to make its several subtle political points that prove it to be a propaganda exercise for the Anne camp in an oblique comparison between William, 'the sun', and his six-year-old nephew and ultimate heir:

For tho the sun has all
His summer's glories on
This day has brighter splendour far
From a little rising star.

William's 'summer glories' were his campaigns.

One of Purcell's most tender airs celebrates the Prince's birth with the high tenor, 'A prince of glorious race descended', which becomes a lyrical string ritornello. The bass solo praises Prince George's courage and then it's the turn of the soprano for Anne, accompanied by oboes and other instruments.

The graces in his mother shine
Of all the beauties, saints and queens
And martyrs of her line.
She's great let Fortune smile or frown
Her vertues make all hearts her own;
She reigns without a crown.

This frankly dangerous text, referring to Anne's 'suffering', her abrogating the crown at the Revolution in favour of William after Mary's death and, by implication, putting her above Mary, Purcell sets without lingering over the words, which are immediately subsumed into praise of the Prince and his war games:

Ah! how pleased he is and gay
When the trumpet strikes his ear.

The final chaconne, the longest section of the ode, is extremely rich, with a variety of voices and instruments anticipating the future in 'When grown what will he do?' There's a final hit at William, evidence perhaps of the influence of John Churchill, the Earl of Marlborough. In theory he had been reinstated in the royal favour since kissing William's hand at the beginning of the year but, like Prince George, he was left behind with no command when William sailed for Flanders.

> *Then Thames shall be the queen of Tyber and Seine*
> *Of Nilus, of Indus and Ganges*
> *And, without foreign aid,*
> *Our fleets be obey'd.*

The text may be by Nahum Tate, but I think it's very unlikely that he, as poet laureate, would have dared such an equivocal ode which offers no praise of the King at all. For his part, Purcell was still finding, or making, new challenges for himself in a form he knew so well.

William had other things on his mind than the intrigues of the rival court, which moved to Windsor at the beginning of August with two troops of Oxford's guards to attend them. The attempt to retake Namur had begun in July. The day after the performance of Purcell's last royal ode the deputy governor of the newly founded Bank of England, Michael Godfrey, who had gone with the governor, Sir James Houblon, to oversee payment for the war, was killed when viewing the trenches in front of the town by a cannon-ball which narrowly missed the King. The siege took a further month of intense fighting, in which Edward Purcell's ensign, George Newby (commissioned only in 1693), was killed, before the express finally reached London with the news that Namur had fallen. A thanksgiving was at once ordered, but neither Purcell nor Blow seems to have contributed an anthem – or, at least, if they did, Gostling wasn't concerned in the performance and it doesn't appear in his manuscript.

The description of the final assault in Luttrell helps to explain Purcell's contributions to the old play by Fletcher revived about this time, *Bonduca, or The British Heroine*: 'the King ordered an attack of fusiliers to be made upon the outworks of the castle and fort, commanded by the lord Cutts, which was very obstinate and bloody; the enemy besides all their firing rowled down great stones from the precipice upon our men; but at length we gained the said works and had near 1000 of our men killed and wounded therein'.

The overture and act tunes to *Bonduca* set the mood: minor, sinister and suggestive of a fretful distractedness. The music is often openly aggressive, leading up to the clarion of 'Britons, strike home'. As if he had sickened even himself of the sound of blood and war, Purcell gives Bonduca the lovely lamenting aria in praise of love and peace, 'O lead me to some peaceful ground', whose 'peaceful ground' is supplied by a string bass.

Bonduca also has one of Purcell's most popular catches, 'Jack thou'rt a toper', which was to be endlessly copied and anthologised. As it doesn't appear in Henry Playford's third edition of *The Pleasant Musical Companion*, published this year, I deduce that the collection must predate *Bonduca*. It contains more than sixty catches, of which over half are by Purcell; the rest are shared among ten other composers or are anonymous. Once again it's the sheer prolificness of Purcell that amazes, yet it also opens up important questions, some of which I've already touched on. Unless a catch was religious, in which case it became a canon, it was designed to be sung in a drinking house. The greater number of them are either drinking songs or expressions of a wide range of dubious attitudes to women, especially wives, that are the reverse side of the extremes of romanticised sexual desire that make up the bulk of the love songs. 'Jack, thou'rt a toper' has the lines:

None but a cuckold bullied by his wife
For coming late, fears domestic strife.

Another in the collection begins 'For once in our lives,/Let us drink to our wives' and there are many more, covering a full range of locker-room stereotypes. It will be argued that these catches meant nothing or were all schoolboyish, harmless fun, and I'm far from condemning them out of any dislike of drink or for being bawdy, as they were condemned (and therefore bowdlerised) later. My concern is only what they reveal of

Purcell's ambiguities. As I've said before, it was entirely his choice to set them and in such quantities. Take, for example:

'Tis woman makes us love,
'Tis love that makes us sad;
'Tis sadness makes us drink,
And drinking makes us mad.

or

To thee, to thee, and to a maid
That kindly on her back will be laid
And laugh and sing and kiss and play,
And wanton all a summer's day,
Such a lass, kind friend, and drinking
Give me, Great Jove, and damn the thinking.

Some are simply jokes, such as the catch said to have been written for John Gostling, 'Of all the instruments', which mocks in a friendly way his liking for the viol. But another hints at a hidden aggression and that Purcell's 'conquering sweetness' of expression didn't arise from a natural softness of temper. His lauded modesty had, I believe, another side: ambition and a sense of being equal to anyone which was an aspect of the universal and increased demand for freedom and equality as the old order crumbled. Money, not just acres, demanded status and the 'sons of art' of the various professions began to have pride in their achievements and to see themselves not as servants but as a new breed of professional. The 'innate modesty' is a disciplined cover for a real self-esteem. One of the catches in the collection shows a bawdy republicanism:

My lady's coachman being married to her maid,
Her ladyship did hear and to him thus she said:
I never had a wench so handsome in my life,
I prithee therefore tell me how you got such a wife.
John stared her in the face and answered very blunt
E'en as my lord got you. How's that? Why by the c—![5]

Against the impression given by these catches must be set the couplet in Robert Gould's final version of his elegy on Purcell as published in his complete works of 1709.

no words he set but what the chastest ear
(And none were chaster than his own) might hear.

Gould's play *The Rival Sisters* was produced in October, but he and Purcell must have met long before this for Gould to lay claim, as he does in this version of the elegy, to great intimacy. Gould was a talented writer, but inclined to a whining self-pity. His picture of Purcell's relationship with his close friends is of physical warmth and charm:

the kindness so diffusive he professed
That I, even I, was numbered with the rest,
Prest in his arms and kneaded to his brest.
How oft he has delighted in my lays,
And thought th'unlearn'd production worth his praise.

The Bertie family, especially James, Earl of Abingdon, were Gould's patrons, as they were to be patrons of Edward Purcell's last years; as already mentioned, they owned Lindsey House next to the Priests in Chelsea, which must have been the channel through which Purcell and Gould met, since Gould spent much of his time in the country. Both Gould and Edward Purcell were residents in houses belonging to Abingdon at Rycote and Wytham respectively. Gould's other connection to Purcell was through the poet Charles Sackville, Earl of Dorset.

Purcell contributed three songs to Gould's play and wrote two or possibly three for *The Mock Marriage* by Thomas Scott. The most interesting is the semi-comic song 'Man is for the woman made'. The others, though charming, are the kind of songs to a ground he could write with deceptive ease. The duet for underage lovers, 'Celemene, pray tell me', which D'Urfey supplied for a production of Southerne's *Oroonoko*, is beautifully turned, but it's the seduction song from a play called *Pausanius, or The Betrayer of his Country* by Richard Norton which shows Purcell in top flight again.

William returned on 12 October, to be met by a court still officially in mourning. Several of the nobility rode out to meet him and escort him to Kensington. He made a point of visiting the Denmarks at once at Camden House, where they were now staying, and his namesake, little William, 'told him that he would accompany him the next campaign in Flanders'. Four days later he went to take his leave of them before setting out on a progress through the Midlands while elections were held for parliament. Kensington must have seemed very empty on this first return after Mary's death.

The King's birthday was celebrated in his absence, but the fireworks were put off until after his return to London on the 13th. On 16 November he visited the Denmarks again, invited them to return to live at St James's and gave the vacant garter to his godson. Although there would never be any warmth in the relationship, the official reconciliation was now complete. It must have been for this that Purcell set the lines:

Lovely Albina's come ashore to enter her just claim,
Ten times more charming than before.
The Belgic lion as he's brave
This beauty will relieve
For nothing but a mean slave
Can live and let her grieve.

In the *Orpheus Britannicus* this is said, presumably by Frances, to be the last song he set 'before his sickness'. The song is singled out in this way, I believe, not only because the fact is probably true but because by the time of its inclusion in 1698 it was politically important, in terms of hoped-for patronage, to underline his connection with Anne. Its first publication in 1696 said that it was the last song he set 'before he died'.[6] This too had political significance, since Anne had by then 'come ashore' at the royal Palace of St James's 'to enter her just claim'. The great master of music seemed to be giving his blessing to the event from beyond the grave.

October was very mild, though September had been cold. D'Urfey had decided on a third part of *Don Quixote*, and the patentees must have hoped that it would be as successful as the other two. D'Urfey asked Purcell to contribute to the music, but Purcell was ill and could manage only one song, the cantata 'From rosie bowers'. Earlier biographers have suggested that Purcell suffered from tuberculosis, but there's no evidence to support this. The picture of him painted during this year by John Closterman shows no signs of consumption – in particular, none of the weight loss associated with the later stages of the disease that is familiar from images of such known sufferers as Keats and D.H. Lawrence, or from personal experience. If anything, the face is rather plump and has a slight double chin. The eyes are perhaps a little protuberant, often a sign of a hyperactive thyroid. To modern eyes it's the face not of a man of thirty-six but of someone ten years older, mature, confident and controlled, even allowing for the ageing effect of a full wig.

In the account of his illness given by Hawkins, Purcell caught cold when locked out by Frances in circumstances very similar to those in the catch 'Jack, thou'rt a toper': he came home late at night heated with wine. Hawkins describes this story as 'a tradition', which must mean it is a Gostling story, but Gostling was then living in St Paul's, and it might have been several days before the news that Purcell was ill reached him. There's no other evidence, but no other story either, and it's one that would fit the case. Purcell isn't the first spouse to be locked out after a row, and Frances, as her subsequent management of his and the family's affairs shows, wasn't a mouse.

Still, the description of the illness as 'a cold' makes me suspect influenza, which in the damp autumn, when the coal fires were beginning to thicken the air, turned to bronchitis or pleurisy and eventually to pneumonia. During his illness, which could have begun and gradually developed in November, he had enough strength of mind and body to compose a cantata in five movements for the third part of *Don Quixote*. The words, with hindsight, are only too prophetic and would have echoed his own as the illness progressed:

> *Ah! 'Tis in vain, 'tis all in vain,*
> *Death and despair must end the fatal pain.*
> *Cold, cold despair, disguis'd like snow and rain,*
> *Falls on my breast: bleak winds in tempests blow.*
> *My veins all shiver, and my fingers glow*
> *My pulse beats a dead march.*

The song opens hopefully with a flowing love recitative for the soprano Letitia Cross as Altisidora, then becomes a cheerful fairy jig until realism breaks in and the singer begins to despair of ever winning the disdainful Strephon. The song is an allegory of the artist's aspiration and inevitable loss – not that I believe Purcell perceived it in these terms, or not perhaps consciously, but the fact that he didn't make a will until the very last moment shows how much he resisted his illness and the idea of imminent death. The song is to a harpsichord ground and it's easy to imagine him dragging himself from his bed to the keyboard to compose it, perhaps, like Mary, feeling temporarily better and then relapsing. The result is a miniature *tour de force* that ranges through all the fluctuations of disappointed love as though he were determined on a superb flourish if it was to be his last.

He was bled by his apothecary and former neighbour from Bowling Alley East, William Eccles, who applied all the remedies available for the period.

> *Art try'd the last efforts but could not save.*[7]

When it was clear that he was dying, Frances sent for her brother John Baptist Peters from his house in St Mary Le Bow to draw up a hasty, formal will in his elegant clerkly hand and, after Purcell had, shakily and messily, signed it, to stamp it with his seal. A neighbour from Marsham Street, John Chaplin, was the third witness. Quite simply, everything was left to 'my loving wife'. He described himself as 'being dangerously ill as to the constitution of my body but in good and perfect mind and memory'. He died later that day. It was the eve of St Cecilia.

Epilogue

PURCELL WAS BURIED beside the organ in Westminster Abbey on the evening of 26 November to his own music for Mary's funeral. If there was a death mask, taken perhaps by Ralph Battell as sub-dean, rather than by the young John Dolben, and Sir Christopher Wren, it has vanished, together with the bust said to have been made from it. Once again the poets took to their pens. The most famous elegy is Dryden's, which was set by Blow and performed at the concert room in York Buildings. Tate provided the words for Daniel Purcell's own brotherly mourning; James Talbot's lament was set to music by Godfrey Finger. The most musically lavish was possibly Jeremiah Clarke's full-scale Purcellian cantata, given on the stage of Drury Lane with Jemmy Bowen, John Freeman, Richard Leveridge and Letitia Cross, trumpets, hautboys and recorders, kettledrum and strings. It ends, after 'Mr Purcell's Farewell', with an 'antick dance'.

Frances disappears from the Marsham Street house almost at once. Either she stayed with friends or in lodgings until she acquired her own house in fashionable Dean's Yard, from where she set about the publication of Purcell's works, primarily to keep herself and the children, but also, I believe, out of a genuine desire to preserve as much as she could. The first, *A Choice Collection of Lessons for the Harpsichord*, was dedicated to Princess Anne, acknowledging her 'generous encouragement' of Purcell's work and her choice of the harpsichord as her preferred instrument. Hawkins poured scorn on Frances Purcell's expressions of grief and loss in her dedication after, according to his version, she had caused her husband's death, but a stormy relationship isn't incompatible with grief at its being over. In 1705 she moved to a house of her brother's in Richmond. Her sister, Amy Howlett, briefly took over Dean's Yard before joining her. Frances died the following year, her sister in 1707 in their brother's house in St Mary Le Bow. Of the death of their mother, Amy Pieters, I've found no record.

Having lost two of her sons in one year, Elizabeth Purcell also moved to Dean's Yard, presumably to the same house as Frances, so she had probably been living with them all the time. Shortly before she died in 1699 she went to Deptford to collect the last of the money owing to her son Charles as purser to the *Tyger*, for tobacco sold to the crew. The address beside her very shaky signature is Dean's Yard, 'at Mr Norris a wheelwright'. No one of that name appears in the rate books. She was buried in St Margaret's, Westminster, with the finest funeral that could be bought.

Her daughter Katherine Sale was given probate, which suggests to me that Edward was away, probably in Ireland, where the Duke of Ormonde had returned after the peace of Ryswick, and where Edward's portrait was done in miniature by Thomas Forster. It was one of a group of twelve presented to the Duke, among them Charles Trelawney, Edward Purcell's first commander, Dr Peter Birch, the Duke's chaplain and vicar of the musicians' church, St Bride's, George Clarke, a correspondent of Edward at the Admiralty, and Dr Richard Adams, a fellow of Magdalen College, Oxford. Edward's subsequent career is documented on his tombstone in Wytham, Essex, but it has a subtext. On the death of Anne Ormonde refused to recognise the succession of George I, was attainted and withdrew to France. These, I believe, are the 'misfortunes' which broke Edward.

Daniel Purcell too seems, according to Jonathan Swift, to have been a non-juror after the death of Queen Anne. His career, although not negligible compared with the rest of his contemporaries, still remained in his brother's shadow. Like Edward, he didn't marry, and they both died in 1717. Only Joseph made the transition to the new King's service successfully; he was made the permanent surgeon of the royal yacht *William and Mary* in 1718 and died on board in 1734. His wife was probably called Sara, and there are several potential candidates, including a Sara Clarke (possibly a relative of the George Clarke at the Admiralty) who married a Joseph Purcell in 1687 at St Giles, Cripplegate. His daughter Sara Partridge administered his estate.

The Purcells' daughter Frances married the poet Leonard Welstead. She died at thirty-six and her daughter Frances at eighteen, which caused her father such grief that friends were seriously concerned for his health. Edward, the Purcells' son, married Anne and had several children, including Henry, Joseph, Edward and Frances. He became organist of St Margaret's, Westminster, and St Clement, Eastcheap, and died in 1740.

Purcell's musical descendants, his pupils, filled the organ lofts throughout the British Isles. Of the performers both Richard Leveridge and Letitia Cross had a spell at the Smock Alley theatre in Dublin. One of his most talented successors, Jeremiah Clarke, killed himself, it was said for love, in 1707. Along with Daniel Purcell, John Weldon and John Eccles, Clarke supplied music for several plays and masques, but by the time of Thomas Tudway's collection of anthems for Robert Harley, Earl of Oxford, made between 1714 and 1720, Tudway was able to lament a noticeable decline in both secular and sacred music. He blames, as Betterton had done, 'want of encouragement', but also the failure of British musicians to compete with the latest arrival of foreigners, especially those trained at Italian and German courts.

Purcell's very pre-eminence may be partly to blame. Charles Burney's father said that for thirty years after Purcell's death no one would listen to anything else, and there's also his own professed admiration for Italian music, but there are other factors too. Jeremy Collier's attack on 'the immorality and profaneness of the English stage' of 1698 is symptomatic of a change in public taste and mores which includes the closeting of women and a new wave of suppression and self-censorship. Dryden himself connived at it in his final prologue and epilogue to the benefit performance of *The Pilgrim* (adapted by Sir John Vanbrugh, with music by Daniel Purcell and Godfrey Finger) given on 25 March 1700, which also contains his last piece of sustained dramatic writing, *The Secular Masque*. The attack on women, and especially the conjunction of women and theatre, reads like an old man's spite. In defence of the stage he blames the court.

a banished court, with lewdness fraught,
The seeds of open vice returning brought.
Thus lodged, (as vice by great example thrives,)
It first debauched the daughters and the wives.
. . . .
The poets who must live by courts or starve,
Were proud so good a government to serve;
And mixing with buffoons and pimps profane
Tainted the stage for some small snip of gain.
. . . .
What would you say if we should first begin
To stop the trade of love behind the scene,
Where actresses make bold with married men?

Church music had always been vulnerable to Puritan attack, and the established clergy's increasing venality, lack of pastoral care and failure to speak out against enclosure and the slavery of industrialised agriculture and manufacture drove a large part of the population into the arms of that wing of the Christian church for whom the only acceptable sacred music was the psalm and the simple hymn. Increasingly, too, sacred and secular music were separated and no longer fed into each other. It was Handel's great achievement to re-fuse them in his *Messiah*.

Sometime between the death of his godson, the Duke of Gloucester, and his own William, according to an anonymous poet, was present at a concert of music by Purcell which included *Dioclesian* and some of the elegiac music for Mary, and reduced the King to unaccustomed tears.

Now godlike Nassaw feels thy sovereign power,
And conquests o'er his soul unknown before:
Prostrate the vanquish't hero lies,
And with each vary'd note unwillingly complies.

Purcell's *Te Deum* and *Jubilate* were heard at the opening of St Paul's. Purcell missed the opening of the chancel and its organ by his old friend Father Smith by less than two years. *Dido and Aeneas* was performed as a series of entertainments inserted into *Measure for Measure* in 1700. Betterton brought over foreign singers and dancers to make up for the dearth of good plays and to draw off the audience from the rival company. Some of them, like Margarita Delpine, stayed on to become part of the musical life of London. Anne, when she became Queen, did much to support the Chapel Royal and sacred music, and indeed the Purcell family, but she preferred plays at court to a box at the theatre with her ladies-in-waiting. Gradually Purcell's magic faded, so that by 1729 the poet Henry Carey could write:

Ev'n heaven-born Purcell now is held in scorn,
Purcell who did a brighter age adorn.

In both literature and painting the domestically viable succeeds the royal and public as the new century progresses. Novels replace plays and, with some exceptions, landscapes, animals and couples strolling in their gardens push out the courtly gods and their attendants. Temperance reduces the catch to a neutered glee. The late, high-Renaissance flowering in Britain which began with Elizabeth I had burned itself out. Rich young men took to the roads of Europe in pursuit of a cultural veneer that would largely absolve them from any sustained support for native art. Not until almost the end of the nineteenth century would Elgar and Shaw revive the British public arts of music and theatre.

Notes

1 Curtain Tune

1 BM (British Museum), Egerton MS 2542, f. 354.

2 PRO (Public Record Office), CSPD 1656.

3 For example *Cupid and Death* (1653) by James Shirley, performed privately for the Portuguese ambassador with music by Matthew Locke and Christopher Gibbons.

4 Dedication to Christopher Simpson's *Chelys minuritionum artificio exornata* (1665), quoted in John Hawkins, *A General History of the Science and Practice of Music* (London, 1853).

5 Berkshire Record Office, New Windsor Registers. The previous strongest candidates for the composer's father and brother were Henry and Thomas, sons of John Purcell, carpenter of Thornborough, Buckinghamshire, but although Henry disappears from the registers and so might be Henry of the Chapel Royal and Abbey, Thomas stays in the parish, marries and has children in the 1670s. John Purcell was also illiterate, which makes him an unlikely father for a groom of the robes.

6 E. H. Fellowes, *Organists and Masters of the Choristers of St George's Chapel in Windsor Castle* (Windsor, 1979).

7 Ibid.

8 John Purcell, MP, is therefore the most likely candidate for the mysterious 'Mr Pursell' in the Middleton/Chirk Castle Accounts as being bought a drink in London in 1660 by the Middletons' steward.

9 See in particular the elegy by Robert Gould affixed to the 1702 *Orpheus Britannicus*, 'On the death of the late famous Mr Henry Purcell'.

10 Edmund Waller, *Upon Her Majesties New Building at Somerset House* (1665). The staff were in lodgings for part of the time.

11 PRO, PCC 1684.

12 See below, ch. 3, for further discussion of his compositions.

2 A Child of the Chapel

1 A misreading of an entry in the Chapter books of the Abbey has led to the supposition that she was leased the house by the Chapter, but a close look at the name shows it to be 'Mrs Finnall' of another musical family.

2 Hawkins, *History of Music.*

3 Westminster Abbey Muniments, 61228A.

4 WRO (Westminster Record Office), Churchwarden's Accounts.

5 See *The Shorter Pepys*, ed. R. Latham (London, 1985), *passim*, for the sheer variety of his musical encounters.

6 From the account of Taswell, a former pupil at the school, quoted in Edward Pine, *The Westminster Singers* (London, 1953–4).

7 Franklin B. Zimmerman, *Henry Purcell*, 2nd edn (Philadelphia, 1983).

8 Roger North, *The Musicall Grammarian*, ed. J. Wilson (London, 1959), 'Musick to Various Intents', 'Ecclesiastical Musick'.

9 Henry Hall, elegy prefixed to 1698 *Orpheus Britannicus*.

10 BL (British Library), Harl. 7338.

11 Alleged by W. H. Cummings, in *Henry Purcell* (London, 1903), to have been in the possession of E. F. Rimbault and to be a 'Birthday Ode'.

12 Josias Priest, the dancing master with whom Henry Purcell was to collaborate so freqently, was one of their targets. Andrew Ashbee, *Records of English Court Music*, v: *1625–1714* (Aldershot, 1991).

13 WRO, rate books of St Martin's in the Fields.

14 *History of Surrey*, Mickleham, where William Wall of the Inner Temple is said to be son of Moses, and that lands in Fridley also descended from William to Temperance Purcell.

3 Sweeter Than Roses

1 Zimmerman, *Henry Purcell*.

2 Fitzwilliam Museum, MS 88.

3 Ashbee, *Records of English Court Music*, i: *1660–1685* (Kent, 1986).

4 *Catch as Catch Can, or The Musical Companion* (1667).

5 Ashbee, *English Court Music*, vol. i.

6 There's a similar confusion in the Westminster School records with respect, I believe, to the two Silas Taylors, uncle and nephew, son of Sylvanus. The elder was at Shrewsbury School.

7 BM, Add. MSS 30930.

8 BL, Add. MSS 31435.

9 North, *Musicall Grammarian*.

4 Thrice Happy

1 PRO, Probate 5, 5023.

2 I am grateful to Maurits Verhoeff for research in Belgian archives.

3 *Aliens in England 1603–1700*, Huguenot Society (Aberdeen, 1902), and houses of Commons and Lords journals.

4 *Vicar General Marriage Licences, 1687–94*, ed. G. Armytage, Harleian Society, vol. 63 (1912).

5 Melusine Wood, *History of Historical Dances* (London, 1964).

6 Reprinted in Hawkins, *History of Music*.

7 WRO, rate books of St Margaret's, Westminster.

8 Zimmerman, *Henry Purcell.*

9 PRO, KB 33.

10 PRO, CSPD 1682.

11 PRO, Calendar of Treasury Books, 1682.

5 Hail, Bright Cecilia

1 Thomas D'Urfey, *Poems* (London, 1683).

2 Corporation of London Record Office, Accounts for the Lord Mayor's Show, miscellaneous MS.

3 Hawkins, *History of Music.*

4 Ian Spink, *English Song: Dowland to Purcell* (London, 1986).

5 BM, RM 20L8.

6 BM, Add. MSS 22100.

7 BM, RM 20L8.

8 North, *Musicall Grammarian.*

9 Narcissus Luttrell, 1683, *A Brief Historical Relation of State Affairs* (Oxford, 1857).

10 Inner Temple Records.

11 Ibid.

12 Greater London Record Office, Sacrament Certificates.

13 He appears in the inventory, along with the other chief supplier, Gerard Weyman of the same parish as John Baptist Pieters, a naturalised Dutchman and relative by marriage of the architect and dramatist Sir John Vanbrugh.

14 John Peeters, *A Family from Flanders* (London, 1985).

15 Fitzwilliam Museum, MS 117.

16 Westminster Abbey Muniments, 33717.

17 John Evelyn, 23 September 1683, *Diary*, ed. G. Russell (London, 1945).

18 It may be that after John Banister's death in 1679 the celebration was taken on by the 'Musical Society'. Other livery companies' records might provide an answer.

19 Registers of St Pancras, Soper Lane.

6 Sighs and Tears

1 Margaret M. Verney, *Memoirs of the Verney Family* (London, 1899).

2 John Dryden, *The Letters of John Dryden*, ed. C. Ward (Durham, NC, 1942).

3 For further discussion of the musical aspects, see Bruce Wood and Andrew Pinnock, 'Unscarr'd by turning times?', *Early Music* (August 1992).

4 Anonymous satire quoted in E. Howe, *The First English Actresses* (Cambridge, 1992).

5 *The Works of Sir Christopher Wren*, Wren Society, vol. vii (1930).

6 Evelyn, 10 May 1684, *Diary*.

7 Caesar's Godlike Sway

1 PRO, KB 24/1.

2 PRO, LC3/28.

3 PRO, ADM 106/2961.

4 Evelyn, 15 October 1685, *Diary*.

5 *Letters of Queen Anne*, ed. B. Curtis Brown (London, 1935).

6 *Letters of James II*, Society of Antiquaries, vol. 58 (1902).

7 Neither is he in other possible registers, St Mary Le Strand and St Clement Danes. His will seems not to have been proved until some questions arose in 1694.

8 Guido M. Gatti, *Musica Dizionario* (Milan, 1968).

9 BM, Add. MSS 33234.

10 BM, Add. MSS 36772.

11 PRO, CSPD 1687, for his pass in June 1687.

8 Harmonia Sacra

1 PRO, Calendar of Treasury Books, 1688.

2 PRO, CSPD 1688.

3 But see W. VanLennep, *The London Stage* (Illinois, 1965), and Zimmerman, *Henry Purcell*, for further information.

4 PRO, CSPD 1688.

5 Ibid., and Evelyn, 10 April 1687 and 7 October 1688, *Diary*.

6 WRO, will of William Eccles, apothecary, probate February 1709.

7 His wife was given a pass for France, which perhaps indicates a French origin. PRO, CSPD 1688.

8 See above, ch. 1, and *Staffordshire Pedigrees*.

9 *Vicar General Marriage Licences, 1687–94*, and Meriol Trevor, *The Shadow of a Crown: The Life of James II* (London, 1988).

10 Charles Dalton, *English Army Lists and Commission Registers 1661–1714*, vols i–vi (London, 1892).

11 Ibid.

12 PRO, CSPD 1688.

9 When Monarchs Unite

1 Aphra Behn, *A Congratulatory Poem to Her Sacred Majesty Queen Mary on Her Arrival in England* (1689).

2 PRO, SP44, fos 165–6.

3 Ashbee, *Records of English Court Music*, ii: *1685–1714* (Kent, 1987); PRO LC2/13.

4 WRO, plan of Westminster Abbey during the coronation of James II.

5 Ashbee, *English Court Music*, vol. v.

6 Gilbert Burnet, *A History of His Own Time* (London, 1818).

7 PRO, CSPD 1689.

8 Luttrell, 17 May 1689, *Relation of State Affairs*.

9 Ibid., 16 December 1687.

10 Burnet, *History of His Own Time*.

11 Ashbee, *English Court Music*, vol. v.

12 PRO, CSPD 1689.

13 Ibid.

10 Ah, the Sweet Delights of Love!

1 Peter Holman, *Four and Twenty Fiddlers* (Oxford, 1993), and Ashbee, *English Court Music*, vol. i.

2 Charlotte Charke, *A Narrative of the Life of Charlotte Charke* (London, 1755).

3 Hawkins, *History of Music*, presumably on the authority of one or more of his contributors, such as William Gostling or Dr Berenclow.

4 Charke, *Life of Charlotte Charke*.

5 Colley Cibber, *An Apology for the Life of Mr Colley Cibber* (London, 1839).

6 PRO, ADM 20/71.

7 John Weaver, *Orchesography; or The Art of Dancing* (London, 1712).

8 For a fuller discussion of this and other matters relating to *Dioclesian*, see Julian Muller, *Words and Music in Henry Purcell's First Semi-opera, 'Dioclesian'* (Lampeter, Dyfed, 1990).

9 Cibber, *An Apology*.

10 Ashbee, *English Court Music*, vol. ii.

11 Fairest Isle

1 Dryden, *Letters*, *passim* for the subscription system.

2 BL, Stowe, MSS 755.

3 PRO, Calendar of Treasury Books, 1703, 1705, 1713–1715, 1718.

4 WRO, rate books of St Margaret's.

5 Registers of St Michael's, Barbados, 2 October 1684.

6 PRO, Probate 6, Adman 1695.

7 Dedication of the *Te Deum* and *Jubilate*, published 1697. Crewe was installed as rector of Lincoln College, Oxford, by Fuller.

8 C. E. Whiting, *Nathaniel, Lord Crewe* (London, 1940).

9 Luttrell, December 1691, *Relation of State Affairs*.

12 'Tis Nature's Voice

1 WRO, rate books of St Margaret's. She is entered wrongly in the poor rate as 'Ann', but correctly in the highways rate as 'Amy'.

2 *Gentleman's Journal* (March 1692).

3 Evelyn, 10 May 1684, *Diary*.

4 Corporation of London Record Office, 036B.

5 Cibber, *An Apology*.

13 Tell Me, Some Pitying Angel

1 He may be the subject of her poem *A Pindaric to Mrs P Who Sings Finely*. *Abdelazer* was revived again in 1695 and Purcell's music may belong to this later date.

2 The memorial has been wrongly attributed to Lady Elizabeth Dryden, the poet's wife, but she could not possibly be 'the Honourable Lady Howard' of Frances Purcell's dedication.

3 Northampton Record Office, Cartwright Family Papers.

4 In her will she leaves everything to her mother, Mrs Elizabeth Hunt, so presumably Hunt wasn't her husband's name but her own, unless 'mother' means 'mother-in-law'.

5 *A Biographical Dictionary of Actors, Actresses, Musicians, Dancers etc. in London 1660–1800*, ed. P. H. Highfill, A. Kalman and E. A. Langhans (Illinois, 1973).

6 Luttrell, 22 July 1693, *Relation of State Affairs*.

7 Dalton, *Army Lists*.

8 PRO, ADM 33/165.

9 *Westminster Abbey Registers*, ed. J. L. Chester, Harleian Society, vol. 10 (1875).

14 Come, Ye Sons of Art, Away

1 *The Literary Works of Matthew Prior*, ed. H. B. Wright and M. K. Spears (Oxford, 1959).

2 Luttrell, Jan–Feb 1694, *Relation of State Affairs*.

3 J. W. Stubbs, *The History of the University of Dublin* (Dublin, 1889).

4 Ibid.

5 See Peter Holman, 'The Isaacs: A Musical Family', *Musical Times*, 128 (1987), for more on them. What looks like Peter's brother Bartholomew was a child under Blow and a pupil of his.

6 Surrey Record Office, Ashtead Manor Accounts, Guildford Room 1/53/1–5.

7 W. H. Cummings, for example.

8 A point also made by Curtis Price in his lecture, 'Henry Purcell', at the South Bank in London (November 1993).

9 As suggested by its mention in the *Gentleman's Journal* of October and November, but Van Lennep, *The London Stage*, suggests September.

10 BL, Harl. 7342.

15 Mourn, All Ye Muses

1 Mons M., *Relation de la Maladie, de la Mort et des Funérailles de Marie Stuart* (Amsterdam, 1695).

2 The Ashtead Accounts are first of all Thomas Howard's, then his widow Diana's, who rented lodgings from Amy Howlett, Frances Purcell's sister, in 1702 until she bought a house in Duke Street. There's also a payment to Frances's maid and, for black and white calico, to Frances herself.

3 PRO, ADM 106/2961.

4 BL, Add. MSS 30934.

5 Playford's bowdlerisation, not mine.

6 Cummings, *Henry Purcell.*

7 Gould, 'On the death of the late famous Mr Henry Purcell'.

Bibliography

Anon. *Ashtead Past and Present*. 1903.

Anon. *The Form of Queen Mary's Funeral*. London, 1695.

Anon. *Musick or a Parlay of Instruments*. London, 1676.

Anon. *Wit for Money*. London, 1692.

Archeologia vol. 58. London, 1902.

Ashbee, A. *Records of English Court Music* vols i, ii. Kent, 1986–7. vol. v. Hampshire, 1991.

Arundel, D. *Henry Purcell*. London, 1927.

Bachiler, J. *The Virgin's Pattern*. London, 1661.

Banister, J. *New Ayres*. London, 1678.

Battell, R. *A Sermon Preached on St Cecilia's Day 1693*. London, 1694.

Beddard, R. *A Kingdom Without a King*. Oxford, 1988.

The Boscobel Tracts. Ed. J. Burns. London, 1843.

Boswell, E. *The Restoration Court Stage*. USA, 1932.

Brown, B. Curtis. *Letters of Queen Anne*. London, 1935.

Buck, W. *Examples of Handwriting*. London, 1965.

Burnet, G. *A History of His Own Time*. London, 1818.

Campbell, M. *Henry Purcell*. London, 1992.

Charke, C. *A Narrative of the Life of Charlotte Charke*. London, 1755.

Churchill, Sir W. *Marlborough. His Life and Times*. London, 1933.

Cibber, C. *An Apology for the Life of Mr Colley Cibber*. London, 1839.

Cibber, C. *A Poem on the Death of Queen Mary*. London, 1695.

Clark, W. *The Early Irish Stage*. Oxford, 1955.

Cowley, A. *Complete Works*. Ed. A. Grossart. London, 1881.
Croft, W. *Musica Sacra*. London, 1724.
Crowne, J. *Calisto*. London, 1675.
Cummings, W. *Henry Purcell*. London, 1903.
Dalton, J. *St George's Chapel Windsor*. London, 1957.
Davenant, C. *The Songs in Circe*. London, 1677.
Davenant, Sir W. *The Cruelty of the Spaniards in Peru*. London, 1658.
Davenant, Sir W. *The First Day's Entertainment at Rutland House*. London, 1657.
Davenant, Sir W. *Sir Francis Drake*, London, 1659.
Davenant, Sir W. *The Siege of Rhodes*, London, 1663.
Davenant, Sir W. and Dryden, J. *The Tempest*. London, 1690.
Dawe, D. *Organists of the City of London 1666–1850*. London, 1983.
Dent, E. *Foundations of English Opera*. USA, 1965.
Downes, J. *Roscius Anglicanus*. Eds. J. Milhous and R. Hume. London, 1987.
Dryden, J. *Albion and Albanius*. London, 1685.
Dryden, J. *Amphitryon*. London, 1690.
Dryden. J. *King Arthur*. London, 1691.
Dryden, J. *The Letters of John Dryden*. Ed. C. Ward. USA, 1942.
Dryden, J. *Poetical Works*. London, 1874.
Duffet, T. *Beauties Triumph*. London, 1676.
D'Urfey, T. *Don Quixote* I, II, III. London, 1694–6.
D'Urfey, T. *The English Stage Italianized*. London, 1727.
D'Urfey, T. *A Fool's Preferment*. London, 1688.
D'Urfey, T. *Love for Money*. London, 1691.
D'Urfey, T. *A New Collection of Songs*. London, 1683.
D'Urfey, T. *New Poems*. London, 1690.
D'Urfey, T. *Songs Compleat*. London, 1719.
Elmes, J. *Memoirs of Sir Christopher Wren*. London, 1823.
Etherege, Sir G. *Plays and Poems*. London, 1888.
Evelyn, J. *Diary*. Ed. G. Russell. London, 1907.
Fea, A. *The Flight of the King*. London, 1898.

Fellowes, E. *Organists and Masters of the Choristers of St George's Chapel in Windsor Castle*. Windsor, 1979.
Fisher, H. *A History of Europe*. London, 1936.
Flatman, T. *Poems and Songs*. London, 1682.
Fuller, T. *Worthies of England*. London, 1662.
Gould, R. *Poems*. London, 1709.
Harding, R. *Matthew Locke*. Oxford, 1971.
Harley, J. *Music in Purcell's London*. London, 1968.
Hamilton, A. *Memoirs of the Comte de Gramont*. Trans H. Walpole. London, 1965.
Hawkins, Sir J. *A General History of the Science and Practice of Music*. London, 1853.
Highfill, P., Kalman A. and Langhans E. *A Biographical Dictionary of Actors, Actresses, Musicians, Dancers etc. in London 1660–1800*. USA, 1973.
Hilton, J. *Catch as Catch Can*. London, 1663.
Hogwood, C. *Music at Court*. London, 1977.
Holland, A. *Henry Purcell*. London, 1948.
Holman, P. *Four and Twenty Fiddlers: the Violin at the English Court 1540–1690*. Oxford, 1993.
Howard, Sir R. *Five New Plays*. London, 1692.
Howe, E. *The First English Actresses: Women and Drama 1660–1700*. Cambridge, 1992.
Hughes, J. *The Boscobel Tracts*. London, 1857.
Hyde, R. *The A to Z of Restoration London*. Kent, 1992.
Inderwick, F. *The Calender of Inner Temple Records 1505–1714*. London.
Jordon, T. *London's Joy*. London, 1681.
Jordon, T. *London's Royal Triumph*. London, 1684.
Jordon, T. *The Triumphs of London*. London, 1683.
Langbaine, G. *Lives of the Poets*. London, 1699.
Langbaine, G. *Momus Triumphans*. London, 1688.
Lee, N. *Theodosius*. London, 1680.
Locke, A. *The Seymour Family*. London, 1911.

Locke, M. *Observations*. London, 1672.

Locke, M. *Psyche, the English Opera*. London, 1675.

Lowe, R. *Thomas Betterton*. London, 1891.

Mace, T. *Musick's Monument*. London, 1676.

Mackinnon, Sir F. *Inner Temple Papers*. London, 1948.

Maidwell, L. *Essay on Education*. USA, 1951.

Milhous, J. and Hume, R. *A Register of English Historical Documents Relating to the Theatre*. London, 1991.

Miller, J. *Charles II*. London, 1991.

Mons M. *Relation de la Maladie, de la Mort et des Funérailles de Marie Stuart*. Amsterdam, 1695.

Motteux, P. *The Gentleman's Journal 1692–4*. London, 1694.

Motteux, P. *Words for a Musical*. London, 1695.

Muller, J. *Words and Music in Henry Purcell's First Semi-opera, 'Dioclesian'*. Lampeter, 1990.

The Muses Mourn. Ed. J. Alden. London, 1958.

New Everyman Dictionary of Music. Blom, E. Revised Cummins, D. London, 1988.

Norris, J. *Poems*. Blackburn, 1872.

North, R. *Roger North on Music*. Ed. J. Wilson. London, 1959.

Paget, J. *Some Records of the Ashtead Estate and of its Howard Possessors*. Unpublished, 1893.

Parmiter, G. *Elizabethan Popish Recusancy at the Inns of Court*. London, 1976.

Pepys, S. *The Shorter Pepys*. Ed. R. Latham. London, 1985.

Peters, J. *A Family from Flanders*. London, 1985.

Pine, G. *Westminster Abbey Singers*. London, 1953–4.

Playford, H. *The Banquet of Musick*. London, 1688–90.

Playford, H. *Deliciae Musicae*. London, 1695–6.

Playford, H. *Harmonia Sacra*. London, 1688, 1693.

Playford, H. *Musick's Handmaid*. London, 1689.

Playford, H. *The Theater of Music*. London, 1685–7.

Playford, H. *Three Elegies Upon the Much Lamented Loss of Queen Mary*. London, 1695.
Playford, H. *Wit and Mirth: or, Pills to Purge Melancholy*. London, 1699.
Playford, J. *Choice Ayres*. London, 1675–9.
Playford, J. *The Dancing Master*. London, 1650–95.
Playford, J. *An Introduction to the Skill of Musick*. London, 1658–94.
Playford, J. *The Musical Companion*. London, 1667–94.
Playford, J. *The Treasury of Musick*. London, 1659–69.
Price, C. *Henry Purcell and the London Stage*. Cambridge, 1984.
Prior, M. *Works*. London, 1740.
Purcell, H. *Dido and Aeneas*. Birmingham, 1961.
Purcell, H. *A Choice Collection of Lessons*. London, 1696.
Purcell, H. *Orpheus Britannicus*. London, 1698, 1702.
Purcell, H. *Songs in The Fairy Queen*. London, 1692.
Purcell, H. *Songs in The Indian Queen*. London, 1695.
Purcell, H. *Sonatas of Three Parts*. London, 1683.
Purcell, H. *The Vocal and Instrumental Musick in the Prophetess, or the History of Dioclesian*. London, 1691.
Reggio, P. *Songs*. London, 1680.
Shadwell, T. *Complete Works*. London, 1927.
Shadwell, T. *The Libertine*. London, 1676.
Shadwell, T. *The Tempest*. London, 1674.
Shakespeare, W. *Measure for Measure*. Altered C. Gildon. London, 1700.
Shirley, J. *Cupid and Death*. London, 1653.
Sloane, E. *Robert Gould*. USA, 1940.
Spink, I. *English Song: Dowland to Purcell*. London, 1974.
Stubbs, J. *The History of the University of Dublin*. Dublin, 1889.
Summers, M. *The Restoration Theatre*. London, 1934.
Talbot, J. *Instructions to a Painter*. London, 1695.
Tate, N. *Brutus of Alba*. London, 1678.
Tate, N. *A Duke and No Duke*. London, 1684.

Tate, N. *Poems*. London, 1684.
Tate, N. *Poems by Several Hands*. London, 1685.
Thomas, H. *The Life of Nahum Tate*. London, 1934.
Van Lennep, W. *The London Stage 1660–1700*. USA, 1965.
Verney, M. *Memoirs of the Verney Family*. London, 1899.
Waller, E. *Upon Her Majesties New Building at Somerset House*. London, 1665.
Waller, E. *The Passion of Dido*. London, 1679.
Weaver, J. *History of Dancing*. London, 1712.
Weaver, J. *History of Mimes*. London, 1728.
Welstead, L. *Works*. London, 1787.
Welwood, J. *Memoirs of the Most Material Transactions in England*. London, 1700.
Westrup, Sir J. *Henry Purcell*. London, 1980.
Whiting, C. *Nathaniel, Lord Crewe*. London, 1940.
Wildeblood, J. and Brinson, P. *The Polite World*. London, 1965.
Wood, Melusine. *Historical Dances*. London, 1952.
Wren, Sir C. *The Works of Sir Christopher Wren* vol vii. London, 1930.
Wright, J. *The Embassy of the Earl of Castelmaine*. London, 1688.
Young, J. *The Journal of James Young* Ed. F. Poynter. London, 1963.
Zimmerman, F. *Henry Purcell*. USA, 1983.

Index

Plays for which Purcell wrote incidental music or songs are marked with an asterisk.